VISIONS OF AMERICA
How We Saw the 1984 Election

VISIONS
OF AMERICA

How We Saw the 1984 Election

WILLIAM A. HENRY III

The Atlantic Monthly Press
BOSTON / NEW YORK

FIRST EDITION

LIBRARY OF CONGRESS CATALOGING IN PUBLICATION DATA

Henry, William A., 1950–
  Visions of America.

  Includes index.
    1. Presidents—United States—Election—1984.
  2. United States—Politics and government—1981–
  I. Title.
  E879.H48 1985   324.973′0927   85-47631
  ISBN 0-87113-012-2

MV

PUBLISHED SIMULTANEOUSLY IN CANADA

PRINTED IN THE UNITED STATES OF AMERICA

*To my wife, who endured
the development of this book,
and to my mother, who endured
the development of its author*

AUTHOR'S NOTE

I BEGAN this book with two notions about campaign coverage: first, that the story ought to be a narrative, with a beginning, a middle, and an end, with characters and settings and foreshadowing and plot, with asides and ironic juxtapositions and the occasional jocular digression; and second, that the real campaign is the string of public events that voters observe, not the hidden web of strategy memos and fund-raising dinners and portentous telephone calls. It has been said, in my view persuasively, that one could effectively chart the course of a campaign by watching the network evening newscasts and reading the major morning newspapers and newsweeklies. That is not what I did for this book: I visited twenty-six states during 1984, was on hand for most major campaign events, talked to dozens of candidates, aides, journalists, and other observers, and unearthed some nuggets of information that I have not seen elsewhere in print. Still, the theory seems compatible with my basic belief, that a campaign drama is best judged from the point of view of its audience, the voters, rather than from the vantage of center stage or the wings. To me, the real excitement of any presidential election comes from the fact that tens of millions — in 1984, nearly a hundred million — Americans participate, and invest their participation with the deep significance of a formal judgment on the quality of their lives. I set out by presuming that voters care about more than a ready grin and a quip, that they make choices out of deep convictions about the nature of the country. Every four years, we collectively define, if not who and what we are, then certainly who and what we yearn to be.

Thus for me the election began and ended, like this book, with Ronald Reagan. Things that happened among Democrats were rich in tension and consequence, and they propel much of the narrative. But Reagan and his redefinition of what to admire in our national character proved to be the irresistible forces of the campaign. Much of the commentary last

[vii]

year focused on the question of whether liberalism was dying. The more positive question was whether something else was being born, or reborn. Yet this is not a pro-Reagan (nor for that matter anti-Reagan) book. It is highly opinionated, even quirky, but its skepticism has been aimed in every direction.

I owe thanks to many people who were interviewed for this book, and to many more who refined my thinking over the years. I am particularly grateful to the campaigns of Walter Mondale, Gary Hart, Jesse Jackson, and John Glenn (notably his staff member John Dorfman) for their occasional hospitality, and for varying degrees of openness from the candidates. I am appreciative of the availability and candor of some of President Reagan's key aides, especially at the Republican National Convention, and for my 1976 and 1980 experience of covering the man himself. Steve Hess and my close friend Andrew Carron, both of the Brookings Institution, strengthened my perceptions of politics and economics.

Among journalists, at CBS I was helped by Dan Rather, Walter Cronkite, Bill Moyers, Don Hewitt, and Van Gordon Sauter, among others; at NBC, by Tom Brokaw, John Chancellor, Chris Wallace, and Reuven Frank foremost among many; at ABC, by David Brinkley, David Hartman, Jeff Greenfield, Sam Donaldson, Lynn Sherr, and Jeff Gralnick; at Cable News Network, by Daniel Schorr, Bernard Shaw, and James A. Miklaszewski; at the "MacNeil-Lehrer Newshour," by Judy Woodruff; at the *Washington Post*, by Benjamin Bradlee and Martin Schram; at the *New York Times*, by Steven Weisman, Maureen Dowd, and Fay Joyce; at *Newsweek*, by Margaret Warner, Rick Manning, and Howard Fineman; at the *New Republic*, by Martin Peretz, Michael Kinsley, and Sidney Blumenthal. I also benefited from the help of Christopher Lydon of WGBH in Boston, Steven Stark of the *Boston Phoenix* et al., Robert Maynard of the *Oakland Tribune*, and the ubiquitous George Will.

At the *Boston Globe*, which molded me during my first decade of professional life, editor emeritus Tom Winship provided years of paternal friendship and shrewd counsel, and more recently a discerning, corrective reading of this book in manuscript. At *Time*, which is my employer now and I hope forever, Henry Grunwald, Ray Cave, Ralph Graves, and Jason McManus made this project possible. They were joined in providing deft editing and challenging questions of my stories about the media and the campaign by John Elson, Walter Isaacson, and Stephen Smith. Among writing colleagues too numerous to mention without fear of omission, I must nonetheless thank Ed Magnuson, George Church, and Kurt Andersen.

Author's Note

Eileen Chiu researched with her customary sagacity under time constraints that make me solely responsible for any errors of fact this book contains. Michael Carlisle of the William Morris Agency nurtured this project from its inception; it would not exist without his kind persistence.

William A. Henry III
March 21, 1985

CONTENTS

I

The Warrior King

FROM the beginning, the 1984 election was not a race that the Democrats hoped to win. Rather, it was a contest that everyone acknowledged Ronald Reagan would have to lose, if change there was to be. No stratagem or gambit seemed sufficient to dislodge him; no alternative candidate offered greater glitter; not even a vast enfranchising movement for blacks and women and the victims of a changing economy and technology could by itself turn him out, for Reagan, in the breadth and geniality and seeming openheartedness of his appeal, had already established himself as the President of all the people. He came into battle with as many political assets as Richard Nixon in 1972 or Lyndon Johnson in 1964, and with another, almost uniquely potent weapon: he was not merely respected or feared but liked. After nearly twenty years of four successive administrations that prompted fretfulness, mistrust, disregard, and outright rage, the country had, as Republicans reveled in pointing out, a chief executive who could talk plausibly of restoring national optimism. In his most effective moments, Reagan appeared to have attained the ultimate goal of every national politician: to embody so thoroughly the myths and traits of the country's idealized image of itself that a vote for Ronald Reagan would be a vote for the real America.

His success seemed, to borrow from Churchill, an enigma wrapped within a mystery. His programs and his rhetoric were often divisive. He was prone to spontaneous, ill-considered, often contradictory remarks — even on fundamental matters of principle — that his aides would then spend the next day retracting. His appointees had a similar propensity for provocative language, and also for pointless confrontations, unseemly business involvements, and startling indiscretions. Repeatedly and explicitly, Reagan's administration undertook to violate the most sacrosanct rule of American governance: it tried to take away from people the benefits they already possessed. Thousands of the physically and mentally disabled were thrown off Social Security, and horror stories made the network news. Five of every six recipients were threatened with reduction or elimination of their food stamps. The elderly on the verge of retirement were told they might have to wait three more years. In the incident that seemed to sum up the insensitivity of the Reagan team, the bureaucrats of the federal school lunch program proposed to count catsup as a vegetable.

None of this seemed to matter in the end. Did Reagan call for tax-exempt status for segregated academies? People refused to believe him a bigot. Did Reagan stonewall away four years of arms-control opportunities? People refused to believe him an inflexible zealot. Did his aides cut deals with corporate polluters and subvert the toxic waste cleanup fund to crass political purposes? People refused to believe him uncaring about the environment. Did his administration add tens of billions of dollars to the incomes of households already earning $80,000 a year or more, and take away tens of billions from households earning $20,000 a year or less? People still thought him compassionate. Barbs about Reagan and his rich friends rang true only to the already converted.

Democrats believed this phenomenon was the result of some mental aberration, some temporary moral blindness, on the part of voters who needed only to be talked around. Congresswoman Patricia Schroeder of Colorado, a key adviser to presidential candidate Gary Hart and a leader among the Democratic party's less doctrinaire, second-look liberals, coined a widely accepted shorthand when she said that Reagan's was a "Teflon" presidency. Like the chemical coating for pots and pans, the metaphor suggested, Reagan's personal aura seemed to guarantee that every mess he came into contact with could be wiped away in seconds, and no residue would stick. One appeal of the image was that Teflon erodes over time; that offered the Democrats hope. But by July 1984, New York's Governor Mario Cuomo, a man whose heart overflows with traditional New Deal liberal compassion, expressed the party's regretfully achieved wisdom when he said, in its convention's keynote address, that the most the Democrats could do was to "separate the salesman from the product," in the hope that the public might forsake Reagan if it were persuaded that Reaganism was somehow unfair or unsound. That easily turned phrase masked the twofold difficulty of the Democrats' task against this bafflingly popular President: first, to win the debate on purely political issues, no small problem for a party whose ultimate standard-bearer, Walter Mondale, felt obliged to apologize for the errors (roughly, too much free spending and too little flag-waving) of the recent past; second, to turn the public's focus exclusively toward politics and away from deeply felt nonpolitical concerns of character, faith, and spirit, the realm in which Reagan had already won the hearts of so many of his countrymen.

Emotionally, Reaganism was a blend of nostalgia; religious simplicity; patriotic myth; old-fashioned stoic heroism; self-assertion balanced by admiration of self-sacrifice; rugged individualism tempered by respect for unforced community-mindedness; deference to traditional authorities, including one's elders; reverence for the family as the mainspring of the society and the moral superior of every other way of living; a belief that truth dwells in faith and inner conviction rather than facts (especially when they contradict one's intuitive certitude); and a general presumption that niceness, affability, normality — being a regular fellow — is the most trustworthy index of decency.

So much for the emotions. The cultural heritage of Reaganism-as-policy was complicated; it embraced the precepts of many mutually antagonistic factions of American conservatism. To intellectuals, Reaganism seemed a muddle of conflicting initiatives, unresolved debates. But Reaganism had never been meant to appeal to intellectuals. It appealed, rather, to Main Street, and specifically to the people reviled in *Main Street* — that is, the middle to lower bourgeoisie, and their latter-day economic peers, the upper to middle peasantry, for whom citizenship has more to do with loyalty than with ideology. Reagan's America was a remembered America and, moreover, one remembered not from skeptical scholarly histories but from that psychic attic of imagery in which purple mountain majesties, amber waves of grain, small-town schoolmarms, the cavalry riding to the rescue, Norman Rockwell Thanksgivings, the flag-raising at Iwo Jima, the World Series, and astronauts landing on the moon somehow seem interlinked because they each in turn have evoked a swelling sense of personal participation in national pride and purpose.

Conveniently for a candidate in the television age, Reagan's remembered America was also the country that is invoked in television advertising, not only his own but the reach-out-and-touch-someone sentimentality of the telephone companies, the rising-sun and noble-struggle tableaux of corporate sponsors of the Olympics, the park-bench and cracker-barrel wisdom treated with comic homage by IBM and other computer companies. It was fitting that this world be reflected in the mass media, because so many of the images that make it up were received by the public from schoolbooks and songs and magazines and calendars, from photographs and radio and television, above all from the richest source of Reagan's own story-telling, the movies. The unifying power of this kind of Americanism was that it had been experienced by the population in common, and had evoked, from the moment it was first perceived until the moment it was retrieved by recollection, an unanalytic, emotional response, based on the sensation that deep down, all true Americans share the same values, sympathies, beliefs, creed.

It was Reagan's ability to summon up this world of memory and illusion, far more than his technical gifts as a speaker, that had made him, in the all but universally accepted characterization, the Great Communicator. His skills were, to be sure, all but flawless. On the 1980 campaign trail he had sometimes delivered the same speech half a dozen times a day, with a catch in his throat and an emotive thickening of his voice on exactly the same syllable each time. For his State of the Union addresses, he read alternately from TelePrompTers on either side of the room, with no perceptible break in rhythm, indeed with no hint that he was reading. He was so adroit at making each word sound as though it had occurred to him at the moment when he spoke that cynics labeled him a far better actor than had ever been realized in Hollywood, where Reagan had never achieved first-rank stardom and had never been nominated for an Academy Award.

But there was more than style to Reagan's persuasive power. There was a passion, there was an urgency, there was a stubborn consistency. He did not merely voice fashionable attitudes. For two decades before he became President, he served as an insistent spokesman for his and his allies' beliefs, even when they were regarded as out of step, out of date, out of the running. Like the two transforming politicians whom he invoked most often — both Democrats, Franklin Roosevelt and John Kennedy — Reagan created the rationale for his apparent timeliness. He invented his inevitability.

———✎———

If any one inclination unites Presidents and their biographers, it is the impulse to search for Rosebud — for the boyhood incident that explains the man, as the lost sled of that name supposedly illuminates the materialism, discontent, and loneliness of the publishing tycoon who is the title character in the Orson Welles film *Citizen Kane.* This sort of psychobiography has its limits. One can say that Ronald Reagan was born in a smallish town in the American heartland to a family of limited education and modest means; yet the same can be said, with only minor variations, of seven of the eight Presidents since Franklin Roosevelt, excepting only John Kennedy — and also of most of their challengers. One can say that Reagan showed early promise but few signs of brilliance, that he longed for great athletic prowess but did not achieve it; those, too, are presidential norms. But there can be meaningful information in the stories that candidates tell about their youth. Richard Nixon touched on several key aspects of his personality, and his presidency, when in his 1968 acceptance speech he pictured himself as a little boy listening to the sounds of trains passing in the night: the isolation, the ambition, the yearning to travel literally as well as spiritually. Jimmy Carter in 1976 described having listened to the radio addresses of Franklin Roosevelt when he was a boy gathered with his family in the rural Georgia evening. He may have meant a subtle comparison between his communal experience and Nixon's solitary one, but he hinted more about his detachment from politics as process, his yearning to minister to the nation's soul. The most vivid glimpse that Ronald Reagan has given of his growing up in Dixon, Illinois, is his recollection of having to drag in the unconscious body of his alcoholic father, Jack, who had passed out on the front step in the winter cold.

This humiliating episode is remarkable enough merely for the fact of Reagan's telling it. Political candidates' recollections of their parents more customarily resemble hagiography, or, when that is untenable, a discreet near-silence. More intriguing still is what meaning Reagan may attach to this flatly described episode, and whether his interpretation has changed during his decades-long political odyssey from liberal Democrat, like his father, to conservative Republican. Confronting a father's alcoholism could be the origin of a deep compassion toward those beset by hard times, personal tragedy, human weakness. Indeed, Reagan often invokes small-town charity, based on intimate knowledge of the needy, as an ideal model for welfare. The giver is ennobled by the sacrifice; the recipient sees his succor as a token of the goodness and worthy example of those higher up the social ladder, and thus as a spur to self-help rather than an inertia-inducing economic entitlement. This sort of compassion is highly judgmental. Help goes only to the deserving poor. Reagan's system of social justice might well offer scant aid to the likes of his own father, a man too undisciplined to give up his drinking and provide better for a family that was, Reagan has written, "damned poor."

Whatever he may have thought of his father, in boyhood or later, Ronald Reagan showed no overt sign of rebellion, at least among the relatively meager memories that he has summoned up for biographies, including his own *Where's the Rest of Me?* The Reagans lived in various flats, mostly over stores; Jack was a merchant who later distributed government food and worked for the WPA. Ronald read Tom Swift science fantasies and Horatio Alger fictions about hard work that paid off, and he lived above all for football. He was a less than zealous student but, in a venturesome move for a youth of his time, place, and social class, he followed the example of his high school fullback and went off to Eureka College, a small, Protestant-affiliated school in downstate Illinois that had been founded in 1855. Reagan paid for his education by working as a dishwasher and lifeguard.

In some ways Eureka sounds like the sort of narrow, even smug, place sketched by Sinclair Lewis in the early scenes of *Elmer Gantry*. But the one professor in Reagan's major, economics and sociology, was a progressive who bemoaned, for example, the tedium of the assembly line. Shaped by his family circumstances, his education, and his times — some of his earliest memories were of wounded and disillusioned soldiers returning from the carnage of World War I, and he entered college on the eve of the Depression — Reagan was, in his own words, "an almost hopeless hemophiliac liberal." His commitment to causes, however, mattered rather less than his career. He did not head to the South or the Dust Bowl to organize farm workers; he did not sign up to fight for the Loyalists in Spain; he did not even seek a more conventional, better-compensated life in law or government or professional politics. Instead, his postcollege years reflected two other great social trends: the rise of the communications media, and the mass migration to California, the land of opportunity.

Some political talents have to be cultivated through a lifetime. The legislative cunning of a Lyndon Johnson or a Tip O'Neill is a skill that ripens, and acquires credibility, with age. But other gifts are inborn, and that seems to explain Ronald Reagan's dexterity with a microphone: he was a natural storyteller. His first consequential job was as a sports announcer, and what distinguished young Dutch, as he then chose to be called, was his ability to spin out colorful, compelling descriptions of games he had not seen. He was a rip-and-read reporter, relying on wire copy. But he would use the spare, minimal stream of facts, the summary of hits and runs and errors, to conjure up the sights and sounds and smells of the ballpark, the ardor and exuberance of an imaginary crowd. To be sure, some of what Reagan conveyed to his hearers may not have been literally true, and there was much that he had no way to determine the truth or falsity of, yet that seems not to have troubled him. He apparently assumed then, and seems to have assumed for the rest of his life, that people seek a symbolic and emotional truth from storytellers, not merely a narrow synopsis.

As Wright Morris wrote of Norman Rockwell, his "special triumph is in the conviction his countrymen share that the mythical world he evokes actually exists. . . . He understands the hunger, and he supplies the nourishment. The hunger is for the Good Old Days — the black-eyed tomboy, the hopeless, lovable pup, the freckle-faced young swain on his first date, the kid with white flannels at his first prom — sensations which we no longer have but still seem to want; dreams of innocence before it went corrupt." These images are among the deepest truths of the American character, far more widely held and more enduring than the dreary specifics of some legislative proposal or welfare program. And they are best expressed in parable or myth, in evocative human terms rather than abstractions. The youthful Reagan who imagined a stirring athletic contest was continuous with the grandfatherly Reagan who went on telling his tales about "bucks" on welfare buying steaks, or food-stamp families purchasing vodka and beer, even after reporters and political rivals demonstrated that the stories could not be true. He understood, from the beginning, that the purpose of listening to a storyteller is not to gain new information, but to recapture experiences that the listeners already have had, to reaffirm views of the world that they already hold.

For a performer who showed such early promise at playing himself, acting might not have seemed an obvious career. But in 1937, when the twenty-six-year-old Reagan obtained a screen test at the Warner studios, no opportunity offered more potential for glamour, fulfillment, and money than becoming an American movie star, and he grabbed at the chance. During the next three decades he made more than fifty films. Most of the time he played some variation of the boy next door. His roles tended to be so innocuous that when he was brought forward as a candidate for governor of California, a studio tycoon quipped, "No, Jimmy Stewart for governor. Reagan for best friend." He had a homespun charm, but not everyone's idea of grace and elegance. When producer Alfred DeLiagre put together a film version of the Broadway comedy *Voice of the Turtle*, he bitterly but unsuccessfully resisted the studio's choice of Reagan as the romantic lead. In conversation soon after Reagan was elected President, DeLiagre explained, "*Voice* was a sophisticated story. It demanded style. Reagan on camera always had the manner of an earnest gas station attendant."

Still, in his early days Reagan was often cast as a privileged playboy. He had rather delicate good looks, a resonant voice free of pronounced regional or class accent, and the excessive good manners that constitute servility in the lower classes but condescension in the upper ones. He carried himself, as he still does, with a kind of sweet, almost naive self-confidence that could make audiences feel protective rather than resentful. He drew on this vulnerability, and perhaps on memories of his father, as an alcoholic dandy in *Dark Victory*, a Bette Davis weepie, in 1939, and again the next year as a doomed football player, George Gipp, in *Knute Rockne, All American.* For decades to come, he made proud if joking reference to his best line as Gipp, a deathbed plea to Coach Rockne to fire up some future team by telling them to "go in there and win it for the Gipper."

A year later, in *King's Row*, a glimpse of life in a small town not unlike the Illinois hamlets where he grew up, Reagan played a happy-go-lucky layabout who suddenly found himself penniless when his inheritance vanished with an absconding bank officer. The film, which remained Reagan's favorite, was earnestly liberal, modern, and Freudian, as Reagan was in those days. It sided with the downtrodden working people, among whom Reagan knew he had belonged throughout his youth. The movie's title was taken from the name of the village where it was set, a self-professed "good place to live" in which the bucolic bustle barely concealed a pervasive cruelty and corruption. Everywhere one looked, there was class warfare, and the helpless, holy poor were losing. In the most sadistic of the plot's many twists, Reagan had both legs amputated, needlessly, by a self-righteous surgeon who disapproved of the erstwhile heir's breezy ways. The words Reagan shrilled on awakening and discovering his condition later became the title of his autobiography: "Where's the rest of me?" In the climactic scene, the depressed and withdrawn Reagan was brought back to reality by a boyhood friend who used reverse psychology, telling him that he was a victim of spite, in the hope that the shock effect would work. Reagan brought off this seemingly implausible scenario by achieving in seconds a self-awareness that many people could not reach in a lifetime: he broke gamely into a grin, looked at his stumps in wonder, and said, "Does he think I live there?" On film, at least, Reagan had proved himself capable of the stoic heroism he would later expect of other victims of fate in real life.

As Reagan aged from pretty youth to leathery manhood, his screen persona changed; to a considerable extent, his more macho roles also reflected his newly conservative politics. His last overtly liberal film was *Bedtime for Bonzo*, now generally invoked by Reagan's critics to sneer at his acting career, but in fact a charming attempt to remake the screwball comedies of the 1930s for a 1951 audience. Reagan played a college professor of psychology, engaged to marry the dean's daughter until the dean learned that the professor's father had been a lifelong criminal. The professor blazed at the suggestion that he, or for that matter his father, was to blame: "He paid his debt to society, as the moralists would put it. . . . My father was born and raised in a slum environment. Given a decent start in life, my father would have gone as far in the right direction as he went in the wrong one." To prove his belief that heredity matters less than environment, the aggrieved professor then "adopted" the college's new chimp and tried to rear him as a human child. Although the experiment led to predictable slapstick absurdities and a plot contrivance in which Bonzo made Reagan look every bit as crooked as his jailbird father, it ended with the chimp showing the very altruism that the professor had been trying to teach him, and thereby proving Reagan innocent and liberalism right.

Within a few years, Reagan was playing quick-triggered vigilantes and gamblers in Westerns, and a brave but morally flawed hardass submarine captain in *Hellcats of the Navy*, the only film he made with his second wife, Nancy. In *Hellcats*, Reagan showed an absolute lack of guilt or pain at killing enemy soldiers. He even left one of his own men to die, supposedly to ensure the safety of the whole crew, moments after learning that the man was his rival for Nancy's love. In his last film, *The Killers*, made in 1963 and based on the Hemingway short story, Reagan played a petty thug masking his lack of real presence by butched-up brusqueness. At the final moment, facing certain death, he looked at a hard-earned wad of money with a wryly lifted eyebrow and a rueful half-smile, subtly indicating at last a touch of intelligence and irony in this two-bit hood.

Reagan's acting was better than his generally mediocre movies: he showed exceptional range, admirable willingness to take risks, finely calibrated adjustments to a character's carriage and gesture, and an understated, uncluttered, naturalistic delivery. He used, to great effect, many of the same movements that he carried over into speechmaking: the cock of the head when trying extra hard to be persuasive; the sharp, downward, dismissive wave of a hand, as if to say, "I don't know," when he heard a question he did not choose to answer; the slight sideways nod that somehow became as expressive as a studied shrug. But to a surprising degree, for a man who later developed the most distinctive political persona since Kennedy's if not Roosevelt's, Reagan lacked star quality. He always brought to mind some other actor: Henry Fonda could have played his part in *King's Row*, Jimmy Stewart his kindly-sucker role in the Western *Tennessee's Partner*. *Bonzo* is a Cary Grant movie without Cary Grant, *Hellcats* a John Wayne movie without John Wayne. That Reagan could be second choice to such diverse players, who for the most part could never have been cast in place of each other, was a measure of his considerable talent at the old-fashioned acting style of submerging one's personality in a role. But not until he entered politics, ironically, did Reagan truly master the style of acting developed by American movie stars — exaggerated and perpetual self-impersonation. He remained acutely sensitive to the limits of his film career. When asked in 1980 whether he was at all unnerved to be on the same stage as a President, Jimmy Carter, Reagan cracked that he had already been on the same stage as John Wayne. The joke served Reagan's immediate purpose of belittling Carter's virility. But it also carried a rueful undertone of acknowledgment that Reagan the actor never achieved what Reagan the President hoped to: the public's recognition that it was in the presence of an archetype of American manhood.

The chief mystery of Reagan's life is his conversion from liberalism to conservatism, and it happened in Hollywood. There are any number of plausible, conventional explanations of why: he became a wealthy man, with an understandable personal interest in minimizing government spending and taxes, and a direct appreciation of the disincentive effect of high marginal tax rates; he made wealthy conservative friends; he lived in a region bursting with optimism, blessed with profits, in which residence alone made real estate millionaires of many ordinary people, thereby affirming the capitalist contention that money was available to anyone plucky enough to try for it; he grew older, and confronted a changing society with the natural skepticism of his age. Reagan himself would say that he simply became wiser about the world, outgrowing immature and ill-informed beliefs. At times he even insists that he has not changed his principles. Instead, he contends that the New Deal programs he admired were right for a limited set of circumstances, which the country has not come close to reexperiencing, or, of late, he has held that the Franklin Roosevelt he admired was the 1932 campaigner who promised to restore fiscal health through lower government spending, not the Keynesian interventionist that Roosevelt became in office. In fact, Reagan's ardor for the New Deal outlasted Roosevelt himself, and began to ebb only in the late 1940s. Two sets of personal experiences, involving his career and his marriage, seem to have made the difference.

Reagan likes to describe himself as the first former union leader to become President. The Screen Actors Guild is, however, a union that stands most of the principles of unionism on their heads. The essential notion of unions is that work, and workers, are interchangeable; actors prize themselves, and are prized by producers and audiences alike, for their uniqueness. Unions prosper by keeping their members employed; the vast majority of SAG members cannot sustain themselves on their acting earnings. Unions seek to set the prevailing wages in their industries; the most steadily sought-after members of SAG tend to be paid at astronomically higher rates than those negotiated by the union. Above all, unions engage in politics chiefly to advance their members' interests; in Reagan's tenure, SAG became involved in politics to the detriment, in some cases destruction, of members' careers.

Into a life that had already almost accidentally reflected many of the social events of the century, in the late 1940s another trend intruded, the growing split between anti-Communist liberals and pro-Soviet sympathizers on the American left. Reagan, an apparently consistent anti-Communist, found himself involved with various peace groups that turned out to be, in his subsequent judgment, Communist fronts. He discovered that several movie-industry groups he belonged to were influenced, if not dominated, by Communists. Approached by federal agents, and perhaps facing pressure or the threat of exposure, Reagan readily chose to cooperate in tracking down and rooting out Communists in Hollywood's unions. For all his purported liberal tolerance, he saw no hint of a civil-liberties issue in the incipient blacklisting. In his mind, the stakes were high: he believed that the Communists sought to "take over" Hollywood, use the movies to reshape American beliefs, and thus alter the country's fundamental nature. This scenario presupposed awesome power for popular literature, and extreme gullibility and lack of conviction among the American people — although, in fairness, the world was in the immediate aftermath of the age of demagogic dictators. The union infighting was bitter and, in Reagan's view, dangerous; for a time he carried a gun.

Reagan cooperated with the House Un-American Activities Committee, declining to name any Communists himself, on the grounds that he was not one and therefore did not know who others were, but counseling fellow performers to create at least the appearance of complying with the investigation. Yet he remained, in his own mind, a liberal. He supported Hubert Humphrey for the Senate in 1948, and Helen Gahagan Douglas against Richard Nixon in 1950. But over the next few years, his careful attempts to tread the middle ground seemed only to sabotage, not protect, his film career. In all probability, Reagan's star would have declined even if the blacklisting issue had never arisen, or if he had been so indifferent to industry politics as to remain untouched. He was a leading man past forty who had never metamorphosed into a larger-than-life hero or into a distinctive character actor. Television, moreover, had thrown the movie industry into turmoil. But in Reagan's mind, and eventually in that of his wife Nancy, his professional difficulties were the result of sniping by residual Communist elements and betrayal by liberals who should have appreciated Reagan's efforts to "purify" the industry for its own good. Unable to get good parts in films, he was forced to work in television, then a considerable step down in prestige. Decades later, when as President he spoke of the Soviet Communists as people who feel entitled to lie and cheat and commit almost any sin to advance their cause, his constituents probably thought of the invasions of Afghanistan and Czechoslovakia, the crackdowns in Poland and among Soviet Jewish dissidents. But some of the journalists and acquaintances who knew Reagan best assumed that he was recalling, at least as vividly, the Communists he had battled in Hollywood, and the humiliations he had suffered there.

The other factor that shaped Reagan's newfound conservatism was the replacement of Jane Wyman by Nancy Davis as the woman at his side. Reagan had married Wyman in 1940, the year he played George Gipp. Their union ended in 1948, the year of Wyman's Oscar-winning performance in *Johnny Belinda*. There seems little doubt about professional rivalry: eighteen years after the breakup, on the night that Reagan was elected governor of California, Wyman reportedly remarked to friends, "That's Ronnie's Oscar." Both partners said that Wyman was more interested in her career than her husband, and Reagan apparently found that insupportable; his next wife, also an actress, gave up her career to raise children. Reagan seems to have had a deep yearning for masculine dominance. He told his son Ron that the most satisfying experience in life was to come up the front walk at the end of work, knowing that behind the door someone had waited all day for the sound of his footsteps. Wyman's independence and ambition had compounded her frank boredom with politics and, eventually, with Reagan. She complained to movie magazine reporters that he harped obsessively on politics; after the divorce, she also told Hollywood friends that she had tired of having him screen over and over his one critically acclaimed performance, in *King's Row*. Above all, Wyman made no public show of deference. When Reagan married again, it was to a woman who was rarely seen except when clinging to his arm or gazing adoringly, in rapt attention, as he spoke. If the overarching issue for the Moral Majority and the New Right is the change in self-definition of women, with all its implications for the family, sexual mores, and the social structure, then the movement's early, consistent, and emotional identification with Ronald Reagan can be readily understood; unlike any presidential nominee since Adlai Stevenson, Reagan had been publicly rejected and humbled by a wife reaching for her own sense of self, and he had based his personal happiness on finding a woman content with her place.

Nancy Davis's influence on Reagan extended far beyond submission, however. The devoted stepdaughter of an archconservative Chicago surgeon, she introduced Reagan to genially stated right-wing views. Although she makes a point of denying that she or Dr. Loyal Davis had any impact on her husband's conversion, the facts are plain: the year before meeting her, Reagan was still voting for liberal Democrats; the year after meeting her, Reagan cast the first in what would become an unbroken string of votes for Republican presidential candidates, for Dwight Eisenhower in 1952. He was still a Democrat, but only just, in 1960 when he headed Democrats for Nixon; he wrote his candidate a letter linking Kennedy's beliefs to the dogmas of Karl Marx. In 1962, Reagan switched his party affiliation to Republican. It would ill befit the image of the assertive male and his helpmeet to admit her political influence; yet those who know Reagan best say his wife has been the most important figure in his life, and one of his most trusted advisers. Moreover, their romance is interwoven with other factors in Reagan's conversion. He first got to know her when she was in danger of being blacklisted because she had been confused with another actress of the same name. As his spouse she encouraged Reagan to refuse movie offers they considered unsuitable, even when financial pressures were acute, and urged him instead to take a contract with General Electric. He was to be host and actor on the televised "GE Theater," and to make appearances on behalf of the company's conservative management. During the time that he worked for GE, Reagan increasingly articulated the capitalist point of view; his free-market beliefs eventually became so rigorous that the company discontinued his speaking and his show. By that time, Reagan was on the verge of pursuing politics, his longtime avocation, as a career.

Ronald Reagan had as familiar a face and voice as anyone in the Senate when he first came before the American people as a campaigner. Yet in purely political terms he burst from obscurity as suddenly, as dramatically, as Wendell Wilkie or Gary Hart, and with far greater staying power. The kindly young man in the movies, grown into the weather-beaten host of "Death Valley Days" during his last job on TV, was called on in 1964 to make a fund-raising speech for Barry Goldwater. For Reagan, the TV address was the point of no return; he labeled himself not merely as Republican but as outside what was then viewed as the Republican mainstream. With Goldwater plainly headed toward a calamitous defeat, and with the impetus in the party expected to shift back toward the center, Reagan ran the risk of damaging what career he had left in Hollywood, and foreclosing what chances he might have in politics. The speech brought in eight million dollars from true believers and persuaded the moneyed right-wingers who would become Reagan's southern California kitchen cabinet that he had the makings of a marketable candidate.

Two years later, in 1966, he ran for governor, and defeated incumbent Pat Brown in a landslide every bit as heavy as the landslide in which Brown had defeated Richard Nixon four years before. Reagan's million-vote victory was hard to explain, even though it came in an off-year election that was generally disappointing for Democrats, against a governor who after eight years may have worn out his welcome with California's notoriously changeable electorate. Goldwaterite conservatism appeared to have been silenced, perhaps forever, by the 1964 results, and Reagan in 1966 was repeatedly, convincingly portrayed by the Democrats as Goldwater thinly disguised: he was linked, correctly, to the John Birch Society and other extreme-right groups. But in 1966 as in every election thereafter, Reagan demonstrated the gift that made him so valuable to conservatives: his personal manner was so reasonable, so affable, that he did not seem like an extremist. He had the knack of saying the most inflammatory things in the least inflammatory way. Writing in the *National Review* in the wake of Goldwater's fiasco, he had counseled the party, "Time now for the soft sell to prove our radicalism was an optical illusion."

His rise and rise continued: in 1968, the one candidate at the Republican convention who maintained a real chance of taking the nomination away from Richard Nixon was not Nelson Rockefeller, the moderates' hope. Rocky had three strikes against him: as a defector from the 1964 campaign, a temporarily dovish liberal, and an indecisive candidate who had withdrawn from and then reentered the race. The true contender was Reagan. Because Nixon was, by birth if not residence, a Californian, and because Nixon's impulse when pressed was to shift toward the center rather than the right, Reagan had no chance to get onto the national ticket as vice-president in 1968 or 1972. But he won overwhelmingly when he sought reelection in California, and by cunning or intuition or mere accident developed the legislative style that would later suit him in Washington: faced with a Democratic and liberal legislature, he was unable to achieve — and therefore did not have to live with the consequences of — the most extreme elements in his program. Judged strictly on his budget, he was something of a phony conservative. As Gerald Ford pointed out during the 1976 primary season, Reagan had been the biggest taxer and spender in the history of California, just as this purported fiscal conservative would later become the biggest deficit spender in the history of the nation. Reagan proved adroit at proposing unattainable goals, and then, instead of negotiating more modest ones, standing aside and letting someone else take the blame. In some ways, his radicalism was indeed an optical illusion.

He also perfected a rhetorical appeal to the optimism and patriotic pride of the middle class, the people who neither depended on government for their livelihood nor earned and spent so much that they needed to lobby government for tax breaks. The middle class's connection with politics, Reagan discerned, was mostly emotional; they would pay their taxes to a regime that made them feel good about the country, and themselves. California, which has stood in the first wave of many social trends, was at the forefront of campus protest that began with a multiplicity of issues, then focused on the Vietnam war. Reagan campaigned against the dissidents. There was not much else he could do to them in real terms, but he could deny the dignity and legitimacy of their attacks on institutions that the middle class held dear. He also grasped, early and almost intuitively, the position that conservatives could sell to the middle class on civil rights. He did not, as Goldwater had, oppose outright the 1964 civil rights legislation; to do that was to label oneself a racist, to a public that had abruptly, in the wake of the televised beatings of Freedom Marchers in the South, repudiated racism as unacceptable. Instead, Reagan and eventually his whole party argued that citizens of the present could not be expected to bear a burden of guilt for the injustices of the past, and that truly open competition, without affirmative action or other ameliorative programs, was the way to racial harmony. The effect would be to preserve the educational and economic advantages of middle-class whites who could comfortably finance suburban schools over urban blacks who could not, but in the name of the free market.

In only one regard did Reagan threaten his rapport with Middle America: time and again he called for the abolition of Social Security, or for making it voluntary, an effective abolition, or for converting it officially to a welfare program rather than an alleged form of workers' insurance. On more than one occasion, he was forced not only to retract his words but to lie and deny that he had spoken them. Elderly members of the middle class wanted to collect benefits without having to come to terms with the disproportion between what they had paid in taxes and what they received in return; liberals were willing to subsidize the non-needy elderly because their support was of value in keeping the program politically inviolable, whereas a welfare program serving only the destitute elderly would be as vulnerable as any other social service; scholars and journalists generally shared the liberals' political assessment, and would help to attack any proposal to narrow Social Security as something it plainly was not, an attempt at further impoverishment of the poor. The situation galled Reagan; early in his presidency he tried to cut the benefits of those who retired early, and he was rejected virtually unanimously by Congress. Sadder but wiser, in 1984 he proposed to give all recipients, regardless of need, a cost-of-living benefit beyond what might be required by law. The larger moral lesson he learned even sooner: he could simply wish away facts, even his own remarks, when they proved inconvenient, and the public would believe him. As Duke University political scientist James David Barber, a scholar of presidencies, wrote in 1982, "Reagan is the first modern President whose contempt for the facts is treated as a charming idiosyncrasy." It was not that journalists were afraid to assail a popular politician, although they didn't, or that grandfatherly storytellers are granted a leeway that technocrats like Jimmy Carter and legal tacticians like Richard Nixon do not enjoy, although Reagan got it. No, Reagan merely grasped a fact of human nature: that when people are asked to believe something unattractive about someone whom they feel they know and like, they will resist.

———————

By the time Reagan left the California governorship in 1974, after two terms, he had crafted a companion appeal to his nice-guy manner and assertion of middle-class verities: a Russophobia that would surely excite right-wingers and that might reach out to a much broader population, freshly embittered by the fall of U.S. client governments to Communist rebels in Saigon and Phnom Penh. Among Reagan's fellow ideologues, détente was widely misunderstood and deeply mistrusted. During the Nixon and Ford presidencies, conservatives frequently telephoned reporters to say that they had seen secret footage of Henry Kissinger at a KGB training camp, or to adduce some other alleged proof of his treason. To these conservatives, trade and tolerance were not means of reducing tension or bolstering the Western alliance, but the pathway to giving the Soviets the tools and technology to destroy the United States. The painful truth about Vietnam, still not universally acknowledged — that for the first time in its history, the United States had indisputably lost a war — heightened the sense among many ordinary Americans that something had gone wrong. The final sign of the need for vigilance, to Reagan's allies, was the mounting evidence of a Soviet military buildup. To them, this was proof that détente was a subterfuge by the Kremlin in order to disarm the West.

The problem for candidate Reagan, which he did not quite master until after 1976, was how to marry the general fear of the Soviets to the optimism and national confidence that had been the essence of his appeal. John Kennedy had faced exactly the same difficulty in 1960, when he attempted to exploit public anxiety over Sputnik, Soviet and Chinese bellicosity, and Fidel Castro's affiliation with Marxism by exhorting his fellow citizens to "get America moving again." Kennedy solved his political problem by making his appeal generational. The World War II leadership had had its day, he said in effect; it would require a fresh start to protect America in a world whose maps were being remade every day. Thus he disassociated himself from fear and failure, and offered his youth and inexperience as actual advantages. That option was not open to Reagan in 1976: he was the oldest candidate in the field, and if he won he would be older than any first-term President since William Henry Harrison, who died in 1841 after just one month in office. Moreover, Reagan's own party had overseen the management of détente and the collapse of the allies in Southeast Asia. Spiritually battered by Watergate, Americans did not yearn for more disappointment. After eight years of Republican austerity under Richard Nixon and Gerald Ford, the electorate was not primed for a guilt-inducing sermon about the economic ill effects wrought by their own fiscal indulgence.

Furthermore, Reagan's antifeminism, puritanism, and piety were out of step with popular culture, and presumably with the mass audience. The 1976 Oscars would go to the previous year's Establishment-baiting *Network*. The most honored films to be released in 1976, *Annie Hall* and *The Goodbye Girl*, would deal unashamedly with sex outside marriage, with drug use, with general disregard for middle-class norms. On television, the most popular series lionized women who preferred jobs to family, like Mary Tyler Moore's character; liberal youth who talked back to their elders, as on "All in the Family"; a childless psychiatrist (played by Bob Newhart) and a lollipop-sucking cop who epitomized masculinity yet often mocked it (on "Kojak"). In romance novels, in soap operas, in other middlebrow entertainments, the talk was getting steamy. The sexual revolution was in full flood, and fundamentalists had not yet organized to lash back. In every way, 1976 was the wrong year for Reagan, athough he had to attempt what seemed certain to be his last shot at the presidency.

Yet, for all his mischances and shortcomings, Reagan very nearly captured his party's nomination in 1976. Gerald Ford, an incumbent President unstained by scandal, except for the inevitable pardon issued to Richard Nixon, could not be sure of his nomination until the first convention ballot was actually over. Had a handful of circumstances, or the press interpretation of them, gone the other way, Reagan might well have won the nomination. He only narrowly lost the New Hampshire primary, by 1300 votes out of 108,000, but he overwhelmingly lost the expectations game imposed by the press. Polls had shown Reagan a favorite in New Hampshire. Primary polls, however, are notoriously unreliable, and at the time they were taken, the news media, especially the *Boston Globe*, had not yet begun what proved to be generally a drumbeat for Ford. Yet Reagan's New Hampshire defeat was evaluated by the press as an explicit rejection, after due consideration, while the defeats of Eugene McCarthy in 1968 and George McGovern in 1972, by much greater margins, had been interpreted as victories. Had Reagan's performance been treated as it deserved to be, as a clear expression of discontent with Ford, money and help would have flowed to him.

As it was, Reagan went on losing for several weeks and was dismissively written off by the pundits. Then, as primary and caucus action shifted to his strong territories in the South and West, areas that are more truly Republican and that the party can generally expect to carry, he started to win. He did not quite catch up before the convention, and on its eve he tried something that astonished political thinkers with its daring and spirit of compromise. He announced his choice of vice-presidential candidate, and the man he named, Pennsylvania Senator Richard Schweiker, was at least a moderate if not, by the standards of Reagan's hard-core adherents, an utter liberal. The gambit did not succeed, and it could have been a disaster. Some conservatives, remembering Reagan's years as a liberal Democrat, his moderate record (as opposed to his rhetoric) in California, and his repeated evidences of acute ambition, branded him an opportunist and a traitor to the movement. Some invoked the Goldwater dictum that it was better to lose while standing firm than to win while compromising principle. As it turned out, Reagan neither lost nor gained much by his maneuver. But he seemingly sensed some ideological change or personal pliancy in Schweiker; as Reagan's first secretary of health and human services a few years later, the erstwhile liberal comfortably and uncomplainingly oversaw Reagan's cuts in social service programs and his attempts to cut more, then resigned to take a lucrative job in the insurance industry, which indirectly did much of its business with his cabinet department.

Between leaving the governorship and running for President, and again between presidential bids, Reagan kept himself before the public with speeches, a newspaper column, and, most usefully, radio, a medium he would continue to use effectively while in the White House. When he was not an active candidate, radio offered Reagan four significant advantages over other forms of reaching out to an audience: it provided an income of up to hundreds of thousands of dollars, far more than from writing or even speechmaking; it took fullest advantage of Reagan's persuasive skills; it allowed Reagan to tailor his remarks to the already converted, because radio stations segment and target their audiences more than newspapers; and because radio commentaries tend to go unrecorded by the national media, unless they appear on a major network, radio enabled Reagan to express his views full force, serene in the knowledge that he was unlikely to be called to account for his most inflammatory proposals. Biographer Ronnie Dugger contends in *On Reagan* that it was an explicit, official policy of Reagan's 1980 campaign staff to deny reporters access to transcripts of Reagan's radio remarks, in order to avert embarrassing reexamination of his views.

A further advantage of the radio work, the newspaper column, and speeches as an overall enterprise was the employment they provided, not only for Reagan, but also for key staffers; this entrepreneurial politicking thus preserved the core group of a campaign-in-exile. Reagan aide Nancy Reynolds conceded to this writer, then later denied, that the Reagan business furthermore provided a vehicle for supporters to bend the campaign finance laws, by "hiring" Reagan to espouse views shared by owners of newspapers or radio stations, or by leaders of groups who brought him in to speak. Without doubt, Reagan took the fullest possible advantage of the loophole: his last paid radio performance, in 1979, aired on the very day that he announced his candidacy for President. (Reagan's supporters contended that the device, even if dubious, was no worse than, say, Walter Mondale's collecting nearly one million dollars in legal and other fees between 1981 and 1984 for what amounted to no-show jobs, particularly with a Washington law firm that bargained on buying future access and prestige.)

When Reagan announced his candidacy, a little less than a year before the 1980 election and only a few weeks before the Iowa caucuses, most reporters, pundits, and even Republican party officials were ready to write him off. He was a defeated contender, four years older, representing a wing of his party that had captured the nomination only once in history, in the 1964 Goldwater debacle. The voters and especially the activists of the party might be leisure-suited Sunbelt real estate salesmen who thrilled to the Reagan message; but the party's intellectual talent and power still lay with the faction that read the *Wall Street Journal* every day, and Reagan was emphatically not the candidate of the *Journal*. Technically, he was the front-runner: he had by far the largest following in polls. But recent elections had not been kind to front-runners, and it became conventional wisdom, despite Reagan's rousing comeback four years before, that as soon as he lost a single event he would be out of the game. That loss happened in the campaign's first formal contest in Iowa, where George Bush won a solid victory in the caucuses after Reagan, on the advice of his aides, had boycotted an all-comers debate. NBC's Tom Pettet declared flatly on the next morning's "Today Show" that Reagan was through as a presidential candidate. A number of columnists were only a shade more equivocal.

They reckoned without five factors that soon buoyed Reagan back to the top, where he stayed. First was the deep reservoir of affection that Reagan had built up among the conservative faithful by carrying the movement's standard during lean years; so long as he was a viable candidate, they saw no reason to accept substitutes, and competitors from his wing of the party soon fell by the wayside. Meanwhile, the less populous eastern moderate wing of the party remained divided for months between John Anderson and George Bush, so that neither one could mount a fully effective challenge to Reagan.

Second was the unpredictable depth and intensity of the public rage provoked by the hostage-taking in Iran and the invasion of Afghanistan; hostage-taking from the *Pueblo* a dozen years before had caused barely a ripple of sentiment, and an earlier, much more consequential Soviet intervention in Afghanistan, in which a puppet regime was first installed, had prompted only a fraction of the feeling that followed the Soviets' later mop-up. President Carter, by goading the American people on both of these issues, did Reagan's work. Carter created the climate of fear, lacking in 1976, that gave force to Reagan's tub-thumping speeches and ominous commercials showing tanks rolling through Moscow's Red Square.

Third was Carter's unwillingness or inability to engineer at least an apparent economic recovery in time for his reelection effort. Reagan's homiletic claims that fiscal overindulgence was sowing the seeds of ruin, and that social spending must be sharply reduced, sounded far more plausible in 1980, while home mortgage interest rates were surging toward 15 percent and business loan rates toward 20 percent, than they had in the relative prosperity of 1976.

Fourth was the public's deep dissatisfaction with Carter, a pensive and petulant man who faced mounting problems with cumulative dismay. Liberals defected to Edward Kennedy; the Iranian government proved intractable, and a military rescue mission to Tehran failed; his brother Billy's financial woes led to highly improper relations with the totalitarian government of Libya. Through it all, Carter conveyed no ease, no flexibility. When he concluded, in the year before the election, that his political career was in trouble, he gave a speech to the American people in which he blamed his own downfall on a national malaise of spirit. The spreading grin that became his trademark in 1976 was rarely to be seen, and when it appeared as he campaigned for reelection, it looked like a nervous tic.

Fifth was the personal charm of Reagan himself: his apparently spontaneous masculinity, his comfort with his identity, his unboastful but unyielding self-confidence. He seemed a leader who would not frighten the American people, because he would not himself be afraid. He would not give up on problems, because he would not decide they were unsolvable. He said what much of the nation felt but could not articulate: that optimists may not always succeed, but that pessimists never do, because pessimists judge that a grand effort is not worth undertaking. Above all, Reagan projected the belief that political leadership is a matter of spirit, not of legislative agendas. Time and again he invoked the name of Franklin Roosevelt, a man who remained anathema to conservative Republicans; the FDR Reagan had in mind was not the socialistic reformer, but the reassuring father figure of the Fireside Chats. Reagan offered himself as the sort of leader whom people want at perilous, and perhaps at all, points in history: an inspiration, a poet laureate, a protector. His election in 1980 seems, in retrospect at least, to have been almost automatic.

Yet along with Reagan's strengths were vulnerabilities that persisted throughout his first term. Even more than other Republicans, Reagan was mistrusted by blacks, and his aides reacted by impetuously dismissing the importance of the black vote. Publicly, Republicans talked of the need for the party to reach out to blacks; privately, they gloated that every registration of a black voter would be more than offset by registration of white racists alarmed by the prospect of social change. In making the party a haven for bigots, Republicans hoped to turn the solidly Democratic South of old into an impregnably Republican South. The risk was that the party would be damned for intolerance, and would alienate otherwise sympathetic moderates.

Reagan was also disliked by an even larger group, new-consciousness women. Many avoided the labels "feminist" or "liberated," but the majority of American women were employed — even a majority of mothers were employed. The mythology of satisfaction through submission no longer had much appeal for them. They wanted at least the option of equal treatment. The majority of women supported the right to choose an abortion, and resented the Reagan administration's efforts to pass a constitutional ban on it. When linked with their potential allies — union members, threatened public employees, vulnerable beneficiaries of welfare programs and worried recipients of Social Security — these disaffected blacks and women could conceivably add up to a sizable opposition. Yet against most of these groups, even against women seeking affirmative action, Reagan could employ the scornful rhetoric that defined them as self-seeking "special interest" lobbies. At his shrewdest and most persuasive, Reagan could make an audience feel that there was something unpatriotic in people's seeking aid and comfort from their government.

Reagan also inspired mistrust among many ordinary Americans by endorsing the ambitions for spiritual conquest of the resurgent religious right. Contemporary America was in the main a secular society. The vast majority of citizens attended some Christian church at least occasionally, and expressed some sort of belief in God. But they did not guide their lives by the Good Book, nor hang on the words of some electronic evangelist. The theologically inert majority was willing to tolerate the perfervid excesses of the believers, so long as the tolerance was returned. But the Christian extremists felt obliged to change the society around them, in some cases by force, in order to make the behavior of others conform to their own convictions about what was right. This passion particularly worried groups who were, or feared they would become, targets: Jews, atheists and agnostics, homosexuals, and the growing numbers of middle-class couples living without benefit of clergy in what used to be called sin. Even people whose own lives would pass muster were reluctant to empower the ultra-Christians, for fear that debate about relatively innocuous and private matters, such as sex, would overwhelm the necessary national debate on issues of state.

Like any incumbent President, Reagan faced other potential embarrassments. His adopted son, Michael, had attempted to cash in on the family name by hiring himself out as a salesman and then offering goods to military PX stores, explicitly trading on his White House connection. The incident, which was said variously to have hurt or infuriated Reagan, resulted in a family feud that lasted three years. The President's own long life provided ample fodder for critics. Recurrent rumors, denied by his aides, held that in the past Reagan had regularly consulted an astrologer and heeded his advice. Reagan had undeniably signed in the 1940s a real estate covenant that specified an area was to remain for whites only. Reagan's crony Alfred Bloomingdale, the husband of one of Nancy Reagan's closest friends, was accused after his death of keeping a mistress to indulge his "Marquis de Sade complex." Another Reagan friend, Charles Wick, who had been appointed to head the United States Information Agency, proved to have a lamentable propensity for secretly taping telephone calls and for pulling rank in a manner far beyond the modest status of his post. Indeed, almost all of Reagan's closest personal associates displayed questionable judgment, from Attorney General William French Smith's involvement in a dubious tax shelter to public-relations aide Michael Deaver's attempt to capitalize on his White House connection by writing a diet book. Journalists referred widely to the administration's "sleaze factor."

The biggest, most nettlesome problem was that much of the American public feared that Reagan might be a trigger-happy warmonger. Like Goldwater, Reagan presented himself not merely as a Westerner but as a Westerner on horseback — in short, a cowboy. His two-fisted approach to foreign policy brought to mind the slogans from Western movies: "Shoot first and ask questions later," "Ten dead Indians for every dead white man," "The only good Indian is a dead Indian." That swaggering rhetoric had provided a certain satisfaction to cinema audiences who knew that the West was already won, but it was considerably less reassuring as a set of precepts for dealing with a Soviet military machine of proven skill in an age of Mutually Assured Destruction through nuclear weaponry. Reagan readily embraced the use of force. He opposed a military draft, not least because it would lead to disruptive protest, but he had no hesitation in committing the lives of the poor blacks and whites who joined the armed services for lack of any alternative employment. Above all, Reagan seemed not to want to tolerate the very existence of the Soviet Union. He sounded determined to make it go away. And however alluring that prospect might be to most Americans, they rejected it as unrealistic and provocative. The enduring perception of Reagan as warlike was retriggered every time he spoke of the Soviets as an "evil empire" or joked, however broadly, about confrontation. A subtler danger of the vision of Reagan as belligerent was that it alone seemed capable of igniting the latent issue of his age. Ordinarily Reagan was immune to the doubts that would otherwise be raised about the judgment and competence of a man past seventy. Yet if, on the most urgent matters, he was seen as inflexible, cantankerous, even irresponsible, then questions about his fitness would cascade forth from reporters and the public.

If Presidents are to be judged by their first hundred days, Ronald Reagan was in general a failure but with one shining symbolic success. The opening weeks of his administration were chaotic and embarrassing. The "sleaze factor" that would come to bedevil the first term was apparent even before Reagan took office. Frank Sinatra, an unabashed associate of gangsters, played a major role in the inaugural celebrations. Jackie Presser, a Teamster official who was already suspect and who would later face formal inquiry, served on the transition team. Raymond Donovan, a former construction executive and key Reagan fund-raiser, was confirmed for office without a full investigation; as was already being hinted around Washington, a more thorough probe would have turned up myriad questions that would have deterred any prudent President from appointing him and that ultimately led to his indictment.

Moreover, despite Reagan's vows of an antidétente foreign policy, his secretary of state, Alexander Haig, was a protégé of Henry Kissinger, and his secretary of defense, Caspar Weinberger, was another veteran of the Nixon and Ford administrations. Indeed, beyond his entourage of old buddies, Reagan brought surprisingly few members of his faction into high places in government. Bickering had started almost immediately among the various cliques on Reagan's staff, some of them ideologically aligned, some just reaching for power. Looming over these minor failings, and reinforcing the notion that Reagan the officeholder would be considerably less decisive than Reagan the candidate, was the growing realization that it was proving impossible to fulfill simultaneously Reagan's tripartite pledge to cut personal income taxes, vastly increase defense spending, and balance the federal budget — except perhaps in the Cloudcuckooland of supply-side economics.

Then came a drifter, like Reagan from the West, like Reagan with his personal vision of America shaped by the movies, like Reagan prepared to be bold. Their paths crossed on the day that raised Reagan's presidency to almost saintly proportions, and that launched, if it did not ensure, Reagan's efforts toward reelection. As the President approached his waiting limousine after a speech to a convention of the real estate and construction industries, with a little knot of aides, reporters, and security men alongside him, a pudgy, moon-faced young man stepped forward from the roped-off press section and fired a gun. Four men were hit; press secretary James Brady, a policeman, and a Secret Service man were left on the ground, seriously but not mortally wounded; Reagan, apparently unhurt, was pushed into the car and taken off, at first for the White House, then abruptly in midroute for a hospital. Once again the bulletin spread: a President had been shot.

———⟨———

In politics, there is one gift that outshines all others, and that is the gift of luck. Ronald Reagan had been generally lucky through life. On the day he was shot, and survived with a smile, he was seen by all the world to be a lucky man. For a nation that had endured nearly two decades of unremitting disappointments and bad news, from the Marxist affiliations of Fidel Castro through the era of assassinations to the dual defeats of Vietnam and Watergate, and then the humiliating Iran hostage crisis, what better symbol of national renewal could there be than an assassination victim who comes through unscathed — a man who faces death with a hearty joke, and wins the confrontation? Reagan arrived at the George Washington University medical center with a bullet in his chest. He joshed to the doctors that he hoped they were all Republicans. When his ashen, terrified wife arrived, he quoted to her a witticism from his adolescence, Jack Dempsey's line to his spouse after a disastrous day in the boxing ring: "Sorry, honey, I forgot to duck." Even on the operating table, he was filled with concern for the men who had been shot with him. On March 30, 1981, Ronald Reagan became for his nation more than the genial grandfather with the stern principles whom they had elected. He acquired the indomitable image of manliness that he had always aspired to — he became another John Wayne.

A contributing factor to Reagan's apparent heroism, surely, was that he had little idea how close he came to death. The bullet that struck him may have hit as he was already being thrust into his car. Had his would-be assassin, John Hinckley, aimed better or fired sooner, the outcome at such close range would likely have been fatal. Even the bullet Hinckley fired, had its trajectory been slightly different, might have hit Reagan's spine, or his heart, which it missed by three inches. Hinckley used a bullet that was supposed to explode and scatter inside the victim's body, causing much more internal damage; but this particular bullet did not explode. Had Reagan not reached a hospital so quickly, he would have been endangered by internal hemorrhaging. Some of the team who worked on him later estimated that even so, he came within ten to fifteen minutes of bleeding to death, or of choking on his own blood. But the extent of Reagan's peril did not become public that afternoon, or indeed for several days. The closest that the American people were brought to that somber story was an erroneous, and quickly corrected, bulletin by Chris Wallace of NBC that the President had undergone open-heart surgery. (What the doctors said was that Reagan had been subjected to "open-chest" surgery. Reporters also announced, as a result of confusion about the meaning of White House statements, that press secretary Brady had been killed, when in fact he survived to make a substantial recovery from brain injuries. The journalists later acknowledged privately that they had been embarrassed by their very first bulletins, which said that Reagan had not been shot at all. Thus they were overeager to redeem themselves by ferreting out bad news, whether real or exaggerated.)

The shooting, or at least its happy aftermath, buoyed the nation's morale and won Reagan a second honeymoon with the Congress, the press, and the citizenry. The next six months brought seemingly ceaseless victory. There were, to be sure, fleeting setbacks: Reagan was forced to withdraw the appointment of Ernest Lefever as a human rights aide, in large part because while ostensibly running a research institute he had shilled for Nestlé in defense of an infant formula that was dubiously adapted to use in the Third World; CIA Director Bill Casey became embroiled in one of the worst of an all-but-endless series of controversies that marked his tenure, this time over the selection, and eventual departure, of a wheeler-dealer named Max Hugel as deputy chief of the intelligence agency; Secretary of State Haig, who had appeared to engage in an unseemly public power squabble with cabinet peers on the day Reagan was shot, kept clashing with White House aides over pointless items of protocol. But Reagan won passage of his budget cuts. He won passage of his tax cuts. He won a seemingly hopeless vote to confirm sale of AWACs computerized planes to the Saudi Arabian government, over the strident opposition of Israel and its sympathizers, and of some Mideast analysts who questioned the long-term stability of the Saudi royal family's regime. Some Democratic congressmen, sensing that there might be a genuine political revolution under way, just as Reagan supporters claimed, either jumped parties, or flirted openly with the idea, or at the least called themselves Boll Weevils and aligned with the Republican voting bloc. Some leading Democratic party elders, and more than a few journalists, began to speculate that the Democrats had lost control of their last vestige of national authority, their majority in the House. *Time*, in a signed analysis by Washington bureau chief Robert Ajemian, speculated that Reagan's maneuvering had brought to an effective end the long and cunning career of House Speaker Tip O'Neill.

Reagan's mastery over Congress proved temporary, and the significance of his budget cuts was as much apparent as real. To be sure, Reagan's proposals reduced the help available to those at the economic margin, mostly the working poor. By the fall of 1982, 750,000 children had been dropped from eligibility for school lunches; 660,000 children had been dropped from Medicaid; 1,000,000 people had lost their food-stamp benefits outright and another 20,000,000 had had them reduced. But as Reagan argued, the "social safety net" stayed in place; some former beneficiaries may have been disheartened, even devastated, but all the major social welfare programs survived. As a result, the savings from these and other reductions — mostly achieved through tightening eligibility requirements — were modest. Reagan was right when he said, "We haven't thrown anyone out in the snow to die." He was wrong when he claimed to have made much headway on welfare spending. In fact, as the gap between his proposed cuts and the size of the annual deficit widened, Reagan's aides occasionally adopted the comic-opera accounting procedure of crediting themselves with the full potential savings from a reduction for each time they had proposed it — if it had been turned down three straight years, they in effect tripled its value.

Reagan's income-tax cuts proved more tangible and enduring, despite

Democratic vows to diminish or delay them. For most workers, the cuts amounted to more than the simultaneous increase in Social Security taxes and thus had a measurable effect in increasing take-home pay. It did not hurt politically that as one moved up the income scale — and thus became more likely both to be Republican and to vote — the percentage-based cuts were worth more. By the time Reagan sought reelection, the tax reductions were fully serving the political purpose that he had intended: they were something the public had wanted, and received, that he could accuse the Democrats of trying to take away.

Of all Reagan's victories in his first year, however, perhaps the most significant politically was one of only marginal economic consequence, one that was barely related to incalculable speculative numbers or incomprehensible legislative details. The action that most demonstrated to the public that Reagan was a hang-tough guy, and to the political cognoscenti that he was a Napoleon of public relations, was his destruction of PATCO, the Professional Air Traffic Controllers Organization. The union went into its confrontation with Reagan charged up with self-righteousness and confident of victory, and it walked out skinned and cleaned; even months later, as they lobbied fruitlessly to get their jobs back, the controllers seemed not to have grasped what had happened to them.

The confrontation had been in the making for months, indeed years. The controllers epitomized, perhaps more than any other union except the Teamsters, the confusion among well-paid but nonprofessional workers about whether they belong to the working or the middle class. Like the Teamsters, PATCO had endorsed Reagan in 1980. The union's members, trained mostly in the military or other publicly funded programs, were Middle American in outlook and comfortably suburban in income. Starting pay was more than $20,000; top pay, for senior employees at big airports, was just shy of $50,000, and overtime was not hard to come by. In that context, most Americans regarded the union's demands as ridiculous: an across-the-board raise of $10,000, plus twice-per-year cost-of-living raises at 150 percent of the actual rate of inflation; a 20 percent cut in working hours to a four-day week; earlier retirement, at a higher percentage of base pay, than any other federal civil servants.

The controllers had several persuasive arguments to make, but were impelled as well by feelings of blue-collar resentment and envy that were persuasive only to them. They performed a job that most Americans considered uncommonly demanding; scholarly studies showed that controllers had more frequent ulcers and stomach disorders, heartbeat irregularities, and other stress-related ailments. If they erred for as little as five seconds, hundreds of lives could be lost. Like many public employees, they believed that they were worth far more than they were paid, but that they were held down economically because their jobs existed only in the government sector. Pilots, who handled only one plane rather than dozens, were often paid at least three times as much. Another major factor in stimulating the aggressive self-importance of the controllers was the belief that they were indispensable to the nation's system of air service. It was inconceivable to them that the government could operate the air traffic stations for any significant length of time without them, let alone replace them if they walked out en masse. All of these emotional points were made over and over by the union's president, Robert Poli, a burly, bearded, condescending, and almost scornful spokesman who would soon become a perfect media foil for Reagan.

The walkout was delayed repeatedly, from May to August, but neither side budged on its demands. Finally, on August 3, Poli and PATCO were ready. Reagan had wanted to warn the controllers that they would be fired even before they struck, but he was persuaded by aides to wait, so that he would not seem abusive and belligerent. The stakes were nearly as high for the President as for the union, and Reagan's political intuition faced one of its most delicate tests. In his 1980 campaign, Reagan made much of the fact that he was the first former national president of a union to be nominated to occupy the White House. Reagan's ability to capture about two-fifths of union households was decisive in getting him elected in 1980, and his party would need those voters again. Moreover, if an ideologically motivated showdown with PATCO shut down or seriously curtailed the nation's air service, the damage to business travel and sales (not to mention the hazards for the financially precarious airlines themselves) would suggest to even conservative executives that Reagan might be dangerously impractical. The general public, including people who counted on air service for long-planned vacations and sudden family emergencies, would judge Reagan's response as much by its fairness as by its toughness.

Set against these risks in pursuing the hard line were some substantial potential rewards. Foremost was the opportunity to invoke a patriotic imperative. As a law-and-order partisan, Reagan felt sure he could make a case strictly on the importance of enforcement. But lashing out at the controllers would serve his larger agenda in at least three ways. First, the highly paid controllers were a perfect symbol of the bigness and supposed inefficiency that Reagan wanted to root out of the federal government. Second, if they could be replaced by willing and equally effective workers who would do the job for less money, it would bear out the conservative arguments that wages were artificially high. Third, the attempt by the controllers to achieve higher pay through an extortionate and illegal strike was only an exaggerated version of the increasingly unpopular determination of local, county, and state employee unions, including teachers, police, and firefighters, to set their pay through arbitration rather than publicly ratified legislative or municipal fiat — thus taking out of the voters' hands perhaps the most significant aspect of government, its cost. In that sense, the standoff with PATCO contained the quintessence of Reaganism.

When Poli led his union out, Reagan opted, instinctively and as it turned out unerringly, for the hard line. With the network cameras recording the night's lead story as he read a statement in the Rose Garden, Reagan recalled that he had spearheaded a strike by the Screen Actors Guild, in the private sector, in 1959, but he read aloud the no-strike pledge that all federal employees must sign. He added, "They are in violation of the law, and if they do not report for work within forty-eight hours, they have forfeited their jobs and will be terminated." Poli told the controllers that Reagan was bluffing, and journalists, who believed the same thing, hinted as much to their readers and viewers. For Reagan, this media skepticism was a blessing. His absolutist action might have been condemned as unrealistic and unjust if reporters had believed he meant it. But by the time the public began to realize that Reagan had no intention of reinstating more than eleven thousand strikers, the nation's air system was already functioning at close to normal levels. Sounding sorrowful while Poli was defiant, principled while Poli appeared greedy, wronged while Poli seemed shameless, Reagan won it all. For the AFL–CIO, which PATCO spurned when help was offered, and which then spurned PATCO when help was needed, the realization came embarrassingly late that Reagan had made fools of the whole labor movement, and that in the next election the unions would have to try to recoup, at whatever peril.

While Reagan was winning on front after front, reporters who covered the White House were frustrated in their attempts to do what they regarded as their job: cut his grandiose figure down to human terms. The closest they could seem to come was to take potshots at Reagan's age: it was a genuine matter of debate whether Reagan was tinting his hair (a *Time* cover on Reaganomics in September of 1981 was among the first major pictures to show Reagan's mane streaked with white); there were repeated efforts to call attention to his deafness; stories cropped up sporadically, more often in private than in print, about Reagan's short hours or somewhat distant managerial style or his tendency to lapse into movie-industry reminiscence of questionable relevance to the matter at hand. It became standard to refer to Reagan as being in his "anecdotage." Only once did his purported noninvolvement become a genuine media issue, however: when U.S. pilots shot down Libyan jets that were straying over U.S. military exercises with seemingly menacing intent, aide Edwin Meese III acknowledged that he let Reagan sleep rather than wake him to report an incident, minor in itself, that could have prompted Libya's erratic dictator Muammar al-Qaddafi into war. The incident touched off snide columns and editorial cartoons. But inasmuch as there was nothing obvious that a sleeping Reagan had left undone, the matter was dropped by the press.

One problem reporters had in piercing the Reagan team's veil was that the public seemed genuinely weary of hating its leaders, and eager to like Reagan for as long as possible. Another was that many of the principal White House correspondents had no special ties to the Reagan camp: unlike previous elections, 1980 had not buoyed to the top a large group of journalists who had covered the successful challenger. Although the *Washington Post* showcased its knowing coverage by Reagan biographer Lou Cannon, the majority of big-league news organizations, from the three major networks to the *New York Times* and *Boston Globe*, held over their old White House correspondents from the Carter years.

Although the Reagan staff was riven by factionalism from the beginning, primarily but not exclusively between right-wing ideologues and more moderate pragmatists, it was some months before the conflict and the alignments became apparent to most reporters. Reagan himself, so prone to error and so disarmingly indifferent to his fluffs (some of them willfully repeated, when a misstatement helped make a point), remained an almost unglimpsed figure for White House reporters. News conferences were as infrequent as in the Watergate days, interviews all but unheard of. The chief complaint, especially among television reporters, was that the Reagan team had mastered the art of determining what the networks' footage and "sound bites" would be, and thereby virtually controlled the public's perception of what was going on, however forceful the contrary judgments that a reporter might try to interpose.

Fittingly, if embarrassingly to the White House press corps, it was a print reporter — and not one permanently on the presidential body watch, as ghoulish reporters refer to their task — who broke open the biggest, and most curious, story about the Reagan administration: the cynicism and candor of the economic and budget process directed by the administration's one acknowledged wonder boy, David Stockman. As director of the Office of Management and Budget, Stockman held cabinet rank; as architect of at least the budgetary side of Reaganomics, Stockman was de facto the domestic policy czar, and perhaps the most influential figure short of Reagan himself; as the focus of a long-researched article for the *Atlantic Monthly* by William Greider, then national editor of the *Washington Post*, Stockman was the most forthcoming and revelatory exponent of Reagan's decision-making to emerge during the entire first term. Item: the elaborate rationale for the tax package was simply a cover for getting money into the hands of the rich, at minimum political cost to the administration and Congress. Item: the prevailing economic theory in the administration depended on who was winning that day, and the economic package as a whole had no coherence. Item: Stockman's own widely praised estimates were expedient and all but imaginary.

What was most breathtaking was Stockman's admission that, by its own stated goal of balancing the budget, Reaganomics was a certain failure, and the process by which it was being carried forward was one of horse-trading, guesswork, and sleight of hand. Said Stockman: "None of us really understands what's going on with all these numbers. . . . There was less there than met the eye." It was reminiscent of the moment when Toto pulls aside the curtain to reveal the wheezing middle-aged man working the controls of the big, imposing balloon that appears to be the Wizard of Oz; there was no omniscience, indeed no plan, hardly even any Reaganomics, just a sonorous bag of wind. When the December issue of the *Atlantic* reached a stunned press corps, they knew they had a story. But the President and his men did something unpredictable, even strange, that soon had the effect of making the story virtually disappear.

In any other administration, Stockman would almost surely have been fired, either to punish disloyalty, or to reprimand stupidity, or to disavow the awkward truths he had revealed. Instead, the young ex-congressman, whose slick manipulation of the congressional budget process and its economic projection devices had come to seem invaluable, was simply taken to see the boss for what was later described by both parties as a visit to the "woodshed." Then he was allowed to stay on at his job. As with the decision to fire the air traffic controllers, Reagan's decision seemed unbelievable. Again as with PATCO, aides floated repeated rumors that at some unspecified point weeks or months off, the decision would be reversed: Stockman would depart after Christmas, then after the next budget, then after midterm elections. But after election day in 1984 he was still by the President's side. By this act of seemingly inconclusive clemency, Reagan avoided either losing his useful assistant or having to admit that what

Greider published was true. By making no definitive statements, and by allowing hints of various outcomes to continue to circulate, Reagan deactivated tension and escaped facing the tattoo of reporters' questions. Reagan was so self-confident that he did not feel obliged to purge Stockman for having caused embarrassment. But he was also shrewd in dealing with reporters: if he did not make a major issue of Stockman's remarks, then the press, too, would sooner or later have to drop its pursuit, or appear to be sustaining a purely media-generated crisis.

The second year of a presidential term is usually a letdown, both for the incumbent, who typically finds Congress increasingly fractious, and for the public, who subside from euphoric belief in a new leader's limitless possibilities to the resigned recognition that he is, after all, just another politician. For Reagan, the spiral downward was particularly steep and bumpy. Apparently as a direct consequence of his economic policies, the nation went through the worst unemployment since the Depression. The jobless rate pushed steadily closer to the explosive level of 10 percent. The news media played the story harder than any other event. Reagan and his aides insisted that the unemployment was everyone else's fault: Democrats and moderate Republicans, for permitting two decades of deficit spending by government and inflationary, anticompetitive concessions to labor; the Federal Reserve system, for clamping down on the money supply to reduce interest rates; corporate management, for failing to invest in research, to redirect production, or to forecast consumer needs — such as smaller, fuel-efficient automobiles to rival European and Japanese import models. But voters, and the news organizations that inform them, traditionally hold Presidents responsible for the state of the economy, whatever the facts may be. *Time* and *Newsweek* carried cover stories about unemployment: *Newsweek* ran page after page of photographs of scruffy children and down-and-outers, poor all their lives, whom Reagan was blamed for having further impoverished. Newspapers ran the monthly unemployment statistics on the front page, and only rarely emphasized the corollary that employment, too, was at record levels; the economy was expanding, but not fast enough to absorb new entrants ranging from the large Baby Boom generational cohort to increasing numbers of married women seeking a second income for their households. By far the most injurious, politically, were the three major networks, ABC, NBC, and CBS, which filled TV screens with familiar yet powerful images: the supermarket line, accompanied by charts to show the steady rise of prices; the smokeless smokestack of a shut-down factory; the seemingly endless throng of plaintive applicants whenever an employer advertised openings; the hardened face of some formerly well-paid laborer, most often a United Auto Workers member, now consigned to some new trade at a wage less than half the old one.

Some reports reflected the view of conservative economists that the old world was changing, and that workers who hoped to prosper in the new one needed retraining, not self-pity. But most stories did not even touch on the general issue of industrial policy, and some that did also pointed out that the supposed high-tech future seemed to replace lucrative union jobs with low-skilled, low-paid, nonunion jobs, many of them exported by American companies to Latin America or Asia. The most antagonistic major news organization was CBS, which had challenged the morality of Reagan's approach almost from its outset, most notably in a Bill Moyers documentary about the cutoff of federal benefits from selected recipients, "People Like Us." CBS was the most skeptical of the networks about the idea of a new, postindustrial economy, the most gloomy about unemployment and suffering. ABC was the most receptive to the Reagan team's view. NBC tended only to announce the latest government statistics, not to analyze and challenge them.

The emphasis on unemployment heightened in print and on all three networks as the 1982 midterm congressional elections approached. Journalists seemingly had concluded that individual suffering was the inevitable price of the sort of economic cleanup that Reagan had proposed, and that if Reagan were to be judged by the American people through the midterm vote, then the choice should be seen at its starkest. The underlying assumption, that the midterm elections could serve as a clear-cut referendum on Reaganism, was adopted by all three networks and the vast majority of print pundits.

Yet the premise was questionable at best. Reagan's name would not appear on any ballot. As Speaker Tip O'Neill had long counseled young House candidates, "All politics is local." The outcome in any individual district was less likely to reflect feelings about the President than judgments about whether an incumbent had accumulated seniority too valuable to lose or instead had reached the end of his effectiveness; whether he had been attentive to his constituents or instead seemed preoccupied with the power plays in Washington. In general, the party that occupies the White House almost always loses congressional seats at midterm. The size of its losses may have something to do with the popularity and performance of the President. But the results are clouded by other factors: how many seats in each house belonging to each party are being opened through death or retirement or an incumbent's defeat in a primary; how many of each party's incumbents are still in their first term, or are representing districts that putatively belong to the opposition party; how many districts have been redrawn, and by legislators of what party; how far out of the norm the results were two years before — how many seats would change hands just to restore the traditional status quo. Political journalists were not, of course, unaware of these considerations. But they had been primed to look for meaning.

On election night in 1980, most reporters had been flummoxed by the magnitude of the Republican victory. Prudent analysts had been describing that presidential race as too close to call, and almost no one seriously entertained the possibility of a major Republican swing in congressional races. But Reagan carried forty-four states. Moreover, in the Senate races, in which there was no John Anderson to draw off moderate votes and only a residue of whatever animus voters felt toward Jimmy Carter, the GOP captured twelve seats to win control of that body for the first time in twenty-six years. In the House, the Republicans narrowed the Democratic majority to its lowest total since Dwight Eisenhower's administration. The results were consistent and comprehensible: a landslide, and perhaps, in the belated conventional wisdom, a "transforming election," the kind that fundamentally alters the alignment of the two parties with the public.

It has often been said of journalists, as it was first said of generals in the French army, that they are always fighting the last battle. They do not discern the dynamic of an election as it is taking place; they recall instead the lesson taught by the previous election, and apply it to the current one. On the night of the 1982 midterm elections, that description seemed perhaps more apt than ever. The interpretive tone for all journalists was set, as usual on modern election nights, by the three major networks, which not only provide the public with its first information, but accumulate far more detailed data than other news-gathering institutions.

To explain what was happening on election night in 1982, as in years before and since, the networks relied heavily on "exit polls." By approaching voters as they left their balloting places and asking them both whom they chose and what demographic categories they fit, researchers were able to assemble a colorful and to some extent reliable snapshot of the nation's overall sentiment. But there were risks: people who vote early in the day, when exit polls are conducted, are not absolutely representative of all voters, so that the networks' analysts had to guess at the size and nature of the total turnout and then weigh some responses more heavily than others; certain groups of voters, notably older and more conservative ones, have a greater tendency to refuse to participate in an exit poll, or even to lie when surveyed, which adds to the possibility of error; in assessing the attitude of particular segments of society, exit polls are especially dicey, because the smaller the subgroup being sampled, the greater the statistical margin of error; and no poll or group of polls is absolutely trustworthy, as was demonstrated in 1982 when all three networks misforecast the same congressional race in Indiana.

Nonetheless, the network spokesmen plunged into analysis. For the viewer of Dan Rather on CBS, Roger Mudd and Tom Brokaw on NBC, and Frank Reynolds, Ted Koppel, and David Brinkley on ABC, the night sounded like six anchors in search of an author. They all seemed sure that somewhere near at hand there was a script, rich in subtext and implication, some overarching and unifying pattern to the behavior of the voters. ABC, dominated by Brinkley's I've-seen-it-all-before weariness of manner, was the least assertive in describing the results, and ended up, by accident, being rightly equivocal. NBC in general presented the results as cautionary for Reagan. His White House aides' jargon in that period had featured variants of "stay the course," as a metaphor for ideological obduracy. Mudd divined that the message instead was, if not to reverse the course, at least to adjust the direction and reduce the speed. CBS was again the most openly critical of the networks — so much so that White House communications chief David Gergen called correspondent Lesley Stahl while the broadcast was in progress to protest its biased tone. Later, top CBS officials acknowledged privately that there was a fair basis for the complaints. But not all of them were penitent. Commentator Bill Moyers said on election night, and again the next day, that the outcome had been a "disaster" for the Republicans, and he feistily held to that view.

Numerically, the final tallies suggested only that, in most races, Reagan was at best a secondary factor. In the Senate, which the Republicans had feared they might lose to a Democratic majority and in which the GOP leadership had virtually conceded the loss of a couple of seats, there was no change — in effect, a Republican triumph. But in the House, the Republicans lost enough seats of party members and Democratic sympathizers that O'Neill and his colleagues could reassert control. That did not matter much. The Democrats proved only marginally more able to impose their will in consultation with the Senate during Reagan's third and fourth years than during the second. And as it turned out, the economic turmoil on which the news media had lavished so much time, and described as the basis for judging Reagan, had all but disappeared from the political debate by election day in 1984. Inflation and interest rates were moderate and holding steady by then. Unemployment had fallen. Gloom had been dispelled and there were measurable signs of optimism — a renewed market for bigger American-made automobiles, an increase in the square footage of the average newly built house. The public's concern would therefore shift from prosperity to somewhat less tangible issues of fairness, pluralism, and peace. And inevitably, as the 1984 election neared, there would be renewed discussion, in the media if not among voters, about who Reagan was: the most analyzed man in America would be assessed again.

The most perplexing question about Reagan was his seemingly elusive character. For all that people felt they could like and trust in him, they agreed he was extremely difficult to get to know. One view was that he was the ultimate cynic, marketing whatever beliefs would sell: he was willfully playing on nativist bigotry, nostalgia for a simpler morality, and the almost theological nationalism of his core constituency on the right, but neither sharing nor caring about such sentiments. He would talk about such questions as opposing abortion and busing, restoring school prayer and churchly influence in politics — but he would talk only in election years, and take meaningful action never. Once in office for a second term, this theory held, he would do what he had done during his first: concentrate on imposing a traditional Republican economic and foreign policy, rather than spend his energies or political capital on inconsequential "social issues."

Proponents of this theory noted that, despite Reagan's often inflammatory public utterances, he had a history of personal tolerance — he was a divorced man whose associates included people given to various sexual peccadilloes, he had fired some aides when he was governor on suspicion of homosexuality but had zealously guarded their privacy by refusing to give names, he had said he took no interest in inquiring into any adult's private sexual behavior, and as governor he signed bills legalizing abortion and no-fault divorce. As Democrats looked for ways to diminish his popularity, they labeled Reagan a "hypocrite." Their litany of proofs: he called for a national return to godliness, but attended church only a handful of times as President, and never arranged to have formal services conducted in the White House; he extolled the values of "family," but rarely saw his grandchildren and clashed publicly with all four of his offspring; he voiced an almost puritanical morality, but he and his wife had been known for vigorous romantic appetites before meeting each other, they gave birth to a normal-sized infant less than seven months after they were married, and their two children both had lived with partners before marriage. All this evidence made a convincing case for a less pious and more cunning Reagan, and to his political opponents, a less admirable but also less dangerous one. If he were not a theological zealot, he would not be likely to press divisive proposals in search of his vision of a more moral America. Indeed, whenever his remarks to some ardent Christian group would set off protest in the larger, secular world, Reagan would readily back down. The message to true believers was that he was one of them; to the rest of society, that he had merely exaggerated or misspoken or been misunderstood.

In some ways Reagan seemed sincerely to be suspended between two worlds, those of Hollywood urbanity and heartland parochialism. To the astonishment of liberal Democrat Warren Beatty, Reagan invited him to screen his movie *Reds*, a romantic epic about dedicated American Communists, at the White House. The film dealt with a naive, idealistic era in Soviet Russia, the time when revolution made a just society seem possible, before Stalin turned the workers' paradise into a police state. But *Reds'* sympathies were unmistakably leftist in a 1980s fashion, and its narrative passages were punctuated by reminiscences from survivors of the story's epoch, some of them unrelentingly "red." Beatty himself favored a massive shift of wealth from the rich to the poor, and from the United States, Europe, and Japan to the Third World. In explaining his view of his favorite Democratic candidate for 1984, Beatty said, "He stands for 'new ideas.' And 'new ideas' means, 'You pay, motherfucker.'"

Intrigued by the invitation from an old acquaintance and ideological foe, Beatty was almost stunned by his experience with Reagan during the film's intermission. "I used a joke in the film," Beatty recalled later, "in which a character says that he used to work in the Sahara Forest. Somebody says to him, 'Don't you mean the Sahara Desert?' The first one answers: 'Now!' Reagan said to me, 'That joke you tell, you know, it's a fag joke. You should tell it like this.' He proceeded to do the whole thing, in great detail, perfect timing, with the lisp and all, and he was right, it was really funny. I brought Diane Keaton over, and asked Reagan to tell her what he had told me. I hoped he might do just a little bit of it. He did the whole thing over again, from the beginning, and I could tell that Diane was really surprised, and really liking him. And then without missing a beat he said, 'You know what's really wrong with the Russians? What's really wrong with the Russians is this.' He started to tell this long story from World War II, about a plane that is shot down, and the gunner is trapped, and the pilot, instead of parachuting out to save himself, cradles the gunner's head in his arms and they go down together. It must have been the plot of some movie he saw, or made, or something. I kept looking at Diane and she kept looking at me and we kept waiting for the punch line. And there wasn't one. And then we realized that he meant every word of what he said about the Russians."

A second view of Reagan held that, however moderate the private Reagan might be on social matters, he was at heart an alarming extremist on spending, taxes, and especially foreign policy, awaiting only the right opportunity to voice the full extent of his ferocity. This depiction took on special importance as the 1984 election neared. Democrats and disaffected Republicans spun out fantasies about what an "untethered" President might attempt in a second term — gutting welfare and entitlement programs; narrowing Social Security (and sapping its political base) by further linking eligibility to income, rather than having it be an almost automatic subsidy to the middle class; above all, restoring America's traditional role as world policeman.

Adherents to this fretful vision of Reagan tended to assume that he revealed himself, in Freudian fashion, in offhand remarks: a casual statement in Boston that he would like to abolish the corporate income tax (an economically plausible but politically untenable position for a populist); a 1978 radio observation that private insurance would serve workers better than Social Security; a joking reference, during the testing of a microphone for a presidential broadcast, to the leaders of Poland as oppressive, no-good "bums." The notion that Reagan was intemperate, and would sooner or later reveal himself to be so, would acquire its greatest currency much later, in August of 1984, after he again joked while testing a microphone, this time saying that he had outlawed the Soviet Union's right to exist and that bombing would commence in five minutes. The reference to bombing got worldwide media play. But perhaps the most characteristic and legitimately worrisome proposition was that the Soviet Union, and by extension communism, has no legitimate right to be. Reagan had opposed Jimmy Carter's ratification of two United Nations documents because they did not guarantee the ownership of private property and safeguard against seizure without adequate compensation; such provisions would, of course, render impossible any effective Marxist revolution.

A third theory of the inner Reagan, held widely among journalists, including top White House correspondents, but almost never conveyed to the public, was that Reagan was simply out of touch with reality. These reporters contended that Reagan might well mean every word he said, including all the contradictory things, but that it did not matter, because he was not in charge of his administration. They did not assert that he was senile or befuddled: if he had been, he could not have handled even his carefully stage-managed public appearances. But they maintained that he was cut off from the decision-making process in a cloud of rhetorical self-righteousness, confusing his belief in less government — and more self-reliance by the people — with his own growing passivity. They cited, as examples, his seemingly affectless indifference to the largest budget deficits in U.S. history, the incoherence and ineffectuality of his administration's approach to arms-control negotiations, the humiliating and apparently purposeless deaths of U.S. soldiers in Beirut, and the insistent and mawkish discussion of the American intervention in Grenada — a minor police action that was hailed, in banana-republic fashion, with more decorations awarded than there had been soldiers in battle.

More personally, believers in his decline cited his falling asleep at meetings, his lapsing into anecdotes and analogies from his movie days, his insistence on reducing complicated technical problems to the sorts of colorful stories about individuals that he used in his speeches. He had come into office bright but far from brilliant, and intellectually lazy: he rarely immersed himself in a problem, and typically wanted every question reduced to a one-page memo. The tightened security after Hinckley's assassination attempt had isolated him from everyday life; his increasing deafness further distanced him from much group discussion, and occasionally incapacitated him at press conferences.

But beyond these conditions, insiders suggested that Reagan suffered from a growing rigidity of mind. Perhaps the first major news organ to touch on this problem, albeit in oblique and tentative fashion, was *Time* in a late 1982 cover story called "How Reagan Decides." The underlying message was that Reagan did not decide at all: he was beguiled into approving the decisions reached by his subordinates, most often through their persuading him that what he was now endorsing was something he had always believed. They could not easily accommodate Reagan to new ideas; but they could induce him to reaffirm what he was told were his old ones.

This theme was picked up later by other reporters, occasionally explicitly, more often implicitly, in dozens of stories about the struggle between White House pragmatists and ideologues. These stories suggested that the shape of Reagan's second term would depend largely on which aides stayed and which left or were eased out; underlying this analysis was the presumption that the victors would guide Reagan's belief, rather than the innermost nature of Reagan's conviction determining which aides would prevail.

Allied to the question of Reagan's mental alertness was that of physical fitness. Although Reagan had promised annual checkups and full disclosure of his condition, beyond his first few months in office so little was revealed that even White House correspondents commented on not knowing what shape Reagan was in. The administration circulated photographs of Reagan riding horseback, chopping wood, pumping iron; for

Parade, the Sunday newspaper supplement, he wrote a full description of his exercise program. Yet reporters speculated, sometimes in print, about whether Reagan had the physical stamina and psychic will to complete a second term.

———

The debate about Reagan's character shaped the discussion of the three broad issues that the Democrats gradually identified as theirs, once the economy began to improve during 1983: *fairness*, or how the pie of national wealth was to be sliced, particularly with regard to tax policy; *pluralism*, which embraced religious tolerance and church-state separation, racial opportunity and multilingualism in the provision of public services, feminism and the Equal Rights Amendment; and *peace*, which included the proposed nuclear weapons freeze, the status of arms-control talks, the general relationship with the Soviet Union, and the depth of American involvement with unstable governments, especially in Lebanon and Central America. In protesting Reagan's handling of these matters, the Democrats depicted him as too sympathetic to the strong and insufficiently compassionate toward the world's also-rans, too ready to use force, too determined to find national and world consensus when mere coexistence would be far more comfortably achieved and maintained. The cunning Reagan was not a frightening enough image for their purposes; the out-of-touch Reagan was an image too dangerous to project, too likely to backfire and generate sympathy; so the party opted for the image of Reagan as a radical, lying in wait until the freedom of a second term.

Fairness is a potent word to Americans, who cheer for the underdog, pride themselves on sportsmanship, revere the free-market system because it permits fair and open competition. As Garry Wills explicated in *Nixon Agonistes*, the central American myth is of life as a footrace in which in theory — although not in reality — all runners start at the same point and strive toward the same finish line. In this formulation, life's winners can be said to deserve to be winners, and life's losers can blame only themselves and their inborn lack of talent for their losing. But in fact fairness is defined by different citizens in differing ways, depending both on their philosophical convictions and on their self-interest. A Reagan Republican's notion of fairness in the economy would center on the issues that Reagan raised in attacking Carter's dealings with the UN: the chance for a gifted, hardworking, or simply lucky person to amass property, and the opportunity to maintain what his or previous generations had accumulated, subject only to such taxes as are deemed appropriate, nonconfiscatory, and necessary to maintain the public good. For Democrats, fairness had an almost entirely opposite meaning: in their lexicon, it was unfair that anyone (perhaps even criminals) should be poor, and they saw as a purpose of government the reapportionment of incomes and assets to narrow any gaps.

To Republicans, a fair income-tax proposal was a flat tax rate, perhaps with some sort of exclusion to protect the very poorest; to Democrats, a fair tax was one that would restore the previous steeply graduated rates, not least by eliminating shelters that Congress had enacted deliberately to nullify the highest effective tax brackets. In the awarding of welfare and entitlements, Democrats envisioned fairness as allowing those at the economic margin a chance of sharing in general middle-class comfort; Republicans believed that the fair thing was to take money away from earners only to ensure the survival of people who could not get by without help, not to augment the well-being of people whose subsistence was already provided by other means.

In the largest sense, Democrats based their vision of fairness on the notion that the national economy was a great interlocking system, belonging to the public collectively, and with government empowered to determine which participants were entitled to which share of the proceeds; Republicans saw the economy as the accumulation of thousands upon millions of individual transactions, reflected in individual income and net-worth statements, with government empowered only to perform certain universally acknowledged duties. When Democrats charged that Reagan's programs were unfair because they benefited the already prosperous instead of the poor, many of the prosperous felt no hint of shame; they believed that they had been carrying an excessive share of the burden of maintaining society. They applauded Reagan's tacit notion of imposing more of the responsibility for maintaining government's most costly services onto citizens most likely to make use of them.

The numbers of the prosperous were growing. As a result of a variety of factors, most notably the sharp increase in the number of two-income households among the Baby Boomers, the fastest-growing economic subset was families with an income in excess of $50,000. Just as the supposedly prototypical nuclear families of working father, nonworking mother, and two children had dwindled to far less than 10 percent of all households, so the cherished 1950s and 1960s image of the middle-income family was declining. The middle, typically defined as those earning between 75 percent and 125 percent of the median family income, was a dwindling class; the upper middle was a growing class, and it was increasingly populated by young (under forty), upwardly mobile professionals, college educated and with sophisticated, materialistic buying tastes, who would make themselves heard. When Democrats raised their voices to cry out to their middle-class constituency, they found the crowd noticeably thinned.

―――✑―――

Pluralism is a grand American tradition, although each widening of its definition has been achieved at the cost of grief and, often, bloodshed. Catholics wedged their way into the common throng in the nineteenth century, Jews in the early twentieth. Blacks waited until a century after emancipation. In the early 1980s, Hispanics had not made it yet; many Anglos in the big border states of Texas and California were determined to hold down the Hispanics' numbers and participation, and thereby limit the influence of an alien culture. Thus both parties, Democrats and Republicans, were suddenly preoccupied with sealing the nation's unsealable borders.

Freethinkers and atheists, although rarely organized or unified, had won their legal battles, if not public tolerance: a succession of church-state separation rulings, most notably the ban on prayer in public schools, had established the Supreme Court's belief that publicly expressed pieties could prove coercive.

The latest group to agitate for equality was not a minority but a majority — women, whose demands and needs were as diverse as their ranks were vast. On two matters, however, more than half of them agreed: they were uneasy about Ronald Reagan, and they favored the Equal Rights Amendment for women, which he opposed. Almost as soon as the 1980 balloting was over and poll analysts spotted Reagan's "gender gap," Democrats began looking to the women's vote to restore them to power, whoever their nominee might be, in 1984.

Traditionally the Democrats have been the party of those seeking entry to full participation in American life, and the Republicans have been the party of those guarding the door. The cobbling together of ethnic coalitions is often credited to Franklin Roosevelt, who did it with the greatest success, but the process started in the nineteenth century. In 1884, an intemperate remark by a Republican clergyman that Democrats were the party of "rum, Romanism and rebellion" — a slur made in the presence of, and not immediately repudiated by, GOP nominee James G. Blaine — caused Irish and other Catholics to rise up in sufficient numbers to ensure the election of the first Democratic President since the onset of the Civil War, Grover Cleveland. Democratic machines in big cities welcomed and exploited the waves of southern and eastern European immigrants in the early twentieth century. In 1928, the Democrats were the first party to propose a Roman Catholic for President, Al Smith, and in

1960 the party elected one, John Kennedy. But as members of the party's coalition moved up in circumstance and self-definition from "them" to "us," from outsider to establishmentarian, many of them dropped away from the Democratic ranks. The party had to keep replacing them, and for a time in the late 1960s and 1970s, the task seemed beyond hope. Women were numerous enough, and frustrated enough in their career quest, to reverse the situation. And unlike the blacks and Hispanics who were also party stalwarts and climbers, women would not trigger a backlash from bigots. Save perhaps for some diehards in the battle of the sexes, no one saw women as a pushy, upstart threat. For Reagan, who opposed an Equal Rights Amendment and instead offered a lame legislative package, who had wanted his wife to give up her career for him, who viewed affirmative action with suspicion and seemed to doubt that any employable person needed, or should get, a helping hand, the disaffection of women posed a formidable threat. And that was before 1983 brought the dual embarrassments of James Watt and Barbara Honegger.

Watt was Reagan's most provocative appointee almost from the day he took office. A lawyer whose chief pursuit, and livelihood, had been the frustration of environmental groups and the promotion of development in even the most isolated wilderness, he infuriated conservationists who believed that the post of interior secretary should belong to one of their own. Watt, moreover, was a gifted rhetorician with an instinct for the kind of extravagant remark or public-relations gesture that would bring his enemies to a helpless rage. While other administrations, of both parties, had tried exclusively to add to federal land holdings, Watt sold some off. While other administrations had regarded Interior as a lobbying agency for the regulation of development, Watt saw his agency as a second Commerce Department, dedicated to bringing publicly held natural resources to their fullest economic potential. He was a major player in the Reagan first term. Honegger, by contrast, was a minor functionary — in the dismissive word of a White House aide, a "munchkin." She had gone from a low-level campaign job to a busywork research project, reviewing federal statutes for sexual bias or discrimination, a duty for which she lacked even the minimal qualification of being a lawyer. What brought both of them to public notice, for the first time for Honegger and the last time for Watt, was their role in suggesting that Ronald Reagan was insensitive to the aims of the disadvantaged, especially women.

Watt's besetting sin was candor. The deed that brought him down was not some heinous assault on the environment, nor the muck of favoritism and deceit at the Environmental Protection Agency, a body he had attempted to disassemble in the guise of supervision, but his accurate description of the impact of affirmative action on the formation of an advisory panel. In introducing the group, he announced that he had found "quality," and moreover had assembled "a black, a woman, two Jews and a cripple." The term "cripple" is no longer in fashion — "handicapped" is the locution of the moment, until that, too, becomes stigmatized and is replaced by some new euphemism — but the other language was unexceptionable. Watt's error was in calling attention to these descriptive traits, and in acknowledging that candidates' fitting such categories was a major reason they were named. By the pieties of affirmative action, people were sought out because they met particular target quotas, and then were presented as though they had been chosen strictly on merit. The rationale was that in a truly just society, all target groups would rise automatically to authority in proportion to their share of the population, so the quota-filling supposedly merely achieved the kind of blind justice that ought to have been the case to begin with.

Watt's assertion that the emperor had no clothes would not normally have been enough to destroy a career. But he had to depart, after painful weeks of limbo, for three reasons. He was already so controversial a figure that the public outcry exhausted his legitimacy. He had become a potential threat to Reagan's reelection. And the national media disliked Watt on policy grounds, especially because of EPA scandals that eventually resulted in mass departures and the conviction of a high-ranking official, Rita Lavelle. Journalists decided that it was time for him to go, and simply would not drop the overplayed story of his offending remarks until he did. It is hard to define how such a consensus gets formed. The same relentless pressure had been applied to force Reagan to drop the would-be diplomat Lefever and, later, Lefever's sponsor, national security adviser Richard Allen. Although Allen was cleared of corrupt intent in accepting a payment made after he helped arrange an interview with Nancy Reagan for a Japanese magazine, his presence in the White House continued to generate such controversy that Reagan accepted his resignation. Similar media lobbying failed to separate Reagan from Edwin Meese, whom he sought to make attorney general, in part because Reagan felt more enduring personal loyalty to Meese. The customary media line was that a high officeholder must be above all suspicion; yet it was the media that generated or buoyed most of the suspicion.

Barbara Honegger burst into view when she quit her duties, apparently not long before she was to be phased out of them, with a long article and accompanying interview in the *Washington Post* saying that Reagan was insincere in his pledge of legislative reform of sex discrimination. Reagan aides then made the grievous tactical error of belittling her in what looked like arrogant and sexist fashion. Suddenly Honegger was news everywhere, making her case on a succession of talk shows. Her claim against Reagan was probably just, although to most people, it had been clear from the outset that the "statutory review" was merely a veil of propriety drawn over a scene of willful indolence. As a scorned bureaucrat with a high opinion of herself not shared by her superiors, Honegger managed to present herself as a victim of sex discrimination of the very type she was hired to research. Only slowly did reporters begin to discover that she had a history of winning advancement by claiming sexual harassment, that she had a graduate degree in parapsychology and believed in an assortment of psychic oddments from "auras" to UFOs, and that she was considerably less calm and reasonable in interviews than she sounded in print.

Reagan's only comebacks against Honegger's attack, and the depth of feminist suspicion that her publicity storm confirmed, were reminders that he had appointed Elizabeth Dole as transportation secretary, Sandra Day O'Connor as a Supreme Court justice, and Margaret Heckler, whom Reagan referred to as "a good girl" when he could not remember her name, as secretary of health and human services. The list was not, and could not be, enough.

Peace would become the most complex issue of the campaign, but not until the 1984 debate was well under way. Jimmy Carter had been able to boast in 1980 that during his term no American lives were lost in combat that the United States voluntarily undertook; until the failed rescue mission for the hostages in Iran, he had been able to claim that no lives at all had been lost in combat. Reagan did not even long to make such a claim. In perhaps the most revealing line of his eventual acceptance speech at the Republican convention, he would repeat a boast that defined this grandpa-with-gumption's vision of leadership: during his term, not one inch of soil had been lost to Communists anywhere in the entire world. He had not raised armies in the night against the Soviet encroachments in Afghanistan and Poland, but he had strengthened American armies for future war. He had reasserted U.S. dominance in its own hemisphere. In Grenada, he had sent U.S. soldiers into combat action against Cuban troops. His aides had authorized action against the Soviets' terroristic ally Libya. In Beirut, in El Salvador, in Nicaragua, the United States had shown that it would act to confound its enemies and defend its friends. Against what in 1983 he called an "evil empire," centered in Moscow, Reagan meant to be the warrior king.

II

Ambitions

THE Democratic party came to the 1984 elections, as it had for fifty years, as the natural majority party of the country. But it also was on the verge of becoming what the courts call a legal fiction. Its numerical strength was tangible; its intellectual identity was not. Democrats held the mayoralties in most big cities and the governorships in a substantial majority of states, and presided over a majority of state legislative bodies. The party's formal, if not ideological, control of the House of Representatives had not been in jeopardy for nearly three decades. Its return to command in the Senate, even though that body overrepresents small states and thus tilts toward Republicans, was widely conceded to be only a matter of time. Yet when Democrats tried to define what the party stood for, as they had done in four successive bitter battles for the presidential nomination and would have to do again in the coming race, they spoke in a cacophony of dissent. Democrats had a united vision of America's past and of their heroic role in it, but they shared no sense of how that past connected to the present and future.

Through much of the twentieth century, the lack of sharply defined ideology in political parties had been regarded as a sort of civic virtue. Democrats and Republicans alike congratulated themselves on embracing a vast, even self-contradictory range of opinions, excluding no one and denying no one the claim of legitimacy. Civic watchdogs and the press joined in this endorsement, treating the all-embracing nature of the parties as proof of tolerance at the heart of the national character, and consensus at the center of the decision-making process. Europeans often viewed the American parties' absence of ideology as a sign that the nation's politics remained mired in a primitive state of power grabbing; Americans, even intellectuals, countered that their society instead had advanced beyond the splintering theoretical strife that bedeviled Europe. To be sure, the Democrats and Republicans differed in serving, respectively, labor and business. On occasion they disagreed profoundly on matters of policy. But for the citizenry, any shift in presidential administration tended to be somewhat obscured by an overwhelming continuity in both domestic and foreign affairs.

The national emphasis on consensus reinforced Democratic strength. For decades, the status quo for both parties was the New Deal agenda, if not in specific programs, then in principles. The reservoir of tradition was the generally Democratic Congress. Disgruntled Republicans long complained that "me, too" was not enough of a party philosophy to provide a chance to win. Their efforts to write a radically conservative platform and nominate a radically conservative candidate failed, however, until 1964; then the nomination of Barry Goldwater proved disastrous. For a time thereafter, Democrats and Republicans alike thought more than ever that the center was the place to strive for, and once-controversial Rooseveltian principles became the universally accepted norms.

Yet for all the apparent success of the Democratic party, it too had split into factions that had emerged in full-blown disputation by the middle 1960s, and that by the eve of the 1984 election barely tolerated each other. It was said that when liberals formed a firing line, they automatically arranged themselves in a circle, and aimed inward.

The Democratic factions all grew out of what was known as the Franklin Roosevelt coalition. That terminology was misleading: all politics is to some extent personal, and even the most beloved officeholders generally have a hard time transferring the loyalty of their supporters to someone else whom they endorse. A large part of Roosevelt's following voted for him simply because he was Roosevelt, with his almost mystical powers to reassure and inspire; at the minimum, these followers and their descendants had to be excluded from the customary calculus of interest blocs who had banded together.

Moreover, the "Roosevelt coalition," to the extent that it coalesced at all, had been shaped and sustained by two epochal events: the Depression and the battle against Hitler in World War II. By far the more important was the Depression. The groups who gathered under the Democratic banner in the 1930s included the suddenly penniless and the always deprived but newly hopeless: labor union members; Southerners, especially hand-to-mouth farmers and farmhands; blacks, Jews, southern and eastern European immigrants, and others who by ethnicity were, or felt themselves to be, outcasts; small businessmen who were neither lucky nor adept enough to stay afloat in hard times; some doctrinaire liberals, even socialists, who preferred affiliating with an American-style political movement rather than any of the various groups that then idealized Stalinist

Russia; and significant numbers of intellectuals and reformers who saw government as an arena for debating and testing ideas, attempting social change, perfecting public behavior. With the exception of thinkers who were drawn to Roosevelt because he believed in government action per se, most of the coalition's members were, by objective economic measures, life's losers. They looked to Roosevelt — and also, as poignant letters in the Roosevelt archives attest, to such hokum artists as Father Coughlin and Huey Long — for the help and hope they no longer believed they could attain by themselves.

By the eve of the 1984 campaign, however, America had been changed utterly, and a terrible beauty born. Prosperity was the norm: two-thirds of the nation's households owned their dwellings, and many of the rest were either saving in anticipation of home ownership or enjoying in retirement the capital gains that homeowning had provided. Pension plans, coupled with Social Security, had transformed the image of retirement from penury to leisure. Unemployment persisted, but it tended to be concentrated among three groups: those of marginal skills, those who insisted on waiting to be recalled to highly paid but unsteady union positions, and those who stubbornly continued to live in depressed areas. New Deal rhetoric about poverty and privation was almost laughably distant from the lives of average citizens. In this new America, life's losers were increasingly viewed, not as victims of circumstance, but as failures with no one to blame but themselves for not having cashed in on opportunity. As wealth spread through the populace, so did the serene selfishness, derived from Calvinism by way of Social Darwinism, that in generations gone by had sheltered the consciences of the well-to-do: the conviction that one's riches were richly deserved, in all probability divinely sent, in reward for hard work and moral virtue.

Against this changed social context, New Deal liberalism looked increasingly dated. Nonetheless, as the Democrats began to think about a 1984 standard-bearer, and about the standard under which he would ask Americans to rally, the party's dominant faction looked unregenerately back to the New Deal. Its oratory was apocalyptic, invoking an imperiled America with apple sellers and homeless beggars on nearly every street corner. Its political strategy was more practical, but rested on the notion of coalition: people were addressed, not as individuals, but as members of demographic groups, and the theme of us-versus-them resounded far more loudly than the theme of Americans-pulling-together. For every identifiable social problem, government was offered as the solution of first resort. Government should even finance studies to unearth new problems that government could address; it should fund pressure groups that would in turn lobby for even more government spending. For this faction, the New Deal represented not only the acme of the political past but also the living spirit of the party's present and future. Any attempt to modify the approach or even the imagery of the party, to respond to newer problems, looked like a betrayal of true Democratic tradition and of the numberless needy it served.

The leaders of this faction were groups and institutions that had come to national power through the New Deal and that would not likely have gained access to power without what the New Deal had achieved. Most prominent among them were national labor union bureaucracies, especially the AFL–CIO and the National Education Association, and the Roman Catholic "ethnics" from big cities of the Northeast and the industrial midwestern "rust belt" — typified by Senator Edward Kennedy, House Speaker Thomas O'Neill, New York Governor Mario Cuomo, and House Ways and Means Committee Chairman Daniel Rostenkowski. They thought of the Democrats as the party of the workingman, and the union hierarchy as his representative. This equation might have suited Britain, where three-quarters of the labor force is unionized, but it ill fitted the United States, where barely a fifth of the labor force belongs to AFL–CIO recognized unions. Even union members, moreover, were often alienated from their leaders, who were perceived as at best self-serving and self-perpetuating, at worst corrupt and tied to organized crime. In the press and in popular culture, the image of labor leaders was scarcely more endearing than that of cigar-chomping ward heelers.

The New Deal faction softened its standpat image, and made vague overtures toward new generations, by aligning with two minor clusters within the party: the radicals who favored sharply increased socialism, and the new-consciousness coalition of feminists, gay-rights activists, communitarians, would-be decriminalizers of marijuana use, and others whose aim in politics was mainly to protect and perhaps legitimize their personal life-styles. Alliances among these disparate groups did not come easy. The socialist goal — to equalize incomes and assets — had been decisively rejected by New Deal Democrats of even modest means when George McGovern embraced it in 1972; as that year's party nominee, McGovern urged a confiscatory inheritance tax on estates in excess of, say, $500,000, and was repudiated by, among others, blue-collar workers, for whom the accumulation of patrimony for one's children was perhaps life's most sacred goal. The Catholic ethnics, who dominated both the big-city machines and the labor movement, generally strove for the utmost propriety in personal behavior, and felt little in common with exotics and experimenters.

[54]

The second major faction in the Democratic party was centrists. On domestic matters, their differences with the New Deal legacy could be summed up in a phrase: let's spend a little less. Centrists voiced few specific disagreements with the party on foreign policy, but they generally viewed the Pentagon's budget requests with less suspicion than the liberal New Dealers and felt less constraint about the use of force to contain communism. Like moderates everywhere, the centrists lacked a grand, inspiriting slogan, beyond the tepid claims of compromise. Yet in their quiet way they could make a plausible case for being true heirs of Roosevelt. Like him, they sought to be architects of consensus. Like him, they believed in collaboration with business, and depicted social welfare programs as part of the overhead cost of maintaining a healthy, stable capitalist country. Like him, they were less interested in the ideological purity of a project than in a businesslike evaluation of its cost-effectiveness. They viewed themselves, in an almost nonpartisan way, as pragmatists.

The most obvious divisions between the centrists and the New Deal liberals showed up in their views of unions and corporations. The centrists regarded labor as only one constituency among several to be consulted in the shaping of economic policy. They paid at most lip service to the idea that union officials represented all working men and women. The centrists preferred the offer of incentives for job development in the private sector to direct employment by government. Centrists were more inclined to be troubled by budget deficits, and to favor crackdowns on program management and spending. Centrists extolled the virtues of the free market. But the division between centrists and ardent liberals was geographic as well as ideological. Old-fashioned centrist Democrats, tied to traditional Democratic organizations, tended to come from the South or the agricultural Midwest, to speak for farmers and small businessmen more than AFL–CIO units, to be Protestant and of Anglo-Saxon, Nordic, or Teutonic stock rather than Roman Catholic and "ethnic."

Because of the southern roots of the centrist wing, it found itself allied with an unwelcome and dwindling but still sizable faction in the party: white supremacists. Many of the party's older officials had at one time openly advocated segregation. None dared do so publicly any longer. Even George Wallace, who had unnerved party officials in four consecutive primary campaigns by carrying northern communities or even whole states through an explicitly racist appeal, had latterly abased himself to win black endorsements. Yet race remained a preoccupation of many white Democrats, and they trusted Southerners to look out for white interests. Jimmy Carter, for all his close ties to black church leaders, discovered in 1976 that he got support from urban white Democrats who felt sure that a Georgian must be a discreet, closeted but committed racist. In Roosevelt's day, the Democrats had managed to attract both white racists and blacks by preaching in public about their shared economic interests, while tolerating in private a divided nation, free in the North, autonomously segregated in the South. Civil rights laws passed since World War II had made that straddle impossible, and white racists perceived the Democrats as having taken the side of the blacks. The numbers of whites who defected to the Republican party had more than outweighed the newly registered Democratic voters who were black; in state after state in the South, the once-helpless Republican organization could win, or at least vigorously contest, most statewide races and many a congressional seat. No Democrat could prudently suggest, aloud, that the party might still offer a home for racists. But an implicit part of the centrists' bid for power was the presumption that they might be able to diminish the outflow.

The party's third major faction was reformers. Within the New Deal context, they had inherited the position of Roosevelt's Brain Trust, the scholars and social innovators whom FDR gathered around him. In the longer sweep of history, the 1984 reformers were the latest generation of a tinkering, perfectionist type of maverick to be found in both parties — fascinated more by the definition of good government and the analysis of how to achieve it than by any emotional or ideological agenda. Perhaps the prototypical reformer had been Grover Cleveland, who, as the only Democratic President over a span of fifty-two years, decimated his own powers by creating the federal civil service. In the twentieth century, reformers had been more prominent in the Republican party than in the Democratic: the pre-presidential Herbert Hoover, Wendell Willkie, Nelson Rockefeller all embodied the reformist personality, while the last Democratic nominee who unmistakably did so was Woodrow Wilson. There were practical reasons why. One traditional target of reformers is entrenched political machines. In the twentieth century, the most effective of those machines generally were run by Democrats.

The reform tradition was so little recognized within the Democratic hierarchy that when a cohesive generation of reformers began to emerge, they were mislabeled and misunderstood. At first, such senators as Bill Bradley of New Jersey, Joseph Biden of Delaware, Paul Tsongas of Massachusetts, and Gary Hart of Colorado, and such governors as Michael Dukakis of Massachusetts, Bruce Babbitt of Arizona, and Jerry Brown of California, were described as conservative or centrist Democrats. Some of these politicians accepted that characterization, but most of them insisted that they were some modified form of New Deal liberal — or, especially if they were Westerners, called themselves "progressive." For a while, the voguish term for them was "second look" liberals, then "neo-" liberals, then, for the more hawkish and free-trade oriented, "neoconservatives." After some of them began to explore the idea of a postindustrial or at least postsmokestack economy, based heavily on high technology and services, they were half-derisively known as "Atari" Democrats. Finally one of the ablest of them, Hart, began to speak in generational terms: these were Democrats who had few if any personal memories of the Depression and World War II, whose formative experiences had been Korea and the Silent Generation of the 1950s and John Kennedy's New Frontier and perhaps Vietnam. They were neither pro– nor anti–New Deal, but simply post–New Deal. Their orientation was not toward meeting the human needs of individuals, but toward defining and solving the problems of America as an economic entity. They felt little interest in either confrontation, or coalition building, or consensus as the political means of enacting programs and passing budgets; they were far more interested in the apolitical questions of what the programs and budgets sought to achieve, and what were the most efficient ways of meeting those goals. They were detached from the battles of the past, compelled by visions of the future.

The fourth major faction had changed least and was potentially the most monolithic of the old Roosevelt constituencies: blacks. Of all the Democratic groups, their assertions were the most candidly self-interested. They wanted more jobs, more training, higher salaries, more quotas in education and hiring. They wanted economic advantages that under the status quo would more likely go to others. Black leaders were no longer willing to wait for a rising tide to lift all boats, nor were they amenable to tergiversations about being helped by programs aimed also at helping other disadvantaged groups. Blacks were ready to say openly that they wanted *for themselves* the opportunities that now belonged to someone else. To justify these provocative claims, they pointed to some compelling facts.

The most striking was the simplest: except for Lyndon Johnson, who ran in the aftermath of the assassination of a young and popular President, no Democratic nominee since Roosevelt had won a majority of the white vote in the country. Truman, Kennedy, and Carter scraped by to their narrow victories because of substantial majorities among blacks. And blacks were rapidly becoming perhaps the largest, certainly the most loyal of the identifiable blocs remaining within the New Deal coalition. Decades of Republican opposition to civil rights bills had eroded what had been a residual tendency for blacks to favor the party of Abraham Lincoln; now, up to 90 percent or more of American blacks voted for Democratic nominees for President. Registration drives and voting-rights laws had lifted black voting up almost to blacks' proportional share of the population, about one in eight. Among Democrats, black voters were nearly one in four. Their rewards for participation had been few: some cabinet and subcabinet appointments, some judgeships, some legislative concessions. With the possible exception of Andrew Young, Jimmy Carter's United Nations ambassador, no black had ever stood in the inmost circle of advisers to a President, or even a party nominee. The smoldering question among black leaders was whether the time had come to run a candidate of their own, to demonstrate both to white officials and to black voters that blacks were a crucial presence in preserving what was left of Franklin Roosevelt's coalition.

In American politics the story of every election begins, at the latest, on the morning after the last one. Any narrative of the 1984 presidential election could plausibly start with the election of Franklin Roosevelt in 1932, or the doomed crusade of Barry Goldwater and his archconservative claque in 1964, or with the seizure of the American embassy in Tehran by terrorists masquerading as "students" in 1979. Given the social forces that were soon to make themselves felt, the chronology could reach back to the ratification of woman suffrage in 1920, or Martin Luther King, Jr.'s "I have a dream" speech on the Washington Mall in 1963. But in tactical terms, the maneuvering began on the morning of November 5, 1980, when Democrats woke up the day after the presidential election — those who had been able to sleep, that is — and surveyed the massive damage. The results were measured in numbers, objective and inarguable. But for each of eight deeply diverse men, the spiritual message implicit in those numbers, the insight into the mood and direction of the American people, had a specific and personal import. To each of them, pondering the party's disarray and how to overcome it, the thought came: you are the one. Bruce Babbitt, the witty Arizona governor who is now often cited as a potential President or vice-president, says, "There is no man who has held significant public office for more than six months who does not look into his mirror at least once a week or so and say, 'Why not?' " One by one, eight men asked themselves that question and gave their hearts to the struggle.

The statistics of the 1980 election were crushing. Carter carried only Georgia, his home state; Minnesota, his running mate's home state; Maryland, the home state of legions of federal bureaucrats whose wages, pensions, and even job security were potentially threatened by Reagan's proposed cuts in government spending; Rhode Island, perhaps the most unionized and Democratic state in the Northeast; West Virginia, a living symbol of poverty, backwardness, and dependency in the South; Hawaii, the only state with a nonwhite majority; and the District of Columbia, overwhelmingly black and accustomed to relying on federal handouts even to pay its firefighters and police. For a sitting President, the repudiation was almost without precedent. But there was more. Whether the fault lay with Jimmy Carter as a personality or more deeply with the party's philosophy, the Democrats had been humbled in the congressional vote as well. In the House, the party lost a disheartening 33 seats. The Senate, which had been under Democratic control for a quarter of a century, and which the party had held on election morning by the seemingly unassailable margin of 59–41, had unthinkably gone Republican, 53–47. Among the dozen Democratic Senate seats lost were those of three former serious presidential candidates — Birch Bayh of Indiana, Frank Church of Idaho, and the 1972 nominee, McGovern of South Dakota.

Most of the losers blamed bad luck, bad timing, the weak top of the ticket, and the inevitable discontent of some of the public toward anyone who has held office for a while. But McGovern saw something sinister at work: the religious right, especially Jerry Falwell's Moral Majority, which McGovern accused of campaigning that was ugly, divisive, un-American, and often willfully untrue. The left would need a counterforce, McGovern declared, and he proclaimed himself the man to lead it. At first his angry words sounded like mere rhetoric, the game if graceless parting shot of a feisty has-been. But McGovern went out onto the lecture circuit and professed to discover a new generation of students who responded to his old exhortations. Perversely but inevitably, the defeat of 1980 led McGovern into the presidential race of 1984.

Another defeated aspirant, Walter Mondale, read the results in a characteristically analytic way. Reagan had won a widespread majority, he saw, but by a narrow margin within most states. Carter had lost badly, but Carter and liberal independent John Anderson together had actually captured a larger popular vote in 1980 than Carter had in 1976. Roughly half the country might still be willing to vote Democratic, particularly for a better candidate than Carter, who neither spoke for nor stirred many of the party's traditional constituencies. Moreover, there remained millions of poor, black, and Hispanic citizens who had not enrolled to vote. Surely a true Democrat, of the old style that America had so long trusted and loved, could hold the loyalists, bring back some of the alienated voters, and enroll enough new voters to win. It needed only a strong, united party, spending its hard-won cash on organization and registration rather than combative primaries and insubstantial TV ads, to restore the days of

Rooseveltian glory. As practical politicians like to say, the numbers were there. And if the party were to spare itself a bear-pit brawl to the last primary and beyond, for the first time since 1964, around whom could it more likely gather than Mondale? Carter was through. But he and his supporters would do everything to block Edward Kennedy, to punish him for having run in the primaries. Scoop Jackson was too old, California Governor Jerry Brown was passé, and no one else had the visibility and stature to claim the nomination by right. If the party were to have the best chance to win, Mondale surely must be the undisputed nominee.

A third campaigner, whose name was not on any 1980 ballot but whose voice had resounded day after day on the hustings, surveyed the results for the way they served his special agenda. Jesse Jackson had been given an airplane and a travel budget by the Carter campaign to rouse the black vote. He succeeded, but as much on his own behalf as Carter's. Audiences swayed and shouted in response to his plea as they had not for any black leader since Martin Luther King, Jr. It began to occur to Jackson that blacks in large numbers were ready, perhaps eager, to give their votes as well as their "amens" to one of their own. A black man could not expect to become President. But he could hope to unify black America behind himself as its spokesman, and he could thereby make blacks, and himself, forces to be reckoned with. Who could calculate what opportunities might follow?

Off on the sidelines, a former southern governor who had once been spoken of by every commentator in the same breath as, and perhaps a little ahead of, Jimmy Carter, read the totals and thought of what might have been. Reubin Askew of Florida probably could have had the vice-presidential nomination in 1972 if he had wanted it. He could have mustered most of the same assets, offered the same appeals, that Carter did in 1976. Askew chose not to run. By 1980, not much had changed, except that he was older, retired from office, with time to brood. The party and the country seemed to be coming his way — more conservative, more business oriented, perhaps more restrictive on abortion. And with the Democrats once again all but shut out in the West in the 1980 tallying, the party needed more than ever to look to the South.

For the other four men, the results brought a more tangible kind of affirmation: while other Democrats were losing in droves, they were holding their seats, and in states that Carter had signally failed to carry. The public, these four reasoned, plainly saw in them and their beliefs some virtue not perceived in other Democrats. For the party to recoup, each of them concluded, he would have to lead. In all, ten Democrats were reelected to the Senate in 1980. Several were ill-suited to making a presidential bid: Daniel Inouye of Hawaii, by reason of his Asian descent; Russell Long of

Louisiana, as a result of his many business associations and secretive temperament; Thomas Eagleton of Missouri, as an afterbang of his withdrawal as the party's vice-presidential nominee in 1972, when it was revealed that he had repeatedly undergone electroshock therapy for depression. Wendell Ford of Kentucky and Patrick Leahy of Vermont had failed to attract much attention, even within the Senate. For the rest, the temptation to see themselves as the Democrats' potential saviors was strong, at times overwhelming. Dale Bumpers of Arkansas flirted with the notion and eventually came to regret not having made a stand. Ernest Hollings, who had finished 200,000 votes ahead of the presidential ticket in South Carolina, decided to run. So did Gary Hart, who had drawn 300,000 more votes than the ticket in Colorado. Hollings believed the Democrats had residual strength in the South; Hart was sure the party could do better if it looked more, and spoke more convincingly, to the West. Two of their colleagues not only survived but won landslides. Alan Cranston of California ran more than 1 million votes ahead of the ticket in Reagan's home state. In Ohio, a state that tilts Republican in presidential elections and that in 1980 elected a House delegation numbering 13 Republicans to 10 Democrats, John Glenn ran 1 million votes ahead of the ticket and 1.6 million ahead of his opponent. Cranston believed himself right on the issues — environment, disarmament, and economic development. Glenn attributed his popularity to his middle-of-the-road outlook, his down-home personal style, and the remembered glamour of his having been an original astronaut.

None of the new contenders started campaigning right away. Mondale, the elder statesman among them, announced he would take a year off to reexamine his beliefs, a gesture so goofy on its face, from a man who had been in public life for two decades, that few people took it seriously enough even to mock it. McGovern went speechifying. Jackson returned to his coercive campaign to force businesses that rely on black trade — fast food and hamburger companies, car manufacturers, distillers and breweries — to turn over more management jobs and distributorships to minorities, or face a Jackson-led black boycott of their products. The rest waited to see what kind of President this Ronald Reagan would turn out to be, and whether a nomination to run against him would seem to be worth having. Waiting with them, at least for a time, was the party's perennial — and perennially unavailable — first choice, Edward Kennedy.

The emotional tug that the Kennedys exert is one of the few enduring facts of national political life. Their story combines two archetypal

American myths: immigrants making good, achieving participation, then dignity, then wealth, then power, and ultimately glory; and the indomitable family, beset by tragedy and suffering and the cruel incursions of the uncontrollable outside, but unfailingly rising anew, held together by love and mutual devotion and the shared sense that life is a struggle of the family against the world. Part of the lure of the Kennedys is their fortune, their physical vigor, their exuberant involvement in all the pursuits of life. But an equal part is their grief, their relentless subjection to all the ills that flesh is heir to, and their quiet capacity to survive and carry on. If the nation does indeed, as so many critics have asserted, yearn for a royal family, and if the Kennedys are the consensus choice for that de facto role, then perhaps it is for the same fundamental reason that the British love the Windsors: come what may, they shoulder the burden of duty, that life may continue.

The Kennedys have figured, in some fashion, in every national election since 1952, when young Congressman John Fitzgerald Kennedy unseated Senator Henry Cabot Lodge, who had simultaneously sought reelection and served as the national campaign chief for President-elect Dwight Eisenhower. In 1956, Kennedy narrowly lost a convention floor fight for the vice-presidential nomination. In 1960, he was elected President. After his assassination in 1963, the party passionately longed to make his brother Robert the vice-presidential nominee for 1964, but President Lyndon Johnson resisted. In 1968, Robert Kennedy ran for President and was apparently on the verge of capturing the nomination when he was assassinated. Many party leaders urged his brother Edward to run in his place, and when he declined, nominee Hubert Humphrey begged him to stand for vice-president, even offering to let him sit out the campaign in safety. In 1972, the bag of dirty tricks known as Watergate was opened because of Nixon administration fears that Edward Kennedy would run; as late as May of that year, White House assistants were attempting to pass disinformation, including forged documents, to reporters, in hopes of smoking out proof of whether Kennedy might still jump into the race. In 1976, it remained true probably until the very day of nominations at the party convention that Kennedy could have won the party's bid just by asking for it. Even his stumbling performance in 1980, when he could not prevail against unpopular Jimmy Carter in the New England neighbor states of Maine and New Hampshire, did not discredit him. He dominated the primaries of the late spring, and by the time of the 1980 convention, the mood in the party and especially the press was that he was somehow the rightful nominee, cheated of his place by Jimmy Carter's deceit. The ticket did not seem legitimate until the climactic moment on the final night of the convention, when Kennedy appeared, oh so reluctantly, to give his blessing. In November, even as the Democratic collapse cost him the chairmanship of the Judiciary Committee in the Senate, and he watched his vanquished friends bid farewell, Kennedy could feel a certain grim satisfaction. Party leaders and elected officials by the score had come to him in 1979, warning that unless he were the nominee, the party faced an electoral disaster. Then, when trouble struck, they sneaked to the Carter camp. Kennedy was not the nominee. And just as they had predicted, there was indeed an electoral disaster that swept away his fair-weather friends.

People who believed themselves to be close to Kennedy — the qualification was necessary because he remained an intensely private man, even with his children — were uncertain what meaning he took away from the buffeting of 1980. Some thought he was through with politics and would not even run for reelection to the Senate in 1982. Others thought that he had never wanted to run for President, had let himself be talked into a campaign against his better judgment, and would happily return to a career as a liberal advocate in the Senate, a club he knew and liked. A number thought that he would run again for the White House, almost certainly in 1984, to avenge his honor or to fulfill a hankering for the job that he supposedly discovered in himself during the latter, better days of the 1980 primary season. As it turned out, Kennedy leaped the first hurdle, reelection to his Massachusetts Senate seat, with just under 70 percent of the vote; his victory, two decades after he first won the job, made him one of the nation's most senior senators at the politically youthful age of fifty. Kennedy faced a weak, unknown opponent and had no prospect of trouble, but several of the would-be candidates for 1984 offered their help. Mondale, the only aspirant who seemed certain to run whether Kennedy did or not, nonetheless showed up to stump with him. Mondale hoped that if Kennedy decided against a bid, he would endorse a faithful fellow liberal. Even if Kennedy did not stay out, they could make common cause for a while. Between them they could control the party machinery, and adjust it to minimize the chance that some unknown could come along to beat both of them.

———✦———

The battle among the factions and their respective operatives — the fund-raisers, publicists, field organizers, media strategists — began, if not in private, at least with little attention from the press and public, during the framing of convention rules and the delegate selection process. Back-corridor chats and deal making in smoke-filled rooms have been replaced, presumably forever, by primaries, caucuses, and other public means for voters to express their opinion. By and large, what voters see and hear about the process is all that there is to know. And the role of political authority figures has been reduced, perhaps eliminated, by television news, commercials, and broadcast debates, which give voters a firsthand sense of who the candidates are. Virtually the only limit to a voter's informed scrutiny and participation is his own patience in learning. Still, the semi-private part of the process can be significant. In 1984, it would be portrayed, with some justice, as an attempt to steal the election.

Two facts shaped the rule-making meetings for 1984. One was that the New Deal liberals, despite their dominance of the party machinery and their self-image as the bearers of the one and true cross, had not had their own untrammeled way in choosing the nominee since 1964. The other was that the Democrats invariably try to rectify what they see as the mistakes or injustices of the last campaign by rejiggering the bylaws for the next. In 1968, the party elders had faced primary challenges by Eugene McCarthy, at heart an independent and reformer, and Robert Kennedy, who had become spokesman for the black and socialist-radical factions. The late Senator Richard Russell of Georgia found himself, to his surprise, supporting Lyndon Johnson's vice-president for the 1968 nomination. Russell explained: "I never thought I would see the day when Hubert Humphrey was the most conservative man running for the Democratic nomination for President." Humphrey was imposed on the party by *force majeure.*

For the 1972 convention, the Democrats decided to try to guarantee that no one would become the nominee the way Humphrey had, without competing in primaries. The party also set radical-reformist quotas for representing blacks, women, and other groups whom the party establishment too often left out. These choices led almost predictably to the nomination of radical faction leader George McGovern, one election later than when a radical might have had a chance to win. For 1976, the party swung back to rules that diminished quotas and restored some of the power of traditional New Deal Democrats; but in a party divided over the Vietnam war, the New Dealers failed to settle on a candidate. The outcome was the nomination of Jimmy Carter, a southern centrist with few ties or obligations to elements of the New Deal coalition.

In 1980, when party elders privately favored the nomination of Edward Kennedy, and when both sentiment and practicality might have led the convention to bolt to him, the last-minute shift proved impossible: long before, Carter's operatives had written in a rule compelling delegates to vote on the first ballot for the candidate they had been chosen to represent. In retrospect, party elders viewed that rule as a mistake; it seemed inflexible, perhaps unjust. So for 1984 they left open the possibility of last-minute defections based on "conscience," and thereby potentially inspirited a dull convention with down-to-the-wire drama and suspense. Contradicting that calculation, however, was a judgment that the major reason Kennedy had remained a disruptive threat in 1980 was that the selection process had gone on too long. What was needed in 1984, party elders concluded, was an irresistible momentum toward consensus. Especially when running against this well-liked Republican incumbent, the party elders judged, the Democrats of 1984 needed to unify quickly and without bitterness.

Three basic decisions shaped the effort by the New Deal mainstream to control the 1984 nomination. The first was to award more than a quarter of the total convention delegate seats needed for nomination to party officials and elected officeholders, who would not have to pledge themselves to any candidate. These "superdelegates" would reflect the will of the New Dealers for two reasons: most of them belonged to, or sympathized with, that faction; and most of them depended for fund-raising and organizational help on elements of the New Deal coalition. In the unlikely event of a repeat of the dilemma of 1980, when the more viable candidate during springtime primaries turned into the less tenable one for the fall, the superdelegates not only could shift their own votes at the convention, but also would be positioned to persuade diehards within their own state delegations of the need to switch allegiance.

The second major party decision was to "front-load" the schedule so that the process would be over almost before it had begun. The first caucus would be held in Iowa in late February, the first primary in New Hampshire eight days later. Within a month thereafter, the selection mechanism would have been completed or at least started for about 40 percent of all delegates. Thus, only a candidate with the contacts, resources, name recognition, and personal following to stage a truly national campaign from the outset would have much of a chance to win. There could be no slow building to a late climax, as McGovern had done in 1972 and Reagan almost did in 1976. A candidate would have to win some victories early or be out of the running.

Both these decisions about rules were fashioned not only to suit the party establishment but to mirror the strengths of two particular candidates, Kennedy and Mondale. They were by far the best-known aspirants, they had by far the best chance to assemble organizations and amass money, they were considered the most known and trusted commodities by party power brokers. Operatives for Kennedy and Mondale controlled the committees that wrote the delegate selection rules, and their frank aim was to shut dark-horse contenders out of the process. In the end, Kennedy chose not to run, but the rules he sponsored suited his secondary purpose: to ensure that a Democrat acceptable to him, not some outsider like Carter, would be the nominee.

The third major decision, perhaps the most fateful and certainly the most controversial, was made by organized labor. Once labor had been considered perhaps the most potent force in American political life. But for nearly two decades, union leaders had been losing the capacity to deliver the votes of their members. A rising tide of insurgent candidacies for union leadership, some of them put down by violence, had prompted the press and public to wonder whether the union hierarchies represented anyone's interests other than their own. On Labor Day, 1983, television networks and newspaper editorialists delivered what had become pro forma stories on the dwindling influence of labor; one of the toughest, by former NBC White House correspondent Judy Woodruff, showed up as the centerpiece of public television's premiere edition of the hour-long "MacNeil/Lehrer Report." These doomsaying appraisals only reconfirmed the determination of Lane Kirkland, president of the AFL–CIO, to thrust his organization into the center of the nominating process. Before the first vote had been cast, labor would designate its candidate. If that candidate won, labor could claim to have been decisive. If he lost, of course, labor might well shoulder the blame. To Kirkland, that risk was less great than it seemed. Labor was in danger of being cut out of party decision-making anyway, and had not seen its first choice nominated since Humphrey in 1968. Moreover, the new party rules seemed certain to tilt the process toward Mondale. Kirkland and his minions believed that they were betting on a winner.

———

In another family, another state, or another generation, Walter Mondale, the quintessential Democrat, might easily have grown up a Republican. He was born in rural Ceylon, Minnesota, in 1928, the year that Herbert Hoover was elected President. His father was a Lutheran minister of modest means but great authority and status in his community. If tragedy or scandal touched the family, Mondale never let it be known. There was never any great doubt that he would be able to attend college and law school, and he apprenticed himself early to prominent men. Fortune smiled on his diligent deference: until his presidential campaign, he had received every office he ever held as a result of appointment, and had never faced election except as an incumbent or a running mate. If ever a

[66]

man were tempted to believe the Republican tenet that success was a product of virtue, Mondale ought to have been the one. If ever a man trod the straight and narrow of white Protestant middle-class proprieties, it was Mondale. But in an age of party demoralization and heightened personal ambition, of weak Democratic organization and strong followings for individuals, Mondale was one of the last politicians who still felt subservient to institutions. He presented himself, and seemingly truly saw himself, as a mere representative of a great government and a noble party. Like his Nordic cousins who have taken so readily to socialism, Mondale responded most deeply to the achievement of collective consciousness and caring, not to the solitary triumphs of the individual.

Mondale's self-image as a mere inheritor, a placeholder for Roosevelt, was dispiritingly apt. Democrats had no Mondaleism to stack up against Reaganism, no movement clamoring for his voice and leadership, no worldview or value system that he alone best expressed. Mondale offered the most practical but least inspirational quality in politics: acceptability. He aroused little passion on his behalf, but equally little passion in opposition. He was even innocuous personally. No one told Walter Mondale anecdotes. His name evoked no aura of glamour in gossip columns. He was noted neither for wit nor for meanness. He had a sound analytic mind, but without a hint of poetry. Above all, he lacked the gallant, headstrong recklessness of a man with a cause. Time and again, his caution had outweighed his ambition. He would take a plunge only if the odds were clearly in his favor.

The most striking contrast between Reagan and Mondale was that Reagan seemed to have lived his entire life to satisfy his sense of himself, while Mondale appeared to have lived chiefly to please and impress others. He was not a comfortable man; even in blue jeans and a plaid shirt, fishing in a Minnesota lake, he carried himself formally. He refused to be photographed enjoying two of his favorite recreations, a glass of Scotch whiskey and a cigar, because he thought them undignified, and he believed that people want a distant majesty in their leaders. He had few known cronies, mostly just contributors, business associates, subordinates, and fellow campaign warriors. He seemed preoccupied with not offending, not slipping, not making mistakes. It was as though he had never outgrown his duty to be a paragon so as not to embarrass his preacher father. Unlike Reagan, he did not seem to savor life.

Mondale was a boy living in cramped, rundown parsonages during the Depression; he was an adolescent during World War II. Admiration for Roosevelt made him a Democrat. But perhaps the seminal events in shaping his career were Hubert Humphrey's election to the U.S. Senate in

1948, and Humphrey's revival of the beleaguered Minnesota Demo-
cratic-Farmer-Labor party. Mondale volunteered in Humphrey's Senate
race, and worked in every Humphrey campaign thereafter. Throughout
his political career, Mondale would be known as Humphrey's protégé.
The two men were far from a match in personality: Humphrey was
exuberant, Mondale dour. Humphrey was privately ribald and fleshly,
Mondale an apparent model of sober rectitude. Humphrey had an un-
quenchable zeal for campaigning, Mondale endured it as a grim necessity.
Nor were they in complete agreement that Mondale was Humphrey's natural political heir. Twice when major jobs came open, the state attorney
generalship in 1961 and then Humphrey's Senate seat when he was
elected vice-president in 1964, Humphrey also had other candidates in
mind. But Mondale maneuvered and connived to make himself the front-
runner, and Humphrey, saving face, gave his imprimatur to accomplished
fact.

As a senator, Mondale was a reliable liberal vote on civil rights and on
Lyndon Johnson's Great Society, and he sided with other Northerners in
moves to break down the chamber's southern squirearchy. Partly in deference to Humphrey, partly in loyalty to Johnson and the party's traditions
of anticommunism, he long supported the Vietnam war. In later years he
said that his slowness to oppose the conflict had been his greatest public
error. It certainly estranged him from a whole stratum of affluent Baby
Boom–generation professionals who regarded Vietnam as a better index
than Social Security of whether a candidate shared their brand of responsible liberalism. But Mondale's delay and moderation in opposing the
war, his hesitation about seeming unpatriotic, made up much of what had
endeared him to the labor movement and other factions of the old New
Deal establishment.

By the time he had served in the Senate for a decade, he was, if not the
beau ideal of the left, certainly one of the short list of generally acknowledged and generally acceptable potential Presidents. He had established
himself as a thoughtful critic of the detached, "imperial" presidency and a
shrewd student of the ways that access and accountability may be best
achieved in a parliamentary rather than presidential system. A skilled and
practiced partisan, he nonetheless urged a more collaborative, noncon-
frontational approach to governance. His mind seemed more responsive
to questions of the mechanics and craft of politics than to the grand,
overarching issues of economics and foreign policy, but the same could
have been said of most of his colleagues. And, unlike most of his colleagues, and in contrast to his general reputation, Mondale had repeatedly
demonstrated moral courage, on occasion at the risk of his career.

Tentative as he had been on Vietnam, Mondale always spoke forthrightly and fervently about the needs of the groups who would remain his special constituencies: the elderly, the black, and the poor. In the late 1960s, he chaired a subcommittee on migratory labor, a problem all but irrelevant to his Minnesota voters but of passionate importance to Mondale. His committee helped bring to prominence the unionization struggles of Cesar Chavez and his fellow organizers. This may have been smart personal politics: it earned the approbation of union leaders, and it established Mondale and the Democrats as friends of the Hispanics long before Latins were generally recognized as a substantial future force in American life. But promoting the union-led boycott of table grapes that were being marketed by anti-union growers was chiefly an act of decency. Arrayed against Mondale were dangerous enemies: the growers; their ally, California Governor Ronald Reagan; and the Pentagon, which shored up the sagging price of grapes by boosting its purchases 350 percent to supply the troops in Vietnam.

In 1972, facing reelection, Mondale led the thankless fight to defend busing as a tactic for integrating schools, against the massed opposition of Southerners, northern urban Democrats, the Nixon administration, and most of the would-be presidential nominees in his own party. Busing was by then being described even by former advocates as an idea whose time had come, and gone — that very phrase was used repeatedly by aides to Massachusetts' ultraliberal Republican Governor Francis W. Sargent as Boston faced court-ordered desegregation. Some critics of the methodology may genuinely have worried about the social dislocation visited upon children who had to travel substantial distances and lengths of time. Most opponents, however, seemed more concerned that mingling with the children of the poor might coarsen the language and behavior of middle-class offspring or slow the pace of their education. Moreover, the egalitarianism underlying busing endangered the most cherished aspirations of the middle class, including many blue-collar Democrats: to earn and save enough money to move to a better neighborhood, with better schools. What was the point of getting ahead if some social engineer kept society's winners from buying their children a head start in the footrace of life? Democrats with ambition, no matter how liberal, were beginning to cave in on busing: Senator Scoop Jackson, a prototypical New Deal Democrat, flatly opposed it, while Senator Edmund Muskie, New York City Mayor (and presidential hopeful) John Lindsay, and even Mondale's mentor Humphrey were waffling in various ways. Mondale, who was up for reelection in 1972 and who had higher hopes for the future, nonetheless held firm. He was hailed for his steadfastness by one of the most influential of doctrinaire liberals, Richard Strout, writing as TRB in the *New Republic:* "For sheer guts we hand it to him. He's put his political life on the line. As we have said before, we rate Mondale of presidential caliber."

Mondale survived the 1972 election, but the image of his bravery somehow did not. People thought of him more as a man who yielded — to party leaders, especially to Humphrey, to labor, to blacks, to the elderly, to all the organized lobbies of the party. Still, he was one of the few national figures who was equally welcome on both sides of the divisive fight over Vietnam policy, among pacifist neo-isolationists like McGovern and among defense-conscious, old-line domino theorists like Jackson. Thus Mondale began to think that 1976 might be the year he could become President. After the 1972 disaster, the party would need a candidate less strident and ideological than McGovern, but the liberals would not be ready to forgive the outright hawks. Like many a liberal before and since, however, Mondale found that his likeliest supporters were reluctant to commit themselves until they knew for certain whether Senator Edward Kennedy would enter the race. Having tested both public response and his own endurance, and having barely budged his name recognition from 1 percent to about 3 percent, Mondale concluded that he could not face what he described as two years, night after night, in look-alike Holiday Inns. He pulled out of the contest. In all probability, 1976 would not have been his year, after all. A shrewd Georgian named Jimmy Carter was already telling everyone who would listen that the 1976 Democratic race would narrow down quickly to two candidates, one of the left and one of the center, because journalists and the public would find that sort of split easier to understand than a multicandidate primary season; that the Democratic candidate of the center would be Carter rather than Jackson, because Carter had made fewer enemies on Vietnam, and because he would endear himself to liberals by nullifying the segregationist insurgency of George Wallace in the South; that the Democratic candidate of the center would capture the nomination, because the party would feel compelled to lure back the once-loyal Democrats who had voted for Richard Nixon in 1972; and that in the wake of Watergate, the Democrats would win. The only thing Carter did not foretell was that as the Democratic candidate of the center he would balance his ticket by reaching out to the left, and would choose Walter Mondale to be his vice-president.

Mondale's withdrawal from the 1976 presidential race might be said to have worked to his advantage: it got him a place on the ticket that he might otherwise have been denied. Yet it raised questions that would haunt him for years. At first, journalists praised his decision not to run as a rare expression of sanity, humility, sound judgment, and moral values in a field aswarm with masochists and egomaniacs. One veteran network news anchor said, "I have known Mondale for years, and always thought of him as an intelligent and personable man, although not a very interesting or original one. That decision of his intrigued me, and made me pay attention thereafter." In time, however, especially among party professionals, the manner of Mondale's pullout led to doubts about whether he had the grim, obsessive fortitude a candidate needs to stay the distance. Even after he had reconciled himself by 1983 to the nights in the Holiday Inns and was running, hard and all but alone in the early going, commentators as sympathetic as Robert Ajemian, Washington bureau chief of *Time*, debated in print whether Mondale had what his mentor Humphrey liked to call "the fire in the belly." He collected money and endorsements humorlessly, almost bloodlessly. He and his aides tried to give the impression that there was no need for a contest, and no purpose in one, that the nomination was Mondale's by right and the party could only be hurt by a competitive struggle. What would Mondale do, critics wondered, in the seemingly unlikely event that he found himself in a real fight?

———✦———

If any opponent was to give Mondale that fight, journalists and other manufacturers of conventional wisdom assumed, it would be John Glenn, the ex-astronaut and Ohio senator. Glenn had been practically invited into the race by elder statesmen and money-raisers among the party centrists, on the theory that he would represent a homespun heroism, and would bring back memories of the last era in which the Democrats had seemed to stand for affirmation and optimism, the presidential term of John Kennedy. Glenn spoke authentically in the marketable terms of Reagan at his most congenial: he urged balance, consensus, and common sense. After nearly a decade in the Senate he remained an outsider, in an age when the public seemed mistrustful of Washington insiders. He had no ideological baggage, no awkward ties to interest groups, no controversy to live down. The corollary, of course, was that he had no natural constituency, except perhaps the plain people. They did not know that he had been a businessman. They barely knew he had been a senator. But they remembered him vividly, two decades later, as an astronaut. They were not quite sure just what feat he had accomplished. Often Glenn found himself introduced as the first man in space (an honor that belonged to the Soviet cosmonaut Yuri Gagarin) or as the first American in space (in reality it was Alan Shepard) or as the first man to orbit the earth (Gagarin again). But whether or not the crowd knew precisely that he was the first American to orbit the earth, for just under five hours on February 20, 1962, they knew he had done something wonderful, and they cheered.

Glenn had rarely if ever shown reluctance to promote his ambitions. After he flew the first nonstop, coast-to-coast supersonic flight in 1957, he was invited to appear on the television game show "Name That Tune." He lasted several weeks as a contestant. A former production executive on the series recalls Glenn as personable but self-assured, even driven, and scrupulously, ostentatiously polite. As an astronaut, Glenn was perhaps the squarest and most public relations–conscious of the original seven Mercury fliers, the readiest to invoke God, country, and family, yet he was also among the most insistent that he be treated as a pilot and not merely a test animal. Although he insisted that he was still a modest small-town Ohio boy, he moved happily, eagerly, into the charmed circle of the Kennedys at the height of their popularity. He eagerly accepted John Kennedy's bid to share in the Mercury program's glory and became a politically useful friend to the President. In the wake of Bobby Kennedy's death, he recalled on national television that he had been invited to the attorney general's Virginia home, Hickory Hill, for dinner, when he and the younger Kennedy brother were virtual strangers — and had accepted. As early as 1964, just two years after his one and only flight into space, Glenn started trying to get himself elected senator from Ohio. It took three attempts, spread over a decade. Yet almost instantly on his arrival in Washington, Glenn was rediscovered by the party as a hot political property. Less than two years after he took office, he was selected by Jimmy Carter as a finalist for the 1976 vice-presidential nomination, and he remained in contention until the party convention, at which he delivered a speech of stupefying dullness and vapidity.

For all his eagerness to get to the Senate, Glenn showed surprisingly little interest in mastering its ways and means once he arrived. Although accident and circumstance occasionally thrust responsibility upon him, especially in closely fought armament and defense debates, he almost never sought to lead a battle. He was not so much ineffectual as uninvolved. To be sure, by the time he was senior enough for some mantle of state to have befallen him, his party was out of power, in the Senate's minority. Yet his unfruitful tenure was the result of more than deference to his party elders. A senior shadow minister in Britain's Labor party, who met Glenn a few months before he announced his candidacy for President, recalled, "I never met a politician who was less interested in politics. Most of the time when elected officials from the States and the United Kingdom get together, the talk is a bubbling caldron of ideas, tactics, issues, and gossip, from the black arts of undoing your enemies to statecraft. Glenn was not interested in any of it. He fell silent almost right off, and it was like a visit to the dentist to keep him involved."

———✐———

Every candidate of consequence has two campaigns going on simultaneously: the private campaign, the behind-closed-doors maneuvering over money and endorsements and strategy, and the public campaign, conducted in and for the news media. Through much of American history, the private campaign was the real campaign. The support of the public mattered far less than the support of the party bosses, and the nominees literally thrust upon the electorate were often people the general public had barely heard of. That began to change in the 1952 election, when popular clamor was a principal factor in the Republicans' decision to nominate Dwight Eisenhower rather than their sentimental favorite, the dogged conservative loyalist Robert Taft. The watershed election was 1960. Even as Theodore White, in his first *Making of the President*, exposed all the backstage agitation, he pointed out that none of it really mattered: the political system he exposed so adroitly was dying, not being born. What had really mattered was what the public saw on primary nights in Wisconsin and West Virginia, when John Kennedy established himself as the people's choice, and legitimized the primary itself as the means of expression of the people's right to choose. By 1984, when primaries or caucuses would take place in every jurisdiction, Walter Mondale's private campaign victories in rigging the delegate selection system could not ensure nomination. His tactical success would count for nothing without the legitimizing rite of triumph in some truly public campaign event.

Several kinds of happenings, diverse in character and circumstance, are embraced under the loosely used rubric of "media." Candidates have the most control over what they call "paid media," or advertising, which consists largely of television commercials. Presidential TV ads are typically standardized throughout the nation at any one moment, but campaign directors replace them every few weeks to develop a preferred sequence of themes and perceptions in the minds of voters. Given the spending limits imposed by federal law during the nominating campaign, few candidates put commercials on the air in any state until the final few weeks before the primary or caucus there. Hence, "paid media" rarely plays much of a part in the early skirmishing in a nominating campaign.

Among the various kinds of "free media," meaning news coverage, the most controlled by candidates are debates, straw polls, and other staged "media events," events that exist only to be covered. A candidate cannot ensure that the interpretation of such events will be congenial to his or her cause. But a campaign staff can ensure that the facts — which in the crucial instance of televised debates will consist of the candidates' words and performance — will go out to voters largely unfiltered. Almost as much under the candidate's control are his own campaign appearances, which furnish pictures, although not usually the text, for local and national television stories. But campaigners find it far harder to manipulate stories that are mostly analysis or commentary, or to deflect stories that result from lobbying by rivals or dissemination of outright disinformation.

To most American citizens, 1983 was a year in which no national election was being held. They were not obliged to vote, and therefore did not pay attention to the maneuverings among party officials, legislative election-law committees, and labor leaders. Nor did they pore over the sparse coverage that even the most elite print and broadcast outlets were rationing out to the first stirrings of the 1984 campaign. But inside the camps of the eight men who yearned for the Democratic nomination, it was understood that the crucial events of 1983 would be media events.

Walter Mondale had the most elaborate and manipulative aspirations. He wanted to persuade reporters that he had assembled the largest and most professional campaign organization in the history of American politics, that his vast and humorless army was invincible. Stories that made this case would not in themselves mean much: they would prompt voters to say to pollsters that they favored Mondale, simply because they would recognize his name and associate it with some positive context. The real value of stories saying that Mondale could not be stopped was to stampede professional politicians, party chieftains, and prominent activists into jumping aboard before the train pulled out of its first station, and to pressure contributors and fund-raisers into making their decisions early. This bandwagon would be doubly effective: it would strengthen Mondale and foreclose human and financial resources that might otherwise be tapped by rivals.

When Mondale and his aides met to discuss press relations, they began with one shrewd insight into the facts of political life: reporters operate more from intuition and extrapolation than from sweeping factual knowledge. If what they see before them, or hear from people they trust, consistently suggests that some version of events is true, journalists will rarely have the time or persistence to check further. By midsummer of 1983, major news organizations had already assigned specific reporters to cover the Mondale campaign. By the end of the year, the entourage had grown into dozens. Most of them referred flatteringly, in stories, to Mondale's masterful "organization." Few asked for the names of Mondale's volunteer chairmen in selected New Hampshire or Iowa counties, towns, and precincts and then called those people to find out how much time they were spending and what they were accomplishing — and very few indeed flew to these localities to see for themselves. As it happened, even by Thanksgiving Mondale had designated precinct chairmen in only 300 of 2600 precincts in Iowa, it was reported much later by *Newsweek* — almost certainly a more formidable organization than his competitors', but hardly the juggernaut that reporters had described.

How were the reporters fooled? Partly by the Mondale staff's own brash self-assurance. Partly by the arrogance of the candidate, who insisted that everything aboard his campaign plane or bus be kept off the record, except by his specifically granted exception, and who enforced his rule by excluding transgressors. Especially, by the ready provision of creature comforts. On the Mondale bus, soda and sandwiches were abundant, time was built in for filing stories and for dinner, arrivals and departures took place more or less on time, and the names of hotels where the entourage would stay overnight were disclosed days, even weeks, in advance. Campaign aides gathered up the reporters' luggage, hunted them out when the bus was about to roll, and scrupulously dug up information as requested — provided, of course, that the campaign was willing to release it. Even when facts were being withheld, the manner of Mondale's aides was, if condescending, also unfailingly polite. Many of the senior advisers to Mondale were Washington veterans, and they understood the hothouse atmosphere inside a campaign entourage: corny in-jokes seem like Wildean wit, minor inconveniences become major affronts, items merely worthy of gossip come to look like world-shaking events. In this circumstance, reporters tend to judge much, sometimes everything, by the way their needs are met. A campaign that coddles the press is presumed to have a candidate who is open, public-spirited, and competent. A campaign that is Spartan and chaotic is, reporters assume, malign or inept or both.

Reporters reinforced each other's canonization of the Mondale staff. Journalists are a clannish lot: they tend by preference to spend more time with each other than with anyone else, and they trust each other's judgment more. However bullish their published or broadcast stories about Mondale, their private assessments during 1983 were even more affirmative. Despite the frequent defeats of front-runners — Lyndon Johnson in 1968, Edmund Muskie in 1972, Edward Kennedy in 1980 — pundits by the score pronounced Mondale unbeatable once Kennedy left the race. At lunches in Washington and New York and Boston, the opinion was voiced, to a chorus of assenting nods, by the political editors of major newspapers, by columnists for such influential magazines as the liberal

New Republic, by top political reporters for the newsweeklies. At a representative party at the home of CBS commentator Bill Moyers, Mondale's apparent invincibility was agreed upon by anchors, top news producers, and their bosses, the news division chiefs of two networks.

———————

Yet in the next breath of these conversations, the sages of the instant analysis would echo, as equally certain truth, the very contention John Glenn's advisers had hoped to transmit to the media: that Glenn alone had the kind of all-American wholesomeness and personal independence needed to defeat Ronald Reagan. Glenn's closest advisers were not wise in the ways of Washington, and like their candidate they had a deep distaste for conventional politics. But they were canny enough to recognize that Glenn's chief weakness was that he appealed to independents, even Republicans, more than to the partisan Democrats who participate in primaries and caucuses. The more Mondale attracted the endorsements and assistance of the New Deal constituencies, and the more he labeled himself the Democrat's Democrat, the more important it became to Glenn to portray himself as a man who could broaden the party's appeal. His claim, accepted more or less uncritically by the news media, was electability. Journalism thrives on conflict, and reporters felt they had to presuppose some obstacle between Mondale and the nomination. They adopted Glenn for the role by consensus. Only Glenn and Mondale were followed with any consistency by most major news organizations. When *Time* prepared a chart showing the dates and prospects for the various primaries and caucuses, only Glenn figured as a realistic challenger to Mondale in any state except the home territories of some of those grouped as "others." And in most of the stories, Glenn's claim of electability was treated as received wisdom or widely held opinion, not as his campaign's fundamental strategy.

In three other regards, however, Glenn's campaign staff made media errors — mistakes that turned into hurtful stories. The first was to hire seasoned professional operatives, tell them they had authority, then ignore their advice and fire them. Glenn brought the professionals into his campaign in an effort to look less provincial. He succeeded only in making himself seem more isolated and, worse, unwilling to do the hard slogging needed to win. One veteran Washington columnist snorted: "He's waiting for the puff of white smoke to come up, like it does for the Pope."

The problem centered, as the campaign did, on Glenn's stiff-necked, insular Senate chief of staff, Bill White, who prided himself on being the only man Glenn would consult or trust. After reluctantly concluding that a large-scale national campaign needed experienced help at raising money and, perhaps more important, at spending it effectively, White recruited field organizer J. Joseph Grandmaison, who had performed the same function, successfully, for George McGovern in 1972 and who had then held a variety of political jobs. Grandmaison pleaded for money to establish organizations in early states; White held off, insisting instead on a campaign conducted through free and paid media. He was certain of Glenn's appeal, and unconvinced of the difficulty of getting supporters to turn out at the voting booth or caucus. White was also fearful that the campaign would run out of money. Despite this determination to husband funds, and despite their rapid influx — by the last quarter of 1983, Glenn was raising contributions faster than Mondale — a principal aide to Grandmaison correctly predicted in early October that the Glenn campaign would be broke by mid-March. Grandmaison argued that emphasizing the early states would produce hopeful results that would in turn bring in more money. White countered that Glenn carried more potential strength in the next phase of primaries, in the South, and ought to hold back some assets. White also resisted suggestions that Glenn reach out to traditional Democratic intellectuals and party elders, about whom White knew next to nothing. In an early meeting, a senior campaign aide suggested that Glenn was seen, unfairly, as a lightweight, and could be helped by a well-publicized series of briefings, which the aide offered to arrange, by such Kennedy- and Johnson-era policymakers as Walt Rostow and William Bundy. White replied, without sarcasm and in genuine bewilderment, "Who is Bill Bundy?"

Glenn's second mistake was in reaching for some issue on which to confront a special-interest group, so as to underline his independence and, by implication, Mondale's excessive deference. He hoped to provoke stories that would show him as a brave man, doing something impolitic out of dedication to principle. The group he chose to confront was homosexuals, and the occasion was a New York City forum, to which he got himself invited, on gay rights legislation. Glenn was not bigoted against homosexuals: he had accepted a professed homosexual as one of his topmost campaign aides. But that fact made his decision all the worse in the eyes of some aides and reporters. They saw what he did as cynical grandstanding. His posture was in itself reasonable: he said he opposed discrimination, but objected to condoning a controversial life-style. The result was not what he sought. The news stories that Glenn generated reached print or air primarily in New York City, where homosexuals have begun to become a political force, or in the suddenly hostile gay press. Worse, despite advice from New York staff and supporters, Glenn had failed to

[77]

grasp that his New York chairman, Manfred Ohrenstein, represented a state legislative district that was heavily homosexual. Ohrenstein, who had been Glenn's only consequential supporter among elected officials in New York, came under increasing pressure from constituents, and soon withdrew from Glenn's campaign.

The third media mishap was not primarily of Glenn's making, but it was by far the worst. *New York Times* columnist William Safire, prompted in part by remarks Glenn had made in private at a dinner party, questioned in print whether Glenn was sufficiently friendly toward Israel. His voting record was not notably objectionable to Israeli sympathizers. Nothing in his personal life, save perhaps that he was a small-town midwestern Christian, could have caused grave concern about prejudice or insensitivity. But Glenn had dared to note in conversation one of the largely unexamined facts of life in Washington: the potent lobbying, single-issue giving, and single-issue voting by American Jews to ensure that the wishes of Israel's government predominate in the shaping of American policy in the Middle East. The effect of this agitation is to enforce, not just an American commitment to the survival of Israel, but an American deference to Israel's judgment of the best means of effecting that survival. Glenn tried to mollify Safire. He made reassuring utterances in reply to reporters. Finally, he changed his schedule to come to New York City to speak to a major Jewish civic meeting, both to profess friendship and to implore forgiveness. Nonetheless, the damage was done, and it was considerable: Glenn was mistrusted residually by Jews, who exert a de facto veto in Democratic politics, and who are of all interest groups the most important in fund-raising; he had also aroused questions in the minds of reporters and news organizations as to whether he had the sensitivity needed in a national leader. And although Jews are quick to deny suggestions that as a group they control or influence the mass media, aides to Glenn ruefully noted that at each of the so-called Magnificent Seven — the *New York Times, Washington Post, Time, Newsweek,* ABC, NBC, and CBS — either the top business figure or the chief news executive was then Jewish.

For other candidates, the problem in 1983 was not so much to shape media perception as to attract any notice at all. Senator Alan Cranston poured resources into straw polls, as Jimmy Carter had done in 1975 and 1979, to create the early appearance of a surge in popularity that the media would report and thereby bring into being. Cranston also decided to make himself a single-issue, nuclear freeze candidate, less because he was sure it would work than because he reasoned that only an issue campaign that struck a nerve with the public was likely to make a hero of a skinny, balding near-septuagenarian who had recently dyed what remained of his hair.

George McGovern, who had pioneered single-issue presidential campaigning in 1972 against the Vietnam war, described himself candidly to journalists as a primarily symbolic candidate, running to compel the party to recognize the left point of view. By all but nullifying himself as a vote seeker, McGovern hoped to persuade the press to treat him as an ideological elder statesman and thus to write about his détentist opinions, especially on Soviet relations, the arms race, and Central America.

Reubin Askew hardly seemed to campaign, and had trouble clarifying why he had entered the race. His primary support groups were strange bedfellows — the anti-abortion movement and some elements of the business community who were attracted to his emphasis on international trade and tariff negotiation.

Ernest Hollings found himself in the oddest and most frustrating relationship of all with the press: they conceded that his conservative stance on defense and moderate one on economic policy was probably the best for the Democrats; they hailed him for offering the most workable approach to resolving federal budget problems — a flat cut of, say, 10 percent on everything except debt service, to share the pain equally; they admired his brain, praised his wit, found him funny and genial and quick to get to the point. But they would not take him seriously as a candidate.

Cranston's travails were understandable; he was too old, and looked it, unlike Reagan. McGovern was tainted by his landslide loss in 1972. Askew, as an opponent of abortion, might be able to make trouble but would never be tolerated by feminists as a genuine contender for the nomination. But what was Hollings's automatic disqualification? Simply that he was a Southerner, like the discredited Carter? That he had a thick, at times incomprehensible, South Carolina accent? That he was a Vietnam war hawk in a party still dominated by those who had been doves? Perhaps. But one newspaper political analyst thought Hollings's problems were far simpler to explain: "It is just that, if the Democrats are going to nominate someone who thinks what he thinks, the person they choose is much more likely to be John Glenn. In effect, that slot in the field is already taken."

Gary Hart faced a similar, slightly more complex conundrum: he was an attractive Westerner with nearly a decade of Senate experience, a moderate-to-liberal voting record, an expertise in defense, which Democrats viewed as the most cuttable part of the federal budget, and a middle-of-the-road posture on foreign policy. He was craggy and telegenic, spoke lucidly and persuasively, and had identified a special constituency to which he could plausibly appeal, the Baby Boom generation, many of them just a decade or so younger than he was himself. Yet Hart was unable until late in 1983 to break out of the pack, and then he did so chiefly in profiles that emphasized the shy, wintry side of his personality rather than his puckishness. For much of the year, his campaign was actively burdened by media stories that he was about to quit for lack of funds and support; the stories, which disheartened his committed backers and discouraged potential others, were "planted," Hart contended, by people in Cranston's camp. He speculated that the Cranston aides were trying to avoid having to share the lucrative fund-raising resources available to a western liberal, foremost among them the drawing power of performers from Hollywood and the music industry. At the turn of the year, Hart complained, "The major coverage that I have been able to get from the national media is this story that I was going to give up, which was harmful, not true, and not adequately checked." In truth, Hart's aides admitted, he was intensely moody and on any given day might well have sounded as though he were on the verge of leaving the contest.

Perhaps the most offbeat, daring — and cunning — media strategy was Jesse Jackson's. Unlike the other aspirants, who declared their candidacies and then spent the rest of the year trying to get reporters to pay attention, Jackson contrived to create the appearance of a genuine draft by the black community, generating intense publicity around the question: will he or won't he run? He would not be the first black to seek the nomination: Shirley Chisholm had run in Democratic primaries and received some convention votes in 1972. But Jackson presented himself as the first black candidate with a chance to make a significant impact, and he did so by creating a dynamic between black audiences and mainstream white reporters. The more black churchgoers and ralliers chanted, "Run, Jesse, run," the more reporters for the mainstream media described Jackson to their audiences as a serious candidate. And the more Jackson's candidacy was legitimized by the media, the more young and poor blacks felt impelled to support him. The position of black establishment leaders, who preferred to deal with Mondale and who distrusted Jackson's personal ambition, grew untenable. With the news media proclaiming Jackson a force, how could blacks themselves write off a candidate from their own community as unable to make an impact? With no alternative candidate to offer, and with black enthusiasm being conveyed on the nightly news, the resisters slowly yielded.

The twentieth anniversary celebrations of Martin Luther King, Jr.'s

March on Washington, climaxed by recollections of his "I have a dream" speech, turned out, despite the organizers' wishes, to provide compelling testimony of the zeal for a Jackson campaign. The reawakened memory of King seemed to deepen the yearning among blacks, and among white liberals and moderates, for a national black leader of passionate style and burning moral conscience. The repeated replaying of footage from the incantatory peroration of King's speech led columnists and commentators to note that, of all politicians, black or white, only Jackson had anything like the same oratorical fire.

By October, Jackson was being covered more or less steadily by major news organizations, an attention extended only to Mondale and Glenn among his rivals. In that month, he became the first of any of the Democrats to receive Middle America's highest insignia of media approval: he occupied, alone, the cover of a weekly issue of *Time* magazine. None of his rivals would appear as the sole cover subject of *Time* until after the nomination race was effectively settled. And the only reason Jackson did not wind up on the cover of *Newsweek* at virtually the same moment is that the newsweekly's editors postponed their assessment of Jackson, simply because *Time* had got there first. Jackson had made himself in effect the black Edward Kennedy — the candidate whose decision to pursue an ambition becomes a pivotal news story in the public mind.

———————

There was no way of telling, that night in October 1983, that what was about to take place was the first important media event of the campaign — a debate that brought all the candidates into direct, public competition in the media capital, New York City. The evening's entertainment had been assembled as a public-relations gesture on behalf of New York's new Democratic governor, Mario Cuomo, and on that basis it had become a command performance for the participants. The event had not even been well run from the candidates' point of view: the audience was made up primarily of their supporters, in approximately equal numbers from each camp, who would cheer on cue; journalists, the group whom the candidates would have preferred to reach, had had to scratch for tickets and in many instances had been turned away. Despite supposedly tight security, supporters of the highly eccentric splinter candidate Lyndon LaRouche had managed to get in, and they would stage a disturbance midway through. Except for cable TV, electronic coverage of the two-hours-plus event would be limited to snippets, mostly on the late-evening local news.

Yet what happened at Town Hall in New York City was the forerunner of what would prove to be a marathon series of debates among the Democratic candidates for President — there would be at least ten more televised over the next eight months — and they would matter, more than in any election ever before, in determining who would win the nomination. Moreover, the themes and conflicts that were soon to be played out under the glare of more intense national scrutiny were already evident that night. The campaign in microcosm was on that Manhattan stage.

The host at Town Hall was Senator Daniel Patrick Moynihan, and the questioners (debate formats owe much to TV talk shows) were campaign-book author Theodore White, retired NBC reporter and anchor Edwin Newman, political scientist James David Barber of Duke University, and former Congresswoman Barbara Jordan of Texas. The roster, aside from its intellectual glitter, provided a neat example of the ticket balancing that New York's Democrats pioneered for the national party. Moynihan is an Irish Catholic, White a Jew, Barber something of a good ole boy (despite his having taught at Yale), and Jordan is not only a woman but black. Nationally, the Democrats may feel prompted to reestablish ties to white Middle America, and to set aside the traditions of currying favor with special interests and ethnic voting blocs. But among New York Democrats — whom Moynihan described, with a minimum of hyperbole, as "the oldest political party in the world" — politics remains, as strongly as ever, synonymous with the assertion of special and ethnic interests.

The front-runner, Walter Mondale, sat in a row with the other candidates, but he acted aloof, condescending. He smiled, leaned back, shrugged expressively, sometimes attempted a dismissive wave at references to his standing ahead of the field or, as the description was sometimes more pettishly phrased, his receiving more attention than anyone else. His goal was to remind the audience of the gulf of experience that separated him from other candidates. As Jimmy Carter's vice-president, he had to expect to be lambasted for each of the many failures of his former boss. So he had decided to embrace his past and emphasize the training it provided, both in practical knowledge and in dealing with the psychological pressures of leadership. Virtually every answer he gave was meant to signal to listeners that he did not just have opinions or theories about what life is like in the White House; he *knew*. Talking about the desirability of a summit with the Soviets, he said, perhaps irrelevantly but in keeping with his agenda, "Most cable traffic might just as well be sent directly to the *New York Times* and *Washington Post*, because it's going to be there tomorrow, anyway. Any telephone calls you might make to the other head of state are monitored by everyone else in the world, so you can't be candid in them."

Mondale spoke proudly of the Camp David accords that had brought at least a temporary peace between Israel and Egypt, although the import of his role in them was open to question, and their value was dubious because the main participants were either dead or fading from power, while tension in the region remained acute. Camp David had been the one generally acknowledged success of the Carter administration, and it was still popular among Jews, who constitute roughly a third of the Democratic vote in New York City. Mondale did not for a moment hesitate to make so specifically targeted an appeal. Before the night was out, he pleaded the cases of teachers, nuclear freezeniks, the labor movement. Describing the people who must be consulted when taking any major governmental initiative, he invoked, in a litany, "blacks, Hispanics, Asians, Indians, women, ethnics." He sounded as though he honestly did view Americans, not as individuals, but as members of defined groups.

Glenn showed none of Mondale's hauteur, but he, too, carried himself in a way meant to suggest that his prominence was natural and irreversible. He had been coached by David Sawyer, a gifted filmmaker who had become one of the most respected and research-conscious political media consultants. To contrast with Mondale, who cast himself as the quintessential professional politician, Glenn presented himself as an antipolitician. Or rather, as more than a politician. Research conducted for his campaign had shown that many people were unaware of anything he had done since he returned nervelessly to earth in his space capsule, a scary 250 miles off course as a result of a manual retrofire error. So he stressed his experience and purported independence and courage during his nine years in the Senate. But he equally emphasized that he had been a military pilot, a war hero, a company president in three private businesses. He thereby adopted the central theme of Carter's campaign in 1976, and Reagan's in 1980: that the problems in Washington are self-generated, and that only an outsider of diverse background can take over and provide government "as good as the American people."

Glenn's trickiest problem was how to seem assertive and forceful enough to lead without sounding peevish and sacrificing the public's natural goodwill toward a hero. Aides kept telling him that he must not attack his opponents personally — that the way to set himself apart from mere politics was to disdain its petty feuding. But Glenn believed that he needed to show flashes of anger to prove his virility, and he had rehearsed two outbursts that he was sure the night's format would give him the opportunity to voice. Sure enough, one came during the crosstalk between candidates. Needled by dark-horse contenders about his votes for some of Reagan's economic programs, and their implication that Glenn was less than a true Democrat, he in effect brushed them aside and directed his answer to Mondale instead. After intoning the almost ritual disclaimer that he would have preferred Democratic alternatives to the Reagan plan, Glenn assailed the Carter-Mondale record of soaring inflation and interest rates, rising deficits, sluggish employment patterns. Something, he said, had to be done, and Reagan's proposals were better than nothing. This attack of course proved the point that Glenn was indeed to the right of the party, especially the party's primary voters, on economic issues. But Glenn's aim was to attract independents in such large numbers that the party would embrace him for his electability. He was accustomed to politics in a state that holds "open" primaries, in which independents are permitted to participate, rather than the "closed" primaries, for Democrats only, that prevail in many other jurisdictions. His style of politics was shaped by what he knew.

Glenn's second outburst was even more studied, and it won the battle of the "sound bite" — it was the most memorable and emotional moment of the night, and was featured prominently in the television and radio accounts. His campaign had been relying heavily on a forthcoming movie, *The Right Stuff*, which was to be released just before Christmas, 1983. Based on Tom Wolfe's novelistic nonfiction, the film would tell the story of the nation's original astronaut program. No single figure would be its hero, but Glenn would come closest, and he would be shown in equal measure as a patriot, a risk taker, a man's man, and a devoted husband. In months to come, the film's commercial fate and Glenn's political fortunes would become entwined, and not for the good of either. But on this night, and until the end of the year, the received opinion would hold that *The Right Stuff* would give Glenn millions of dollars' worth of free publicity. Apprehensive of this prospect, Cuomo, in support of Mondale, had sneered at Glenn as a "celluloid candidate." The acerbic phrase, a prime example of Cuomo's gift for finding the lethal *mot juste*, had so compromised him that he bypassed the debate, although he was the nominal host. Glenn, honestly outraged, had practiced the voicing of his anger until it was word-perfect. It was "not on film," he said, that he risked his life on dozens of missions as a pilot. He was not on film when he hurtled into space. He had been proud to serve his country, and grateful for what he learned as a career officer. Cuomo's slur was not just malicious but obtusely wrongheaded, Glenn charged: everyone knew that the real celluloid candidate already occupied the White House. Reagan was the actor. Glenn's bravery was real.

Of the candidates seeking attention rather than endeavoring to exploit it, Gary Hart seemed perhaps the least comfortable. By nature an intellectual and a scholar, Hart was determined to present himself in terms of simple polarities that voters can absorb: optimistic versus pessimistic, new versus old, strong versus weak, and, a touch more subtly, technological and scientific versus ideological and hidebound. But he could barely curb his impulse toward academic hedging and qualification in confronting complex ideas. When he got a chance to question Glenn, he began a long, rambling, seemingly undirected discussion about the "shock of Sputnik," "postindustrialism," "international competition," and, it eventually turned out, the state of economic and technological adaptation in America. The question, let alone the answer, was the basis for a book. Hart was so long-winded that the audience started to fidget and mutter audibly, and he blurted out, with his trademark nervous grin, "I'm coming to the question. "

The funniest moments of the night came from Alan Cranston. Just as he started to speak about nuclear weapons, the one issue on which he hoped to base his campaign, the stage-spanning banner that read "New York Presidential Forum" suddenly fell down. Cranston, a fey and poised speaker, greeted the mishap with just the right blend of mock consternation and aplomb. He got a far bigger laugh, however, with a sally he had prepared especially for the press. During the portion of the evening when the candidates questioned each other, he turned to Hollings and asked why reporters had not given more exposure to candidates who were not front-runners. After the audience had finished its appreciative chuckle, Hollings replied that journalists pay too much heed to the technical side of politics, and not enough to candidates' visions of America.

Hollings's vision, as it happened, was that the nation was overstuffed, overindulgent, overreliant on help from others. He renewed his call for "shared sacrifice," for an across-the-board percentage cut in spending. In his most inspirational moment, he articulated a phrase that eventually would be lifted by one after another of his rivals: "The question is not whether you are better off than you were four years ago, but whether we are better off as a nation."

This shrewdly turned counterpunch to Reagan caught the audience's attention less, however, than Hollings's wry description of the plight of also-ran candidates. He said of reporters: "They have always gone to the mechanics — who's your pollster, how much money you have — and they don't want to discuss issues until you're like Mo Udall [the ultimately forlorn second-place finisher in eight primaries in 1976]. And then they go say you had a lot of wit and humor — 'Wasn't he nice?' "

In fact, the debate provided little serious discussion of issues, even in this format that the candidates largely controlled. McGovern and Hollings clashed over arms-control treaties: Hollings asserted that the Soviets were persistent cheaters on existing agreements; McGovern replied that it didn't matter, because neither side could afford to go on building ever more complex weapons, and no sane chief of state on either side would ever use them anyway. Askew, urging the traditional free market in international trade, a posture increasingly associated with Republicans, attacked Mondale's support of "domestic content" legislation, which would effectively bar most foreign-car imports in order to buttress the uncompetitively high wages and benefits of American laborers. But for the most part, the seven white men of the October debate agreed on: a foreign policy that would be vigorously anti-Communist but less hostile toward the Soviets; a domestic policy that would retain New Deal and Great Society programs but would slow the rate of government spending. Except for McGovern, none of the candidates wanted to cut the defense budget. They differed only on the size of the desired increase. In their closing statements, the candidates did not emphasize issues, but visions. Mondale's invoked an America in which excluded groups would participate anew. Glenn saw a nation pulling together rather than polarized by selfishness; the party, he warned, "must not give in to special interests." Hart pleaded for recognition that the world has changed, and that politics must change with it: "new leadership" must provide "great ideas." Hart's, of all the candidates' themes, was the one most cunningly aimed to answer the nostalgic appeal of Reaganism, which held that the nation's problems stemmed from having turned away from the faiths and morals of our forefathers, and that the problems of the future could best be solved by looking to the best of the past. By evening's end, the alignment of the candidates was clear: Mondale spoke for the old New Deal coalition; Glenn, Hollings, and Askew for the centrists; Hart for the technocratic wing of the reformers; Cranston and McGovern for their pacifist-isolationist wing. And unless Jackson entered the race, Mondale alone would speak for the blacks.

III

Subtractions

CHRISTMAS is normally a caesura in the endless turmoil of politics, a time when voices are lowered because the electorate, enwrapped in hearthside affections and concerns, is presumed not to be listening. On the eve of a presidential election year, Christmas is the last lull before the tumult in Iowa and in the proverbial snows of New Hampshire. But during the Christmas season of 1983, two unpredicted events took place that radically altered perceptions of what was to come. One was an errand of mercy. The other was a failed movie. One made a candidacy. The other doomed one.

The errand of mercy took Jesse Jackson, black candidate for President, to Syria, implacable foe of the United States, to plead for the release of an injured airman, Robert Goodman, who had been shot down over Lebanon. The episode was fraught with risk, and only a candidate of Jackson's unshakable confidence, or perhaps utter desperation, would have attempted it. American voters have a deep and justifiable suspicion of private diplomacy. When it works, it usually reflects only the desire of some foreign power to use a good-hearted citizen to embarrass his own government in Washington. Thus Jackson knew that the public and especially the press might well be skeptical, even critical, if he succeeded. If he failed, the damage to his hopes would be almost beyond repair. Jews who already resented his ties to Arab leaders would proclaim that even the Arabs' friends could not trust them, and that Jackson had been made a dupe. The Reagan administration and in all likelihood his fellow Democrats, especially his rivals for leadership of the black community, would brand him naive and ineffectual, unready to leap without prior training into the highest office in the land. And the American citizenry might turn on him for having reminded them of the bitter helplessness they felt when fifty-two of their countrymen had been held hostage by Islamic forces for more than a year in Tehran. To be sure, Jackson had, or thought he had, hints from Syria's government that Goodman would be freed, as a gesture of Third World solidarity, as a boon to Arab sympathizers in the United States, and as a way to humiliate the Reagan administration. But, in this situation, promises were unreliable and any confrontation might only endanger Goodman's life. For Jackson, perhaps the strongest argument for his all-or-nothing gamble was that he felt he had a special claim to save Goodman: the airman was black.

For days the newspapers and nightly newscasts were filled with reports that Jackson would go to Damascus, that he had gone, that he was negotiating. Had he been directing the media coverage himself, he could not have asked for more. His trip was dramatic, its purpose readily comprehensible to even the least-informed news consumer, and it came during the dearth of competing news at the turn of the year. When the suspense culminated in triumph, he and Goodman made the front pages of hundreds of newspapers, the network newscasts at every hour, the talk shows for days to come. A black had rescued a black: the image appealed across racial and ideological lines. Whites, especially conservatives, liked Jackson's emphasis on self-reliance and even on an implicit separatism for the black community. Blacks cheered the notion of a racial kinsman who had achieved what the President of the United States could not. The return of Goodman to American soil, and his display to millions by means of television, were artfully stage-managed. He was young, handsome, articulate, unassuming. His family was represented by his stunningly beautiful, youthful, impassioned mother. His wife, who is white, was for the most part kept discreetly offscreen.

In the musical *Dreamgirls*, which had premiered on Broadway almost exactly two years before Jackson's trip, and which remained a sellout hit, black singers and musicians who are seeking success measure it by whether they achieve a "crossover," whether they reach beyond the black market to the much larger and more lucrative white one. For all of these artists, the moral crisis is whether to adulterate their style, stripping it of much of its blackness and integrity, to reach the pinnacle, or to remain true to their roots at the cost of fame and wealth. For Jesse Jackson, the rescue of Robert Goodman was the way in which he achieved "crossover." His specific identity as a person, beyond the mere fact of his being black, began to register with white voters. But for Jesse Jackson, there was no crisis of conscience and compromise. He welcomed white support, but he spoke to black America.

He was not, like many rival black leaders, a product of the comfortable middle class. He was not afraid to shout and to sweat. He could speak the language of the ghetto, and despite his peaceful slogans and ready smile he had the violent potential of a coiled spring — he surged with energy about to explode. His manner had the menace of a man who is ready to back up his words with actions. Jesse Jackson was born a bastard, to a teenage mother who had intended to have an abortion until her minister dissuaded her. He grew up in semirural poverty in South Carolina, at the height of the Jim Crow laws; he was nearly thirteen when the Supreme Court made the first step toward desegregating schools, in its *Brown v. Board of Education* decision. An apt student in an area beset with privation, he made it north to college in the fashion of many poor blacks, on a football scholarship to the University of Illinois. But he soon found the North's racism as painful as the South's, and retreated to the black North Carolina Agricultural and Technical State University in Greensboro. He had no illusions about what he faced. He said later, "I grew up under apartheid." It rankled him to have failed to conquer the North's system of living, and after graduation he went back to Illinois, to the Chicago Theological Seminary. Yet the South still called to him, and it had become the crucible of social change. In 1965, after watching on television the beatings of civil rights marchers in Selma, Alabama, Jackson joined the Southern Christian Leadership Conference to work for Martin Luther King, Jr. He was just twenty-six when, three years later, King was gunned down in Memphis.

From that moment, if not before, Jackson had the conviction that he was the chosen instrument to carry forward King's plan. He told reporters the day after the assassination that he had been with King as he died, that he had cradled the fallen leader in his arms, that his clothes were stained with King's blood. Those images were potent, almost biblical. But they were not true. King's widow and his older, closer aides denied Jackson's claim, and in time he came to admit that he had been speaking some sort of metaphor, not fact. Jackson's political ambitions, both within the remains of King's organization and among blacks at large, were opposed by his former colleagues, and especially by King's widow, Coretta, who considered herself the one rightful guardian of her husband's legacy. The King family pointedly opposed Jackson's candidacy for President.

Yet in spiritual terms, Jackson's claim was just. Within a couple of months after King's death, Jackson found the sermon and the rhetoric that would buoy poor and hopeless blacks as no other leader could. He took on the generally unwanted job of "mayor" of Resurrection City, the shantytown of tents set up on Washington Mall to fulfill one of King's dreams for the Poor People's Campaign. Jackson told the bedraggled squatters to say, "I am somebody." King had preached about heaven on earth. Jackson preached about earthly pride and dignity. Over the years, he endeared himself to conservatives because of his rhyming, alliterative, street-rap-style injunctions to youth to learn in school, search for a job, work with diligence, and make it on their own. He endorsed affirmative action and public-works programs, and his Operation PUSH corporations qualified him as a poverty entrepreneur, but his chief concern was making the businesses that profited from blacks be more responsive to their needs. A successful negotiation with Jackson would lead to positive publicity; a breakdown in talks, he warned, could lead to a boycott. His approach, he acknowledged, was little short of blackmail, but it worked.

The private Jackson was urbane, assured, although with pockets of ignorance. He knew what a well-informed layman would know about economic theory, foreign policy, the federal budget. He lacked both the legalistic detail and especially the historical context that were deeply imprinted on his rivals; he was no scholar of government. He was also at best slipshod as a manager of PUSH's federal grant money, and he contrived to provide himself a six-figure income while pleading the case of the poor. He was something of a racial separatist, and some people thought he might be a bigot. He seemed to prefer black reporters to whites and would say to those he favored, "Let's talk black talk," assuming they were recruits in his black-power crusade. He spoke slightingly, often, of Jews and seemed convinced that they were out to ruin him — as, indeed, many were — for his outspoken support of the Palestine Liberation Organization and its claims to at least a portion of the Jewish homeland. Critics of the private Jackson thought him manipulative, perhaps cynical, certainly power-mad. Even supporters said he was disorganized, impulsive, and heedless.

The public Jackson was without question the most exciting personality in American politics. From Mississippi towns to Chicago tenements to Los Angeles churches, he brought the message of black empowerment. In the age-old struggle between those blacks who want to assimilate for advancement and those blacks who want to unite politically to force change, Jackson was the clarion voice of self-assertion. He spoke with a husky-throated fervor, a melodic lilt, a strummed-bass beat and urgency. His words were old-fashioned, periphrastic, like a compendium of invocations from William Jennings Bryan. Their import was hypnotic: "Hands that picked cotton will now pick the President. There's a freedom train coming but you have to be registered to ride. Get on board! Get on board! We can move from the guttermost to the uttermost. From the slave ship to the championship. From the outhouse to the statehouse to the courthouse to the White House." His defiant, pathetic assertion of 1968 became an antiphonal cry of liberation. "I am," he would shout. "I am," the crowd chanted back. "Somebody," he would say. "Somebody," they answered, verse after verse, making his ambition their own.

As horizons were expanding for Jesse Jackson at the end of 1983, they were contracting for John Glenn. While Jackson was making a crossover from a known constituency to a broader base, and thus compelling the attention of the media, Glenn was discovering that his expected constituency was evanescent and that the media were repenting their earlier enthusiasm. Much had gone at least mildly wrong for Glenn, and not much had gone right. He was attracting the support and contributions of southern and Texas conservatives, but they were scarcely enough to win him the party's nomination. His standing in the polls, which had risen through most of the year, had leveled off, even declined. People who had liked the idea of a more conservative, genuinely heroic Democrat had found, on closer examination, that Glenn gave no very clear idea of what sort of alternative to Ronald Reagan he would be. Yet all of those problems were manageable, all within the parameters of his grand strategy. What was not within his power to recoup was the public's seeming conviction that *The Right Stuff* was the wrong stuff.

The film was ballyhooed enough. *Newsweek* gave it the cover, with a solo photograph of Ed Harris, the look-alike actor playing Glenn; *Time* offered a lavish spread inside. Newspapers and television treated the film as a major event, both artistic and political. Critics wrote upbeat, even ecstatic reviews: the movie was hailed as epitomizing a new national spirit of patriotism, a reawakening of traditional derring-do masculinity, a just pride at our feats in space. Praise was heaped on the high-intensity performances, the supercharged visual style, the emotive story-telling. And the most widely quoted scene featured Glenn at his most admirable. Despite his keen ambition and deep sense of duty, he put one commitment ahead of that to his country: his lifelong devotion to his wife, Annie. A brave and decent woman who was all but universally adored by reporters who came to know her through Glenn's campaigns, she was, at the time he was an astronaut, an acute and agonized stutterer. With Vice-President Lyndon Johnson on her doorstep one day, demanding that she let a crowd of milling reporters in, a panicky Annie Glenn begged her husband to tell her what to do. He urged her to stand up to the vice-president, refuse his demands. And she did. The fact that Johnson had few remaining admirers made the Glenns' defiant protection of their privacy all the more appealing. There seemed no way that *The Right Stuff* could miss drawing millions of viewers, and no way that those viewers would not revere John Glenn.

All the Democratic candidates insisted, of course, that the film had nothing to do with the campaign, Glenn somewhat disingenuously and smugly, the others in what sounded like wishful thinking. Almost the only dissenting note was sounded by a Mondale aide who said his colleagues did not regard the film as a problem, because they thought it made Glenn look old. Indeed, Harris, the actor, looked considerably younger than the forty that Glenn was when he went into space; Glenn, more than two decades later, showed most if not all of his sixty-two years. The poignant difference between the face of youth and the face of age, coupled with the public's sublime unawareness of what if anything Glenn had done to fulfill his youthful promise, might have combined to give some people a vague sense that Glenn had been something of a loser.

As it turned out, Glenn's problem was not how people interpreted the film but the fact that they did not see it at all. *The Right Stuff* was perhaps the biggest box-office bomb of the Christmas season. Market research had shown, before it was released, that people were not eager to go, and apparently nothing that they heard about the film, however positive, could move them. Even when the film was rereleased in late winter after being nominated for a raft of Oscars, it remained a dud. No one was quite sure why. Perhaps the early 1960s just seemed too long ago — an emotional high point, with all its Kennedy and Camelot mystique, for the Baby Boom generation who ran studios and wrote reviews, but almost meaningless for the twelve-to-twenty-four-year-olds who dominate the moviegoing public. Perhaps the accomplishments of the Mercury astronauts, and the bravery it took to achieve them, paled beside the courage of those who rocketed to the moon a few years later, or those who left the safety of a NASA shuttle capsule to walk alone in space. Perhaps the public was simply less infatuated with the whole notion of space travel, skeptical about its cost, bored with its logistical whizbangery — certainly the television networks gave spaceflight far less euphoric coverage than in NASA's heyday. Perhaps the very notion of group adventure is inherently less interesting to Americans than a feat of rugged individualism. Perhaps one segment of the public simply felt a movie could not begin to match the drama of real-life television coverage of space travel, while another segment felt that a movie based on truth could not be as exciting as *Star Wars*.

That the hoped-for boost from the movie never materialized was not the most crushing blow to Glenn. A presidential campaign based on a movie tie-in, after all, would seem shallow and misguided to begin with. Rather, the public's explicit rejection of the film belied the reservoir of adulation for astronauts that Glenn and his aides had counted on. Had Glenn not begun as an astronaut, he probably would not have become a senator. Had he not served as an astronaut, he almost certainly would not have run for President. Glenn's past was not, of course, a qualification for the office. But it was supposed to give him an entrée to public notice, a hallmark to distinguish him from his rivals with the voters and with the press. Had *The Right Stuff* never existed, his campaign would have had the same assets and liabilities. Yet the failure of the movie seemed to symbolize all the misguided, optimistic assumptions that underlay his campaign, all the reliance on goodwill and inattention to detail. From the day the film opened, Glenn's high-flying orbit began to decay and his hopes wobbled toward earth.

There are two schools of thought in American journalism about how reporters ought to behave toward political leaders. One school holds that it is improper, even disgraceful, that journalists should be bigger celebrities than the people whom they cover, and insists on due deference to high officialdom. When this sort of journalist conducts a public interview with a major officeholder, he may want to set the record straight, to provide needed context, to follow up an inconclusive answer with a further elucidation of a problem. But he will be meticulously polite. The other school holds that journalists act as surrogates for the people, and that in a democracy, the people are entitled to batter their leaders any way they please. Both schools were represented, indeed epitomized, at the first televised debate of the campaign, at the Dartmouth College campus in Hanover, New Hampshire, on January 15, 1984. Congressional Democrats, spearheaded by Representative Charles Schumer of Brooklyn, created the forum. The first half was moderated with restraint and decorum by ABC "Nightline" anchor Ted Koppel. The second half became a free-for-all in which the most no-holds-barred brawler was syndicated talk show host Phil Donahue. It was a measure both of the contrast in the two newsmen's styles and of the comparative visibility of their jobs versus the candidates' that much of the postdebate press commentary centered on the manner of the emcees, not on the men seeking to run the country. Koppel chided, nudged, encouraged. Even his most ticklish questions were softly spoken. Donahue did not evoke much response, but he demanded to hear it like a customer quarreling with a clerk after a too-long wait in line. For viewers the experience was akin to going to a play only to discover that after a first act by Neil Simon comes a second by Edward Albee.

Nonetheless, for a public at long last ready to be curious, now that the calendar indicated the election year had actually arrived, there was much to learn. As he had in New York City, Mondale took the belittling manner of *noblesse oblige*. The more his rivals challenged him, the more he strove for the serene and beatific smile of a confident leader who knows that this abuse is part of what he must bear. He deflected questions meant to make him commit himself, to define tax and budget plans and legislative agenda. He acted less like a candidate than a President-elect pledging to put off every issue until it has received appropriate study. Glenn, in another rehearsed bout of anger, lurched to his feet late in the debate to denounce Mondale's polite obtuseness as "gobbledygook" that cheated the public and imperiled the party's future. The complaint was valid; the delivery nonetheless seemed inauthentic. Jesse Jackson, at pains to portray himself as something more than an old-fashioned welfare Democrat, emphasized the value of pressuring business to stop the flow of manufacturing jobs to cheaper venues abroad. He urged narrowing the budget deficit, not by cutting spending, but by lobbying Western Europe and Japan to pay for more of their own defense, thereby freeing funds spent by the United States on NATO and Pacific defenses. McGovern, who seemed to be campaigning for a quasi-official designation as elder statesman and peacemaker more than for the presidency, sought a lowering of voices and suggested that a pileup on a front-runner who might well become the nominee was scarcely in the party's interest. Hollings spoke with his customary lucidity but, like Cranston and Askew, he failed to attract much attention. Among party officials and reporters, the debate, while considered inconclusive and inconsequential, was scored as a victory for Gary Hart. His generational theme was at least distinctive. His call for new ideas and new leadership, while self-serving, seemed the most graceful way of pointing out that the party of FDR's New Deal had lost its relevance to much of the American people. His stress on the way new technology points to new economic realities made sense both to intellectuals and to blue-collar auto and steel workers, who had begun to grasp, or at least suspect, that their layoffs were no longer merely cyclical, but might in some cases last forever. For Hart and for most of his rivals, however, the problem remained that there was room in the campaign's dynamic for only one significant alternative to Mondale. If Glenn were falling, would he fall far and fast enough to give anyone a chance at catching the front-runner?

The snow had been so heavy the night before, that the assorted small planes of Walter Mondale's campaign had had to land an hour's drive or more away from the RON — "rest of night stopover" — at the Howard Johnson motel in White River Junction, Vermont. But on the morning of

January 25, ten days after the New Hampshire debate and five weeks before the New Hampshire primary, the sun shone bright on Walter Mondale. He was conducting what seemed like a victory march, accompanied
by a busload of about three dozen reporters, photographers, TV producers, and sound and camera technicians — few of whom got to speak to
him, despite standing within earshot throughout the day. At night, President Reagan gave his State of the Union address, and Mondale commented in response to Reagan for his traveling audience of reporters; the
next morning, he supplied the same service, by satellite TV hookup, to
local broadcast stations around the country. Except for events in Washington and Mondale's replies, it was, the entourage agreed, a fairly typical
day on the hustings in New Hampshire.

Mondale first appeared in the aging industrial city of Claremont, at a
senior citizens' center and then at the local high school. Next his entourage traveled by bus to Keene, where he windmilled his way through a
crisply modern shopping mall with pricey food counters and trendy toys,
and spoke to volunteers at a jammed-to-overflowing room in his grubby
local campaign headquarters. The primary purpose of the day's schedule
was to provide varied "photo opportunities," especially for TV reporters:
Mondale with the old, Mondale with the young; Mondale with the suburban affluent, Mondale with the working poor; Mondale meeting the people, Mondale inspiriting the faithful inner circle. By agreement between
the campaign and its Secret Service aides, the main effort of Mondale's
bodyguards seemed to be to push the print people out of the way (even if
it meant they could not hear what the candidate was saying), to ensure
plenty of running room for the cameramen. To be sure, the print reporters
were not necessarily missing a story. Most of them had heard Mondale's
routine before and were merely holding themselves in readiness for some
driblet of news. Walter Robinson of the *Boston Globe*, one of seven reporters his newspaper had assigned to the campaign, explained his quiet
compliance with the Secret Service shoving: "A lot of the time, we are
not even attempting to report these repetitive events. We are maintaining a 'body watch' in case Mondale gets shot, and he and everyone else
knows it."

Mondale had little to say beyond pleasantries. His few brief speeches
sounded like a coach's pep talks at halftime. He meticulously avoided
claiming victory as a foregone conclusion, but he scarcely acknowledged
that there were any other Democrats in the race. Veterans in the entourage noted groaningly his use of the weather joke (if he had brought such
improved conditions on an eighteen-hour visit as a candidate, imagine
what he could do as President), the patronage joke (the mayor who picked

him up during last night's snowstorm, driving to a distant airport to do so, would doubtless become "at least secretary of state"), and the you're-all-invited-to-the-inauguration joke (the same mayor would pick up the tab).

Reporters deputed to Mondale considered themselves to have the best campaign assignment. Most, perhaps all, of them assumed they would be following him until November, and some believed it possible they might then accompany him to the White House beat. Each of them knew, however, that the continuation of this prominent exposure was contingent on the Mondale campaign's success, and in private moments some of them acknowledged the possibility that career self-interest could make them too sympathetic to Mondale. There was little sign, however, that the reporters were becoming bonded to Mondale as a man. He deflected dinner invitations, corridor chitchat, and virtually every other opportunity, except formal interviews and press conferences, for him and reporters to get to know each other. His press secretary, Maxine Isaacs, was schoolmarmish to reporters. Brit Hume of ABC asked one day when Mondale's position paper on taxes would be ready for the press to see; Isaacs shook her head and said, in a tone of much-tried patience, "When it's ready." Isaacs nonetheless met the press's obvious needs, and Mondale generally granted interview requests by major publications, although he frequently turned down offers of live interview time on television, a medium he distrusted. In a late-January interview that Mondale, uncharacteristically, requested with Thomas Winship, editor of the *Boston Globe*, he let his guard down just a bit, and hinted for a moment that he sensed there might be some chink in what looked like the unbreachable wall of his ascendancy. Looking out a hotel window at Boston's pleasantly preserved proportions, Mondale said to Winship, "Keep up the charm of Boston. Don't ever let it become a high-rise city." Then, gazing north, toward New Hampshire, he said softly, "I never could get a handle on that state. There's so much meanness up there."

While Mondale headed west to another stop on his hectic tour, Gary Hart slipped into Boston on the morning of January 26. No chartered aircraft carried him from Washington; he took a commercial flight. No entourage of aides came with him, only his press secretary, Kathy Bushkin. No local officials met him at the gate, no cheering throngs holding placards, just a paid New England field organizer and two college-student volunteers. Hart was not even the only presidential candidate aboard the plane; Ernest Hollings took the same flight and made his exit before Hart. Both of them were preceded down the ramp by another celebrity who got a warm reception from the campaign aides — boxer Sugar Ray Leonard, whose fame was not only better established than the senators' but maybe more likely to endure beyond the first few primaries.

Hart was widely viewed, perhaps even by himself, as a candidate primarily for 1988 whose purpose in running in 1984 was to get some practice, build name recognition, and perhaps enlist a lasting network of backers. The young men who met him had little optimism about his prospects. One said, "It's a learning experience, and after this Hart will still be a senator, maybe a more important one." The candidate's schedule for the day offered further evidence that his quest was disorganized and perhaps halfhearted. He stopped first at Brandeis University, where he hoped to enlist students as volunteers for the New Hampshire primary. As his young organizers readily acknowledged, that kind of recruitment effort should have taken place months before. "In fact," one said, "we did have some people going up last fall, but they lost interest." There was little sign that Hart renewed their enthusiasm now. He drew a standing-room-only crowd of about seven hundred students to hear him speak and answer questions for more than an hour at lunchtime. But most other candidates, who visited Brandeis as guests of an ongoing campaign forum, had drawn a like number. The students seemed attentive but impassive, and much of the crowd gradually drifted away.

Hart spoke as usual of "new ideas" and of the need for a "new generation of leadership" — but whether he meant their generation or his own was not quite clear. The examples of worthy causes that he cited all seemed to date from his own formative era in national politics, as manager of George McGovern's 1972 presidential campaign. Hart praised the civil rights, ecology, and antiwar movements repeatedly, to at best tepid applause. He sounded like a conventional, indeed doctrinaire, liberal reformer. He spoke elliptically about redefining military goals but took scant opportunity to display his knowledge of both hardware and policy. He seemed to fire up the crowd only when he made a blatant pitch about the importance of political involvement among the young. To strengthen that appeal, he stayed for more than an hour to attend a university-sponsored cocktail party and a private session with student journalists. Barely a month before the New Hampshire primary, Hart was having to humble himself enough to implore coverage from a college newspaper.

His second engagement was at the Fletcher School of Diplomacy, a largely graduate institution cosponsored by Harvard and by Tufts, where Hart's daughter Andrea was a junior. Hart suddenly caught fire. The initially skeptical crowd was stunned by his wit, articulation, and knowledge on matters ranging from arms technology to Soviet bargaining tactics to Third World political movements. Despite his deft performance, however, Hart failed to win over a substantial portion of the crowd. They made it plain that they considered him too détentist toward the Soviets, not warlike enough.

By conventional political standards, the day proved a failure. Hart attracted plenty of major media attention — but precious little coverage. He was accompanied for all or part of the day by reporters from the *New York Times, Washington Post,* Associated Press, *Time,* and his hometown *Denver Post.* His Brandeis speech drew reporters from all of Boston's major newspapers and television stations, and from the Boston offices of all three commercial TV networks. Still, all his work resulted in only brief, routine local stories and no national ones. In frustration at his mangled schedule, Hart canceled his best prospect of the day for exposure in the Massachusetts–New Hampshire TV market: a live interview on the 10:00 P.M. television news show of Boston's PBS station, WGBH, a program anchored by Christopher Lydon, a respected former *New York Times* national political correspondent. Hart's annoyance was understandable: a pointless visit to the North Shore Press Club, a gathering of about four dozen less-than-high-voltage bureaucrats, primarily in public relations rather than journalism, had taken him halfway to New Hampshire, where he was scheduled to arise before dawn the next morning to shake hands at factory gates. To return for Lydon's show — and Lydon refused to do the interview in advance, on tape — would have cost Hart several hours of sleep. One of Mondale's most enviable advantages as a front-runner was to be able to afford the caliber of schedulers who would not so squander their man's energies.

Hart sensed the day had gone badly, and he seemed reconciled to the likelihood of an early defeat for his hopes. Like many a politician before him, he put the onus for much of his trouble on what he described as the pack mentality of the national press. Hart praised local TV and print reporters, by contrast, for not feeling so obliged to show off their political erudition by passing judgment on a candidate's electability. Instead, Hart contended in an interview at day's end, the local press was more interested in getting across a candidate's ideas — in simply explaining who he was and why he was running. "There has been a good deal of high-quality local coverage. In Dubuque or Colorado Springs, I am treated as a viable candidate. The reporter does not feel the need to characterize my campaign as faltering, halting, stumbling, or any of the rest of those gratuitous words. Routinely, even in the tiniest papers, that is the coverage: three-quarters quotes from what I said, and they get it right, and at most a mention that I am 'one of the dark horse candidates.' I do not mind being called a dark horse, but I do mind being called an also-ran or all the rest of it. One has to do with how well you are known, the other with how well you are doing." Unlike, say, Jimmy Carter or Walter Mondale, Hart made no cocky vows about how long his candidacy would be around. He did not present himself as an underappreciated talent, but as yet another victim of commonplace sins of the press.

He conceded, a little grudgingly, a major failing in his own campaign: that he was coming across more as a promoter of the need for new ideas than as an actual proponent of any. Some of the problem, he noted, was that worthwhile new ideas rarely reduce themselves comfortably to slogans, or even to the lengthier confines of campaign news stories. "Military reform, for example, is complex and detailed, and does not lend itself to the needs of people who file six hundred to eight hundred words a day. My ideas are on record in my position papers and my book, and I am not going to do them a disservice by boiling them down." The conversation was vintage Hart, thoroughly illustrative of his native stubbornness. It seemed to satisfy him simply to define a problem, to understand the nature of the threat it posed to his ambitions; he rarely bent his will to resolving the difficulty by compromise.

Despite his complaints and misgivings about reporters, Hart was doing little to win them over. He traveled apart from them, except for interviews, while Kathy Bushkin proffered sandwiches and press releases in the press van. The handful of reporters who had some continuing experience with his campaign said Hart had made little or no effort to engage them in intellectual debate, to argue his beliefs or even challenge their performance. When prodded, in conversation, Hart acknowledged that he rather resented the press's interest in him as a personality, a celebrity, not just as a thinker. If the price of contesting the presidency was having strangers pass judgment on his honesty and likability, he was not sure he wanted to pay it. " 'Hart, cool and distant' is the thing that I have hanging around my neck," he complained. "And it all comes from one Mickey Kaus story in the *Washington Monthly* that went into everyone's clip file and by imitation became dogma. What happened was that Kaus saw me in Denver at a dinner and I was on the edge of the room, talking to a few people, instead of working my way through the crowd in the middle. He said I did not even mingle with the people in my own state. Well, they all know me. They have worked with me for ten years. I didn't have to do that. I do not think I am aloof. I think I am very easygoing and funny." As though on cue, the aides in the car with Hart waited one beat, then all started to laugh, exaggeratedly, in gentle mockery. A second or so later, belatedly getting the joke on himself, Hart laughed too.

The morning after Hart and Hollings arrived in Boston so humbly, another commercial-sized airliner surged in on a runway at Boston's Logan

Airport to deliver the entourage of the man who remained Mondale's only acknowledged serious rival, John Glenn. The big plane was chartered. The waiting crowd was made up chiefly of aides to top conservative Massachusetts Democrats, including the president of the state senate. The ensuing motorcade, swift, noisy, and efficient, hurtled Glenn into town to speak at the city's venerable Faneuil Hall. Money was still coming into Glenn's coffers, although at a slowing rate; polls still showed him a potential victor against Ronald Reagan, and his entourage remained about as big as Mondale's. Yet the candidate himself looked beaten, his face flattened to a wispy cartoon outline of itself, his boiled-egg eyes pouchy and devoid of a twinkle. The smart money that had been betting on him as the next President had been moving away, and Glenn knew it. So did the aides around him. And so did the reporters accompanying him; they said among themselves that it would take a miracle to keep their tour going beyond mid-March. The public had not yet cast a single vote. No one had uncovered any scandal disqualifying Glenn, or even pointed up any lapse of judgment or knowledge that showed him unfit to be President. Public opinion polls on issues continued to show him perhaps the closest figure in either party to the outlook of the citizens. Nonetheless, by the curious, osmotic process of establishing conventional wisdom among political leaders and the media, it had become evident that Glenn was on the decline.

The past few days had been particularly trying for Glenn. He had appeared to lay waste his two chief assets, amiability and integrity. His confrontation with Mondale during the Dartmouth debate — climaxing with Glenn's challenge, "Is this going to be a Democratic party that promises everything to everyone?" — had communicated his themes of lowered expectations and less government, but had done so peevishly. To create the appearance that this sally had given him a "victory" in the debate, Glenn's campaign touted polls taken immediately afterward that purportedly showed people had become more favorable to him. And to reinforce that assertion, the campaign staff began airing commercials that seemed to depict people commending Glenn's handling of himself at the debate. Word quickly leaked, however, that the people who appeared in the commercials had been interviewed before the debate ever took place. Glenn's media consultant, David Sawyer, attempted to explain away the deception in several ways, ultimately by contending that all the people who were seen on camera had been contacted again after the debate and had reaffirmed their endorsements. That defense failed, and in short order the ads were withdrawn, but not before they tarnished Glenn's reputation for decency, and thereby prompted reporters to speak of Glenn's apparent "desperation."

Sawyer then made Glenn seem even trickier with a crude attempt to manipulate the news media. The consultant showed to selected reporters what he said were tapes of highly negative commercials about Mondale that Glenn was about to air. The reporters predictably wrote stories that contained the substance of the attacks on Mondale. When the Glenn ads actually aired, they turned out to be much milder. The reporters, having done the dirty work of conveying the nastier, ultimately unspoken messages, were then supposed to reverse tack and write articles praising the Glenn campaign for moderation and statesmanship. The scheming backfired and further poisoned relations between Glenn and some reporters. Chris Black of the *Boston Globe*, the biggest newspaper not only in Massachusetts but also in New Hampshire, and thus a pivotal force in the primary, typified sentiment when she said, "I feel used."

Reporters had also gone onto the warpath in protest of the chaotic and often almost sadistic nature of Glenn's schedule, which was wearing him down as much as them. Trying to campaign simultaneously in Iowa and New Hampshire, where he had to maintain credibility, and in Florida, Alabama, and Georgia, where he hoped actually to win, Glenn was on the road as much as eighteen hours a day. Moreover, his schedulers and support staff lacked the efficiency and meticulousness about detail that made Mondale's equally arduous schedule at least bearable. One reporter recalled a day that started at 7:00 A.M. and afforded no opportunity to eat, let alone write or file, until 10:00 P.M., fifteen hours later. Said the regretful newsman: "We were getting abusive with the candidate."

In the catalogue of setbacks, among the most costly and certainly the most painful for Glenn had come just a day before he arrived in Boston for his big speech. Belatedly and reluctantly, he had accepted the fact that his longtime aide and friend Bill White was not competent to run a presidential campaign, and had asked him to step aside. The ouster, so late in the pre-primary maneuvering, amounted to a public confession that Glenn was in trouble. White's departure, and the selection of Gerry Vento, a veteran Boston political operative, to replace him, made the front pages of major newspapers, the evening newscasts on the networks, and the campaign roundup articles in the newsweeklies.

Such sober news all but crowded out of national notice the day's events in Boston. And for Glenn, that fact was perhaps the worst of all the bad news, because he had chosen this time and place to attempt to redefine, and reignite, his campaign. In 1980, when Senator Edward Kennedy's presidential bid was flagging, Kennedy traveled to Georgetown University to try to explain, too late, why he was in the race. Although Kennedy did not capture the nomination, he regained his dignity, and many of the reporters who followed him rated the Georgetown speech his finest hour.

Like Kennedy, Glenn had based his campaign on a claim of electability, not on any ideology or even mythology. Like Kennedy, he needed to persuade voters that his quest was motivated not merely by ambition but also by belief in some vision of America. Thus he began by explaining, to the overflow crowd at Faneuil Hall and to the press gallery and TV crews who were his real audience, that he was making a "personal statement," of the kind that some candidates do at the outset of a campaign, and that nearly every party nominee does in his acceptance speech. Glenn described the social contract that links politicians and their people: "In the final analysis, voters do not go to the polls to elect a policy or program. They go to elect a President. And when it comes to choosing a President, I believe candidates should be judged, not on their facility for showmanship, but on their capacity for leadership. Leadership, of course, is composed of many things. It is experience and it is values; it is knowledge and it is character. Partly, it's the candidate's views. But mostly, it's the candidate's vision."

Portraying Reagan as the preferred candidate of big business and the rich, and Mondale as the pledged advocate of the black and the poor, Glenn invoked the traditional pietism of centrists, that they alone stand for the needs of the nation as a whole. "I intend to be President of all the people. I am tired of presidential elections that decide little more than which set of entrenched interests will gain the most power and wield the most influence. I am tired of seeing presidential candidates kowtowing to the captains of industry or bowing before the barons of labor, shamelessly promising either to get the government off their back or on their side."

Guided by David Sawyer, who had been guided in turn by his market research, Glenn played upon what had proved to be the most potent theme for expressing public hopes and anxieties, the urgent importance of the future. In some senses, of course, all elections are about the future — about what candidates and their parties say they will do. But recent American presidential elections had sounded more like referenda about the past, about what had been done. In 1968, the voters' emotions had focused on protest movements and the seeming breakdown in traditional authority, embodied in the rallying cry "law and order." In 1972, voters were asked by both sides to think about the Vietnam war, and to certify or reject the nation's insistence on "peace with honor," which promised at least the semblance of a military victory. In 1976, candidates' customary rhetoric about honesty and decency took on deeper meaning, as voters reacted to Watergate and the subsequent pardon of Richard Nixon. In 1980, voters vented their frustration at the hostage stalemate in Iran, long lines at gasoline pumps, and the general sense of national humiliation encapsulated in Reagan's brilliant summation, "Are you better off now than you were four years ago?" In 1984, no comparably all-consuming event or experience preoccupied the voters, and that in itself seemed to bode well for incumbents. But the voters displayed an underlying fretfulness about the direction of the nation, which seemed to be losing its world political power, its control over nuclear weapons and technology, and perhaps its economic stability and comfort. Thus every candidate addressed himself in some fashion to envisioning what the future might be like, and how it might be cheered for or coped with.

To Mondale and Jackson, the future would be a time when changing demographics could reempower the old New Deal coalition and restore the paternalistic liberalism of government. There would be more blacks, more Hispanics, more Asian and other nonwhite immigrants, while the white share of the population would diminish. There would be, absolutely and especially proportionately, many more elderly voters reliant on Social Security. And there would be many more economically imperiled laborers in fading smokestack industries who would in fear turn back to the Democratic party.

To Hart, the future would be a time of new leadership and new ideas, and, more specifically, a time of sweeping adjustments that could nonetheless easily be made by a more flexible post–World War II generation. They would accept the transformation to a high-tech, service-oriented, computer-literate economy. They would take an attitude of tolerance and pluralism in social and sexual matters. They would accommodate themselves to a Third World that might develop politically along nondemocratic, noncapitalist lines, and they would not insist on measuring every indigenous movement in little countries as a defeat or failure for the United States in its bipolar competition with the Soviets.

To Reagan, by contrast, the future would look like the remembered best of the past, an era of renewed American imperium, to be achieved by restoring the moral and religious values that supposedly had empowered America in the past. Reagan's vision of history was not a straight-line progression, but the swinging of a pendulum between a center of well-rewarded godliness and extremes of timidity and moral turpitude. When America faltered, it was only experiencing God's punishment for its sins.

Measured against these evocative and in most cases metaphysically rooted visions, Glenn's on-the-one-hand-this-on-the-other-hand-that moderation seemed pallid, all but bankrupt. His delivery of the speech in Faneuil Hall was stirring, his rhetoric shapely. But he defined his beliefs only in terms of finding some meritorious middle ground between excoriated extremes: "I say it's time to draw a curtain on the politics of the past. . . . In 1984, I say we should not be forced to choose between a President who wants to take even more from those who have suffered and a challenger who would take us back to the days of runaway spending. I reject the idea that we must choose between being fiscally responsible and being morally responsible. I say we must do both. . . . The current administration lacks the foresight, imagination, and vision needed to restore America's preeminence and lead this nation into the world of tomorrow. And I believe that weakness is equally evident in those Democratic candidates who seek to meet the new problems of the 1980s with recycled programs from the '60s and '70s. . . . To those whose vision is confined to yesterday's polls and who say that the contest for our party's nomination is over, I reply: the people have not yet spoken, and the race has just begun." Despite the ringing defiance of those words, for Glenn the race was indeed almost over. The people had not yet spoken, but they had looked at Glenn and found him wanting. Common sense was a needed quality in a leader, and something to admire. But it was not much of a flag to rally around.

———✦———

It takes a politician of nerve and deftness to subordinate a presidential State of the Union address to a mere announcement for reelection. It takes a master showman to invest the most predictable and foreordained of events with the melodrama that keeps people waiting beforehand, and impels them to talk things over after the fact. Ronald Reagan, most amiable yet in his way brashest of statesmen, was determined to milk his last-in-a-lifetime candidacy for all the attention he could get, and while the Democrats skirmished in their busy manner in January, the chief executive at his ease dominated the public prints and airwaves.

He had more or less committed himself in October to seeking reelection, when he allowed his close friend and eventual campaign chairman, Senator Paul Laxalt of Nevada, to take formal steps toward qualifying for federal matching funds. He had clearly passed the word among at least senior aides well before Christmas that he planned to run again: White House chief of staff James Baker turned down a chance to become commissioner of baseball, a job he might otherwise have welcomed, because he knew — and implied publicly — that he would be needed for a second term. Reagan welcomed the accolades of Republicans who said his presence on the ticket was essential to maintaining the party's control of the Senate; had he not been running, he would have been morally obliged to alert likely candidates of his decision, and he did not.

Yet there remained reasons, which Reagan cunningly exploited, to think that he might not try for another term. He was old: if reelected, he would complete a second term less than three weeks before his seventy-eighth birthday. His wife, Nancy, was rumored to be ill and had undeniably lost weight; she had feared for his safety since the assassination attempt, disliked much of the White House and Washington power struggling, and wanted to be sure her husband would not leave office with the discredit of defeat. Reagan could fairly claim to have achieved much of his legislative agenda, and to have scant prospects for enacting the rest. For another, younger man, the decision not to run again would be an admission of defeat. Reagan, however, could honorably retire. At opportunity after opportunity to commit himself, he resisted, enticing reporters and pundits into speculation. Virtually until the minute of his announcement, opinion about his plans was divided. Among those savvy observers who thought Reagan might well opt out of the race were CBS News anchor Dan Rather and *Newsweek*'s Washington bureau chief, Mel Elfin.

Reagan could have settled the matter during his State of the Union speech, but he equivocated again. He was thus able to claim credit for not having politicized a formal constitutional duty. He also collected double television time. He won clearance from all three commercial networks for a second national address four days later, to announce his plans.

The State of the Union speech was predictably self-congratulatory, and it incorporated deferential references to most of the interest blocs Reagan had distressed as President — environmentalists, civil rights groups, arms-control advocates, feminists. On its face, the text was a campaign speech. Yet it skirted the topic of reelection adroitly enough, and in tone was just austere and detached enough, to keep doubts about Reagan's intentions alive until the following Sunday night. Then the veil lifted. Looking somber, he recalled the problems he had inherited, described with studied humility the corrections he had made, and implored votes for another four years with the plea, "Our work is not finished."

Tradition is a word of singularly flexible meaning in the realm of politics. The tradition of Presidents not running for third terms, which ended with Franklin Roosevelt, had begun with George Washington. The tradition of convention acceptance speeches began with Franklin Roosevelt. The tradition of the New Hampshire primary as the first-in-the-nation campaign event dates back only to 1952. And the Iowa caucuses, by now institutionalized, began only in 1976. Their history, although short, is rich. Jimmy Carter became a national figure by winning a plurality of Iowa participants in 1976, and he ravaged the hopes of Edward Kennedy by defeating him there in 1980, although in both years — indeed, in seven of eight elections between 1952 and 1980 — the state voted Republican in November. George Bush topped Ronald Reagan in Iowa in 1980, prompting journalists to report that Reagan's political career was through. For 1984, the candidates and their supporters collectively spent millions of dollars, and the TV networks and print organizations dispatched hundreds of reporters, to codify the result as meaningful and to guard against surprise.

Political scientists, who generally deplore the disproportionate influence exerted by early primaries and caucuses, often attack the states involved as being demographically "unrepresentative." In Iowa, for example, only about half of the three million population live in urban areas, versus about three-quarters of the national population, and little more than 2 percent are black or Hispanic, versus more than 18 percent of Americans nationally. The state is heavily agricultural; in the late 1970s, heyday of the farm business, Iowa boasted the nation's highest per capita concentration of net-worth millionaires.

Beyond those reasons for caution, there was a sound basis for skepticism about Democrats, and among the reporters covering them, about the validity of the Iowa caucuses as a measure of 1984 voter sentiment. Iowans would likely turn out in small numbers: an incumbent President did not face a contest this time; only one party had any kind of race going; the Democrats offered a confusing and as yet ill-publicized eight-man field; and the best-financed candidate, Mondale, had every motive to damp down enthusiasm to vote among the general electorate, so as to maximize the impact of the known supporters whom he and his labor union allies could count on delivering to their precinct meetings. Caucuses, even at their best, tend to test organizational strength and acumen, not the ability to attract voters en masse.

But journalists and candidates alike were eager, after all the preliminary maneuvering, for some hint, however tentative, of genuine public response. Whatever their limitations, however excessive the accompanying hoopla, the Iowa caucuses would give everyone a genuine political event. They would at last provide real news, not just polls and predictions, and would set a legitimate standard for winnowing the field.

The candidates had to perform, not only numerically, but in accordance with "expectations," a set of obiter dicta that sometimes seem to be — and to a considerable extent are — the result of some journalistic cabal. Through reading or hearing each other's stories and through conversing at the journalistic clan's accepted watering holes, the relative handful of leading national political reporters, six dozen or so by the most generous estimate, collectively establish a judgment about what would constitute a good or bad performance for a particular candidate in a particular set of circumstances. It is part of the game to write or air stories condemning the practice of imposing expectations. But the language of political reporting, replete with "musts" and "had tos" and "neededs," relentlessly sustains the mystique of momentum and necessity.

In Iowa, the expectations were as clear as ever. Walter Mondale, the favorite, "had to" win big. He had been hurt by his rivals' relentless accusation that he was beholden to "special interests." Perhaps the most injurious formation of the charge had been made by Gary Hart, who in a televised debate, sponsored by the *Des Moines Register*, asked Mondale whether he could name even one major domestic issue on which he had willingly crossed labor. Mondale declined, both during the debate and in repeated press conferences later, to emphasize differences with people whose support he had sought and accepted. He viewed Hart's question as a trap, not because it would point him up as obligated to labor, but because it might lure him into alienating his friends. By the time he relented, under pressure from his staff, and noted a few significant disputes, the damage had been done — as much by Mondale's overattentiveness to the feelings of labor as by the absence of any specific reply. If Mondale won anything less than a landslide in Iowa, the journalistic interpretation of his falling below "expectations" would doubtless peg him as too submissive and dependent.

For Glenn, the "need" was to finish second, or at the very worst third, if he hoped to continue to be regarded as the major alternative to Mondale. Iowa was considered Glenn's sort of state, midwestern, somewhat conservative, down-to-earth, square, patriotic. For Cranston and Hart, the goal was to place third, in order to be positioned to supplant Glenn as the main challenger if he continued to slip. Hollings had invested most of his time in New Hampshire rather than Iowa. Jackson was waiting for states with significant black populations. Askew mildly hoped for a meaningful boost from right-to-lifers, and McGovern, who had touchingly urged Iowans to vote their consciences rather than their beliefs about a candidate's electability, looked for a substantial enough sympathy vote to justify his staying in the race.

By those varied standards, Hart and McGovern won the Iowa caucuses, Mondale broke even, and Glenn lost dismally. And indeed, that is how the story was played in the days following the first official event of the nominating process. Numerically, Mondale captured a crushing 48.9 percent of the vote, three times as much as his nearest challenger. Attracting half the voters in an eight-candidate race, in a process that also allowed participants to label themselves uncommitted, was one of the most overwhelming successes in the history of modern campaigning. And initially Mondale got full credit for his achievement. But as commentators and reporters looked for something else to say, they turned to the assessment of Mondale's rivals, and perceived "victories" more "unexpected" — and thus in some undefinable way even bigger — than Mondale's Bunyanesque triumph.

Hart, the commentators said, had emerged from nowhere (meaning from somewhere other than their prognostication lists) to finish second with 16.5 percent of the caucus vote. McGovern, essentially a symbolic candidate, had finished third, at 10 percent, suggesting that there was a still-fervent force of radical idealists within the party. Uncommitted voters, 9.4 percent of the total, had placed fourth. None of the other candidates had distinguished himself at all, and Glenn, who had placed sixth, was particularly humiliated. This fading, wounded hero could no longer claim to be the chief alternative to Mondale. Instead, the candidate of the establishment faced a young, telegenic, articulate, informed outsider, with a shrewd understanding of the rhythms of a national campaign. By the time the three networks had signed off on caucus night, Mondale had already begun to see the ironic result of his landslide. He had been pushed back from a stately procession, followed by assorted stragglers, into a throng.

———

Gary Hart was in the shower on the night of February 20 when he received word that he had placed second in Iowa's caucuses. He was not even in Iowa — he had already gone on to New Hampshire — and had not made adequate arrangements for an electronic hookup so that he could claim "victory" on behalf of his supporters. Caucuses are so difficult to poll that he seemed to be as surprised as anyone by his showing. Yet when word was shouted in to him, he responded, "If I'm second in Iowa, that means I get to be President."

The next morning, Hart told reporters that he considered himself to be in a two-candidate race, and he strongly implied that he and Mondale deserved to be treated on an equal footing. Mondale, to be sure, had enormous assets: more money, more endorsements, more organization, more support in polls than any other candidate. But Mondale also had devastating negatives, Hart said: overdependence on special interests, especially the labor leadership; a close association with the failures of Jimmy Carter; an unabashed commitment to the repudiated spending policies of the past. One of Mondale's own aides had inadvertently provided, in an injudiciously phrased bit of praise, the most precise indictment of the front-runner: "He dares to be cautious." Hart hammered away at that theme: Mondale was not his own man, he would lose to Reagan, and the party therefore must not let the nominating process close down fast.

The message began to take hold. Hart had a genuine organization in New Hampshire, some of it bound to him by friendships dating to the McGovern campaign, much of it made up of the "ruthless house-wives" — in the phrase of *Boston Globe* editorial page editor Martin Nolan — who spearhead nearly every liberal or reform movement in the state. Unencumbered by Mondale's commitments to labor or Glenn's ob-ligations to smokestack industries back in Ohio, Hart had been able to make the right noises to the housewives about environmental issues, espe-cially the iniquity of the "acid rain" that results from airborne industrial pollution. His emphasis on high-tech solutions to economic programs meshed with New Hampshire's experience — rapid growth and one of the lowest unemployment rates in the nation, largely as a result of the booming computer business. His emphasis on military reform appealed to normally irreconcilable groups: the hawks, with their concern for a strong and efficient armed force, and the doves, with their mistrust of waste and excess in the Pentagon budget.

Still, in the eight days between the Iowa caucuses and New Hamp-shire's primary, virtually no one predicted publicly that Hart could win. Contemporary political analysis and reporting consists in large part of quoting polls, and the polls were unanimous. Mondale enjoyed an un-beatable lead. Polling a multicandidate race in a primary is notoriously tricky, and pollsters customarily append cautions that laymen routinely ignore. It is hard to predict the size of the turnout, harder still to gauge which groups are most likely to participate. Voter expressions of prefer-ence are often meaninglessly weak, sometimes no more than a result of name recognition. Ephemeral news events, and such intangibles as the dy-namics and momentum of a race, often exert a decisive last-minute influ-ence. In New Hampshire, the significant news that Hart might suddenly constitute a viable alternative to Glenn and Mondale was only beginning to sink in with voters, too late for the impact to be measurable much be-fore primary day.

Knowing all this, journalists might have acted prudently, might have avoided making predictions. Instead, even after they had begun to ac-knowledge in private that something unpredictable seemed to be happen-ing, they went right on asserting the conventional wisdom in print and on air. By Sunday night before the Tuesday voting, there was so great a sense of movement toward Hart that Frank Lynn of the *New York Times* said, to a barroom tableful of journalists, including Hays Gorey of *Time* and

Bob Healy of the *Boston Globe*, "Let's face it, none of us would be too surprised if Hart won this whole thing, would we?" The next day, ABC News let the audience in on the secret, or part of it, by reporting that last-minute "tracking polls" showed a brisk improvement for Hart. Yet in their final stories before the polls opened, even the biggest names ignored such evidence in favor of asserting once again the "fact" of Mondale's unshakability. His campaign's manipulation of the press continued to work. David Broder of the *Washington Post*, the Pulitzer Prize-winning dean of political commentators, forecast that Mondale's lead was holding steady. The three networks described Mondale as a likely or all but certain winner. The most egregiously wrong, though, was the *New York Times*, which played on page one its own poll showing Mondale with the biggest nationwide lead of any nonincumbent candidate in history. The poll was probably accurate, in the literal sense, but it reflected the opinions of people in states where primaries or caucuses were still weeks, even months, away; they had no considered judgment, only an inclination to parrot back what the press had been telling them was inevitable. The possibility of an upset was hinted at, but only just, in stories by Jim Perry in the *Wall Street Journal*, Bob Healy in the *Boston Globe*, and Tom Ottenad in the *Saint Louis Post-Dispatch*. Nearly all the news consumers in America were utterly unprepared for what happened.

The results were electrifying. Hart, who had been virtually unknown ten days before the voting, won 38 percent. Mondale drew just 28 percent. Hart's support had apparently doubled in the final few days, while Mondale's had dropped long term by nearly half. Reagan had reminded Democrats that he was a formidable opponent: he drew more votes as a write-in among Democrats than three of the major Democratic candidates on the ballot. But Hart had shown himself if anything more impressive: he drew even more write-in votes on the Republican side than Reagan did on the Democratic.

Hart outpointed Mondale among virtually every subgroup, whether assorted by age or region or religion or ethnicity. He was especially strong among a group that did not yet have a name: younger, more educated, more affluent, suburbanized, and generally independent voters, who were beginning to constitute the "swing" vote in many elections. Mondale was rewarded, or perhaps punished, for his loyalty to the elderly, the ill-educated, and the poor: those groups, almost alone, consistently preferred him to his rivals.

If the news media had been slow to recognize what was going to happen, they were quick — in the eyes of many people, too quick — to spread the word once it had happened. All three networks conducted extensive exit polls of voters leaving their balloting places. In past presidential elections, those polls had served only to illuminate voter behavior. But in New Hampshire, and in every primary thereafter, exit polls were used to forecast results. By midday, the Hart landslide was apparent, and network analysts tipped off their pals in the print media to be ready to assess a major upset. At 6:30 P.M. EST on primary night, some ninety minutes before the polls closed, all three networks "estimated" that Hart would win a surprise victory by a wide margin. The word *estimate* was a subterfuge to enable the networks to predict elections in progress while claiming not to do so. Both the euphemism and the practice it served were denounced by Representative Tim Wirth of Colorado, chairman of the House Communications Subcommittee, which had been holding extensive hearings on the propriety of exit polls. The networks remained defiant; they were thrilled that their costly technology had succeeded in detecting astonishing political news.

Exit polls remained at best crude and inexact, however, in defining why people voted as they did. The numbers could indicate, with varying margins of error, how Mondale fared among blue-collar Catholics or Hart among college graduates, but the poll results did not explain whether the stunning shift in outlook reflected mostly Hart's strength or mostly Mondale's weakness. An especially revealing poll statistic, reported by Lou Harris on ABC on primary night, was that 88 percent of voters, regardless of the candidate they chose, rejected the idea that a Mondale victory in New Hampshire should mean that the race was effectively over. Whatever voters felt, they seemed to want more time to let their feelings ripen.

Nonetheless, the news media conducted their quadrennial ritual of pronouncing morning-after obsequies for the New Hampshire also-rans. The candidates, short of money and help and fearing they would soon be bereft of dignity, agreed. Cranston pulled out. Askew pulled out. Hollings, who had envisioned with such clarity in the New York debate the fate awaiting him, pulled out and was praised for his wit and humor, and was told he had been nice. He departed with a graceful, rueful exit line. "Nothing," he told reporters, "happened to me on the way to the White House."

IV

Marathon

THE results in New Hampshire were startling. What followed for the next two weeks was unprecedented. No one, no matter how long his memory, was able to recall anything in politics to compare with the mania of exuberance about Gary Hart that swept America. Prairie fire, Hart's delighted partisans called it. Mass hysteria, Mondale's panicky troops replied. Americans who could not have cared less about Gary Hart now could not get enough of him. He was compared to a panoply of heroes, mythic and real, and most often to the last beloved Democrat, John Kennedy. People saw in Hart the same quick humor. They saw a man who could imbue the country with strength and hope and the energy to plunge into the future. They saw common sense and judgment and vision. Liberals saw a renewed, legitimized liberalism. Conservatives saw a tough, skeptical conservatism. Moderates saw a freedom from cant and extremism, a belief in efficacy and practicality rather than ideology.

Electoral politics in democracies characteristically lends itself to a repeated cycle of rapturous romance followed by crushing disappointment. Voters attach themselves to candidates about whom they know little (and sometimes to candidates about whom they overlook much) and endow them with all the qualities and attributes that are longed for in a leader. They dream that they can experience the ideal form of representative government, in which the chosen executive embodies all the values of all the people. Each loyalist, regarding himself as expressing the society's truest, most enlightened values, remolds the candidate to his own vision of perfection. Eventually, and inevitably, the passionate partisan comes to feel betrayed when he finds that his vividly imagined hero is in fact someone quite different and, unforgivably, just another politician. Electoral fervor can prompt otherwise meek and decent people to make hysterical telephone calls to newspapers, or to start up shouting matches with friends or strangers, or to commit vindictive dirty tricks. They react so intensely, not merely to assert their social or economic attitudes, but to protect their dreams.

The incandescence of the American people's response to Gary Hart was a measure of the national longing for a leader. After two decades of disappointment, watching five consecutive Presidents leave office in death or disgrace or ridicule, the citizenry ached for optimism. Mondale could not offer it. No matter how strenuously he proclaimed the boundless possibilities of the future, the public disbelieved him when, in the next breath, he hailed the unblemished virtues of the recent past. With a stubbornness born of his sense of moral duty, Mondale insisted on trying to lecture the public out of its rejection of paternalistic government. The more he sensed resistance, the more he belabored his views. At times he seemed to scold. A vote for any philosophy other than his own, he said self-righteously, would be a vote for self-interest and greed. Mondale, acting like the gloomy, ascetic Norse clergymen from whose line he sprang, seemingly could not bring himself to promise that life would be better. He pledged only that mankind could become better. Like Jimmy Carter, he transmitted the unwelcome message that the failures of government were generated not by government but by a malaise in the American people.

Reagan, by contrast, was optimism incarnate, but his rosy vision of the future unnerved many Americans who did not share his idealization of the past. His explanation of the nation's problems held that whatever could not be attributed to the malefactions of the Evil Empire in the East could be debited instead to the ungodliness of Americans themselves. Accordingly he offered not hope but disquiet to Jews, nonfundamentalist Christians, secular humanists, and all those who prefer to believe that God helps those who help themselves. At his most literal, Reagan seemed to urge an economically passive and militarily aggressive theocracy, in some ways not unlike Khomeini's Iran.

Hart, or at least the idea of Hart, appealed powerfully to people who had no interest in debating the past and longed to address vast, systematic challenges for the future. The new front-runner said almost nothing specific or quantifiable when he called for new ideas. Yet in a sense he said everything. Implicitly, "new ideas" meant that new social arrangements, new ways of living other than the one-earner nuclear family dominated by the decision-making daddy, were here to stay. "New ideas" strongly suggested that the workers in dying smokestack industries would have to stop expecting intervention and handouts and would have to find places for themselves, at whatever cost in dislocation and pay cuts, in the emerging high-tech economy. "New ideas" opened up vistas of tax reform, environmental and ecological innovation, a complete rethinking of the defense budget. "New ideas" seemed to imply a place at the table for women, for blacks, for Hispanics and others, but not necessarily through the old-fashioned methods of deal making, coalition building, quota setting. "New ideas" was the ultimate rallying cry of rationalists: throw out the familiar, often corrupt arrangements, and make policy based on necessity, fairness, and common sense. For all those who viewed themselves as net supporters of government rather than net recipients from it, Hart's message apparently promised the prospect of lower government cost, better government performance, more precisely targeted government spending. Even the lucky beneficiaries of subsidies to the middle class could persuade themselves, justifiably or not, that their particular pet programs would of course survive any reasonable, "idea"-based scrutiny.

Few voters could articulate what they found attractive in Hart, beyond mentioning his physical charisma and perhaps his disaffection from the shopworn ideologies of both parties. But they sensed something different and responded to it. Within days Hart was transformed from an unknown to a contender, holding the potential, in polls anyway, to defeat Ronald Reagan, something that Mondale had rarely if ever seemed equipped to do. Hart responded to his transformation with an intuitive mastery of image and style. Vanished was the shy, awkward senator who stood at the edge of a party in his hometown. Here onstage was a warm, wide-grinned, witty conquering hero.

His first burst of brilliance came the morning after the New Hampshire primary. Mondale had left the state, before the polls closed, to campaign in Maine, and his staff never adequately explained why. One version they offered was that he had expected to win up until the last minute, and had not wanted to stay around and hog credit from his organizers and volunteers. Another was that he knew he was in trouble and wanted to try to minimize the attention paid to his defeat. A variant, maybe less lame, was that he had known he needed every possible minute of stumping to salvage his dwindling chances in Maine. In retrospect, it seems that the truest explanation was the simplest: Mondale had been scheduled to leave, and his campaign had been too bureaucratic and unwieldy to respond to changing circumstances. Hart, by contrast, thanked New Hampshire's voters in person on primary night. And the next day, instead of heading to Maine or some other state with an upcoming vote, he toured New Hampshire to thank them again. The trip was a triumph of public relations, a blend of humility and self-assertion. It provided exuberant footage and reinforced the recognition of Hart as a winner. Yet virtually no one in the press accused Hart of gloating or grandstanding. His unorthodox gesture was accepted as a sign of genuine gratitude.

Everything about Hart seemed to point up Mondale's weaknesses. Hart, tall and rangy, one day wore a lumberjack shirt and blue jeans and chopped wood for the cameras. Mondale invariably campaigned in a dark gray suit, a white or blue shirt, and a muted tie — his aides called the look a "full Norwegian" — and he often resembled an undertaker. Hart spoke naturally in the quick, elliptical style suited to television, and embraced TV as a campaign tool. To cope with the speeded-up schedule that Mondale had imposed on the primaries, Hart had to try to be everywhere at once. He responded by jetting into cities that were TV markets, often two or three per day, at noon, early evening, perhaps late at night, during times when newscasts were on live. He would bound off the jet, itself a symbol of glamour and excitement, and grant planeside interviews to one or more channels, perhaps to all of them in quick succession.

Within hours, even minutes, Hart would take off again, having created the illusion of a day's presence. Mondale, by contrast, distrusted television and usually sounded on it as though he were delivering a speech, not conducting a conversation. He kept showing up at rallies, at union halls, at factory gates, following the rituals and exuding the mannerisms of old-style politics. He openly curried favor with prominent local politicians; he seemed somewhat distant from the people themselves. Mondale and his aides denied any panic; the primary and caucus schedule, they said, had been so artfully contrived that no Johnny-come-lately could last long. Hart's deft retort: no party would dare nominate a candidate who could not prove himself the choice of the people. Hart rode the crest of a self-sustaining wave of excitement. Mondale more than ever seemed to be claiming the right to the nomination without facing up to a fight. In the cinematic imagery that Reagan's presidency had further popularized, Hart was Gary Cooper as Sergeant York, facing impossible odds and prevailing by sheer courage and cunning. Mondale was the self-serving banker-villain in some Frank Capra movie, sitting on his assets and refusing to play fair.

As politicians and pundits watched in bafflement, and the public watched with sheer, unthinking exuberance at the spectacle of victory, Hart swept into Maine, five days after New Hampshire, and won the caucuses there. Into Vermont, two days later, and won the nonbinding primary by 70 percent to Mondale's 20 percent. Into Wyoming, a state even more Western than his own Colorado, but one where he had scant organization, and won the caucuses by 61 percent to Mondale's 36 percent. The numbers of delegates Hart was taking were small — far fewer than the number Mondale already held, just among members of the House pledged to him. But the repudiation of Mondale was so swift and so nearly universal that unless he could recoup somewhere on what everyone in politics called Super Tuesday — the confluence of five primaries and four state caucuses on one delegate-rich day — then, just two weeks after he had come to the New Hampshire primary as the surest of sure things, he seemed certain to drop out.

Mondale appeared all but helpless to save himself, but he had one urgent hope: the news media always, *always*, reflexively attack a front-runner. Reporters usually regard it as unmanly to batter a loser, but feel a macho necessity to confront a man who might become President. Hart, knowing this, had spurned the laurels of front-runnerdom at every opportunity. No matter how many states I win, he would say, Mondale created the schedule, Mondale has more money, Mondale controls labor, Mondale commands the support of all the politicians, and he therefore must be the front-runner. For a few days, the strategy worked. But as it became the conventional wisdom that Mondale was in peril of exclusion from the race, he began to receive the sympathetic if condescending coverage customarily accorded an apparent loser, and it became only a matter of time before Hart would have to face the fusillades.

———

While Hart and Mondale battled for primacy, the other three candidates still in the race campaigned in a kind of serenity, cheered by their adherents, all but written off by the press and the larger public. The least attended of them was McGovern. His entourage had never been large nor his staff well organized: on many days in January and February, no one had answered the telephone at his Washington headquarters. He had made his effort seem all the more quixotic after the New Hampshire primary, by announcing that he would quit on Super Tuesday, March 13, unless he finished at least second in the Massachusetts primary that day. The pledge was, by conventional political standards, almost perverse. Nearly any other politician, knowing how quickly voters desert an apparent loser, would insist he was irrevocably in the contest, right up to the moment of his withdrawal. Some analysts thought McGovern was simply trying to arrange an orderly exit for himself while striking a blow for realism in campaigning. The target he cited was indeed the very minimum that a serious candidate would be expected to achieve in order to continue, although even that appeared to be well beyond McGovern's capacity. Others thought that McGovern hoped to tap an evident reservoir of affection for him in Massachusetts, the only state he had carried in the 1972 general election, and that he was attempting a form of emotional blackmail with liberals who had supported him then: in this view, the last-ditch appeal was a sincere attempt to stay in the race a little longer, if only to exert some influence on the eventual nominee. Cynics and conspiracy theorists, with whom Massachusetts politics abounds, speculated that McGovern was trying to help Mondale, whom he increasingly seemed to favor over his 1972 campaign manager Hart. If McGovern drew off liberal and activist votes in the Bay State, Mondale might win there, despite his dismal poll standings; at the least, Mondale might lose less badly.

Unlike McGovern, Glenn continued to campaign, not on behalf of some cause or idea, but to promote his own battered hope. Humbled and all but broke, he clung to the claim that he alone among Democrats was best equipped to reach out beyond the party and defeat Reagan in November. His strategy had always been based on his presumed strength in the heartland, in the second and third tiers of primaries in the South and Midwest. Thus he had labored diligently to depict Mondale, and then Hart, as ultraliberal captives of the interests of pacifists, big northeastern cities, and labor unions. The message had failed to do him much good in Iowa and New Hampshire, however, and it meant that on Super Tuesday he had no chance of victory in the liberal, urban, unionized primary states of Rhode Island and Massachusetts. Hence he had to rely on the three southern states to be contested in primaries on that same day, Georgia, Alabama, and Florida. In the early, exuberant days Glenn had hoped to win at least two of them. Now his polls suggested that goal had receded beyond reach, so he began to speak of "doing well" in the South, with the definition of that phrase deliberately left vague. He hoped that the overall outcome on Super Tuesday would be mixed enough for him to claim a plausible basis for continuing. His advisers, more resigned to the likelihood of defeat, acknowledged that without an outright victory somewhere, Glenn would find it hard to rally the money and help to fight on.

Traveling with Glenn were most of the same reporters who had been in his retinue since the glory days, but their stories about him were no longer getting much play in print or on air. Their editors had concluded that Glenn's bubble had burst. *Time* ran a poignant photo that reflected the tone of coverage: the candidate stood alone in a big, bare headquarters office, looking pensively out the window. The image was sympathetic but devastating. The reporters did not generally challenge their employers' dismissive judgment: an assumption of doom seeped through Glenn's own organization, and the candidate himself seemed to be motivated more by the desire to go down trying than by a belief he could win. Oddly, as Glenn diminished in political stature, he grew to nearly heroic proportions in the affections of the journalists around him. By his sweet simplicity, his courtesy, his increasing openness, and his grace in the face of humiliation, he won perhaps the fondest press following of any of the candidates. Glenn and his wife, Annie, mingled with reporters, and one night led them in a sing-along. The Glenns lined up at the end of each major swing to shake hands with the regulars in the press entourage and thank them for coming along. The reporters in turn saw Annie Glenn as combining the best of the old and new versions of womanhood. She and Glenn had been sweethearts since they were little more than toddlers, and she had given her life unstintingly to his career. Even more than Nancy Reagan, Annie Glenn personified wifely devotion. Still, she remained very much her own person, committed and at times outspoken. She embodied personal courage: her severe stutter had for years left her almost mute, but with her husband's coaching and encouragement she had almost completely overcome the handicap. Except when weary, most often at the end of the day, she now spoke clearly, commandingly. And reporters found her words all the more affecting for knowing how painfully they had been achieved. Nonetheless, in the stories they delivered to the voting public, journalists rarely spoke of either of the Glenns' valor and dignity. John Glenn came across instead as a dispirited bumbler, flailing his arms as his legs sank into the quicksand of defeat.

The third candidate, Jackson, could fairly claim not yet to have been tested with the electorate at large. He sought to unify blacks by giving them one of their own to vote for. If he had made scant impact in the first five states to hold primaries or caucuses, it was hardly surprising: the black share of the populace in those states ranged from a high of 1.4 percent in Iowa to a low of 0.22 percent in Vermont. For Jackson, who was not seeking to win the nomination but rather to prove a black man's right to contest it seriously, the first valid measure would come in Georgia and Alabama, where blacks were more than a quarter of the population, and in Florida, where they were nearly 14 percent. Yet in the minds, and in the public utterances, of many in the press, Jackson's candidacy had already been judged a failure. He had been dismissed because he had lost the support of a group he never claimed to own, white liberals. He had been declared defeated because of words and gestures that offended the white media establishment — without any discerning consideration of whether he had offended the supporters he was truly counting on, the black masses.

From the beginning, white editors had not known quite what to do with Jackson. Many of them knew him, and had come to respect his sophistication in dealing with the centers of power. He was as much at ease in a three-piece pinstripe suit as in blue jeans or a bush jacket; he spoke as fluently in a soft, educated voice, free of dialect, as in the hoarse cadences of the cotton field and the urban ghetto. He could come into a meeting to argue the merits of quotas, yet congratulate the all-white group that greeted him for sincerity in not including token blacks. Beyond question, Jesse Jackson had the social skills to deal with white folks.

News organizations were tormented over whom to assign to cover his campaign. To assign a white reporter would be to deny racism, to hold Jackson to the same standards as other candidates, and, in all likelihood, to maintain the news outlet's pecking order: campaign reporting jobs were plums, and relatively few black reporters were judged to have "proved themselves ready." But if Jackson appealed, by intention, primarily to blacks, could white reporters adequately appreciate the nuances and contexts of his rhetoric, and would they have the contacts needed to judge whether his pitch was being well received? Moreover, if Jackson was demonstrating that blacks were ready to run for President, how could blacks not be ready to cover such a race? Most of the newspapers decided in favor of assigning black reporters at least part of the time. The TV networks opted for mostly biracial arrangements — a black correspondent accompanied by a white field producer or vice versa. Jackson visibly preferred the company of black reporters, although some feared he was only trying to co-opt them; they noted with disappointment that if he had a story he wanted to leak, he tended to go to the reporters whose media employers wielded the most power, regardless of race. Still, it was commonplace for Jackson to pull aside one or more of the blacks in his press entourage for a chat.

The ground rules for these conversations had never really been established, in part because Jackson, for all his intuitive gifts in politics, had almost no knowledge of the mechanics of campaigning. Jackson's code phrase, "Let's talk black talk," could be taken by both sides to signal that what was taking place was something less formal than an on-the-record interview. But in the absence of an explicit agreement that Jackson's remarks were off the record, reporters regarded them as available for some sort of future use. Indeed, many journalists questioned whether there should ever be such a thing as off-the-record contact with a candidate for President (although reporters aboard Mondale's plane and bus had long since obediently submitted to his blanket off-the-record rule). Once a man declared himself ready for the highest office, the journalist-militants reasoned, anything he did or said was legitimate news, and he had no right to shortchange the public by trying to control the press. Thus when Milton Coleman, a *Washington Post* reporter, was invited into one of Jackson's chats one winter day, he did not feel honor-bound to conceal what he heard. But he and his bosses at the *Post* seemed unsure whether what

Jackson said was news. Either that, or they were fearful of its consequences.

During this "black talk" with Coleman, Jackson repeatedly referred to Jews as "Hymies" and described New York City as "Hymietown." These racial slurs were comparable to someone else's calling Jackson a "coon" or "nigger." Their newsworthiness should have been beyond question. Jackson, a candidate who called upon the nation to redress the effects of past prejudice, had spoken in the language of prejudice himself. Jackson, whose "rainbow coalition" purported to reunite blacks and white liberals, had disparaged the white ethnic group who had once been the blacks' most stalwart ally. Jackson, whose sympathy for displaced Palestinians prompted supporters of Israel to mistrust him, had now provided what they could seize on as proof of his enmity toward Jews.

The broader subject of the hostility between black and Jewish leaders had been news for more than a decade. Their antagonism began when blacks ousted whites from leadership roles in the NAACP and other civil rights groups. It worsened when the ghetto riots of the 1960s led to looting of neighborhood stores owned by whites, many of them Jews who had indulged indigent customers with credit. Then black leaders began to urge "community control" of schools in New York and other cities, repudiating the heavily Jewish bureaucracy of principals and teachers. A growing infatuation with Islam as an indigenously black faith had further disaffected blacks from Israel. (Historically, of course, Islam had been initially as alien to the animist tribes of Africa as Christianity, which some black leaders dismissed as an imposed, "slave" religion.) And Jews had bitterly opposed the black push for affirmative-action quotas in hiring, promotion, and especially college and graduate school admission. Some Jews simply resisted, on principle, any compromise in standards. Others feared that pro-black quotas, and any allocations for other ethnic groups that might follow, would eventually diminish the number of places available to Jews, who attend four-year colleges in a ratio roughly twice the national norm. By itself, Jackson's language had sounded appallingly injudicious on the lips of a national leader. In the context of recent social history, his remarks were incendiary.

Yet the "Hymie" story did not appear on the front page the next morning. Indeed, it did not appear anywhere at all for many days. When at last the *Post* printed the controversial quotations, Coleman did not even write the story. The information became a brief aside, deep in the body of a profile by another writer. The *Post* and Coleman could not adequately explain the delay. Later, editor Benjamin Bradlee said, "There's a whole collection of things out there waiting for the proper framework. This did not become significant until we decided to talk about blacks and

Jews. A lot of things are only interesting until there is a framework, and, after that, they become important." The treatment of the story may have had something to do with the fact that the *Post* has a predominantly white, suburban readership but sits in the heart of downtown in a primarily black and frequently resentful city. Coleman's hesitation may have had something to do with his being black; but Coleman and the *Post* were not alone in hesitating. Once the fact of Jackson's slurring language percolated into print, other reporters for major news organizations confirmed that they, too, had been hearing the candidate talk that way, and in some cases had alerted their editors. Jackson's opponents in the Zionist community, furious that they had had to wait so long to receive such potent ammunition against him, accused black and white-liberal reporters of having protected him in deference to his race.

Whatever the fairness of that claim, the kindly treatment soon stopped. It took the nation's news media a week or so after publication to conclude that the "Hymie" talk was a major issue. And then it became the only issue for Jackson. Reporters confronted him at every stop. Barbara Walters asked Jackson to confirm or deny the story during a televised debate. Jackson used the locutions of Richard Nixon and his aides during Watergate: he claimed not to "recall" having made such remarks. The regulars in his press entourage rejected this equivocation as a lie. By the weekend before the New Hampshire primary, Jackson had been almost entirely discredited with white liberals, among whom he had theretofore been making modest inroads, and he was finding it almost impossible to persuade the press and public that he had anything left to say. So he confessed, melodramatically, before a mostly Jewish audience in a synagogue. He repented and asked forgiveness. His performance, in the utmost self-condemning traditions of the black evangelical church, moved some who heard him to tears. But most journalists judged his penitence to be too little and too late. CBS News anchor Dan Rather concluded privately that Jackson was probably finished. So did *Boston Globe* editorial page editor Martin Nolan. Only slowly, over the weeks between New Hampshire and Super Tuesday, did polls begin to reveal that Jackson's black constituency did not share the white journalists' reverence for the pious niceties of political speech. Jackson, reassured, responded by directing his campaign more specifically than before at his black brethren, above all on the campuses and in the churches.

—————

Ebenezer Baptist Church is a modest, ramshackle building, a humble workingman's echo of cathedrals: its floors are wood or brick or linoleum, not stone, its stained-glass windows are simple rectangles of opaque pastel glass, and the entrance to its congregation hall is reached by climbing un-adorned schoolhouse-style interior stairs. Only modest plaques, of the kind favored by bowling leagues, hint to the churchgoer that he is enter-ing a place rich in history. Most of them honor the members of the family of the church's longtime preacher, Martin Luther King, Sr. From this building, in April 1968, his murdered son Martin Jr. was buried, his coffin drawn on a wagon hitched to mules. The younger King had dreamed of the day when a black man could run meaningfully for President, and it might have gratified him that one of his disciples was doing it. It surely would have pleased him that the crucial pilgrimage for that disciple was to his mentor's family church. On the Sunday morning when Jesse Jackson's husky voice reverberated through Ebenezer Baptist in fulfillment of the dream, few members of the King family were there to listen. They were not ready to pass on the torch of leadership to Jesse Jackson or any other black man. Daddy King, whose support had been described as the differ-ence between victory and defeat by John Kennedy and Jimmy Carter, was supporting Walter Mondale. So was Martin Jr.'s widow, Coretta, so was Mayor Andrew Young, so were many in the Atlanta black establishment. Yet the faithful of Ebenezer Baptist, like the faithful in church after church, shouted and swayed that morning, in a kind of ecstasy. Jesse Jackson was not a memory but a man, and he had won their hearts.

He was accompanied by Secret Service men and dozens of reporters. They had converged on Atlanta, two days before Super Tuesday, to hear the candidates debate in the grand old theater that had housed the 1939 world premiere of the movie *Gone with the Wind*. For romance and irony of setting, the only event to rival the debate was Jackson's journey to Ebenezer Baptist. He had come to turn the other cheek, in Christian hu-mility, to his repudiators, black America's first family.

To white ears his speech might have sounded megalomaniacal. As his throbbing voice accelerated in energy and volume and incantatory fervor, as his metaphors became ever more richly lyrical, he compared himself more and more explicitly to Jesus Christ. That equation, the preacher as messiah, is something of a tradition in black evangelism. But Jackson found the comparison especially helpful, and he sustained it. Thus, he suggested, it was he, Jesse Jackson, who had wandered in the desert, who had been betrayed by those close to him, who had suffered rejection. And it was he, Jesse Jackson, who would offer redemption and deliverance of the new chosen people to a new promised land. He stopped short of sacri-lege. He offered no miracle, except himself. "For Jesse Jackson to be run-ning for President," he said in his climax, "is truly miraculous." The congregation, which had shouted and applauded and glared at the impassive white journalists, sounded a thunderclap of approval. Not only was it a miracle. It was *their* miracle. Whoever opposed him, whatever he had said to a reporter, they would support him, for his triumph meant *they* had overcome.

———

If Super Tuesday on March 13 had been planned as the focal event of the primary season, then it appeared that Georgia, almost by accident, had become the focal state. By the time of the debate in Atlanta on March 11 — the only televised encounter among all the remaining candidates between New Hampshire and the Super Tuesday voting — the others had more or less ceded Massachusetts, Rhode Island, and probably Florida to Hart. Hart's leads in polls in those states ranged from solid to seemingly insurmountable. Mondale, Glenn, and even Jackson fancied their chances in Alabama, but the place was held in such low regard, for its history of poverty and prejudice, that its affirmation could scarcely be decisive.

Georgia, however, was the hub of the New South. Its capital was a center of culture and commerce, its universities excelled at more than football, its race relations reflected realism if not reconciliation, and its electorate favored progressives. In many ways it resembled the rapidly expanding, newly prosperous Southwest, where Democrats consistently fared badly. A Democrat who proved popular in Georgia could reasonably claim to have a chance at appealing to the nation.

The Atlanta headquarters of the four principal candidates, abuzz in the hours before the debate, mirrored the images that the press had built up about each camp. Mondale's, on two floors of a small office building on the respectable fringe of downtown, was crammed full with dozens of unsmiling, no-nonsense political veterans, virtually all of them white. The men were mostly young, close-cropped, wearing white shirts. The women were trim but drab. Some said they had volunteered on behalf of the teachers or other union groups. Several were professional campaign operatives, guns for hire. The walls were almost completely covered with lists, instructions, favorable cartoons and editorials. Visitors were questioned closely, and the big stacks of computer printouts, from which telephone solicitors were working in back rooms, were zealously guarded.

Jackson operated from a big, bare space, brightened by banks of flowers and women dressed in their Sunday best. Three young girls sat at a table by the doorway greeting newcomers, and a few people loitered in front of a huge, detailed map of Atlanta, but no one seemed to do any work. A sign instructed volunteers: KEEP LINES OPEN. LIMIT PERSONAL CALLS. NO LONG DISTANCE. BE TRUTHFUL.

Glenn's office, inaccessibly tucked into a highrise along a highway in Buckhead, the poshest part of town, appeared almost sleepy. Its staffers seemed older and more southern than at Mondale's suite, and they radiated none of the Mondale team's grim intensity.

To reach Hart headquarters, visitors and volunteers had to travel out of town altogether, to a courtyard shopping center in the prosperous old town of Decatur. Even then, the office was easy to miss: its all but unmarked entrance was a doorway about five feet wide, jammed with bundles of leaflets, behind which a grimy corridor led to a hopelessly overcrowded room. On the wall was a giant calendar: its first day, the start of the universe, was the day of the New Hampshire primary. Most of the dozen people tripping over each other's telephone wires were students, and most had begun to support Hart within the past two weeks. One of them explained patiently, to a reporter from the Tokyo newspaper *Akahata* who was less than fluent in English, "Nobody wants to throw old people off Social Security, but the facts are that I am thirty and it's not going to be around when I am sixty-five." The Japanese reporter, baffled but dutiful, repeated, "You are sixty-five," and started to write it down.

———

NBC News anchor John Chancellor opened the Atlanta debate by summing up the uncomfortable position in which most of the candidates found themselves — Mondale having been "clobbered," Glenn not leading anyplace according to the polls, Jackson facing a cutoff of federal funds unless he topped 20 percent in at least one primary. Then the candidates replied with exaggeratedly upbeat assertions of the Democratic party's prospects, based on Ronald Reagan's presumed sins. Mondale characteristically stressed labor's favorite issue, the imbalance of trade. Hart renewed his lament about the nine million structurally unemployed Americans who needed to be retrained. Jackson spoke anew about the "misery index" of the downtrodden. Glenn warned of a gap between the United States and its competitors in research and development. This political white noise continued until discussion focused on defense. Glenn attacked Mondale and especially Hart for not supporting big enough Pentagon budget increases. "My opponents would cut beyond all reality," he said, although the difference between him and them amounted to all of 2 percent. Hart, thrust into combat for the first time since his ascension, fumbled his reply. McGovern then attacked Hart from the opposite direction, for not using his expertise on military matters to propose deep

Pentagon budget cuts. The front-runner found himself in a cross fire. Jackson dryly observed, "Everybody's sneaking on Gary." Worse was to come.

Chancellor asked a hypothetical question — based loosely on the actual Soviet military downing of a Korean Air Lines passenger jet that had strayed into Soviet airspace — about what an American President would do in similar circumstances. He presupposed that U.S. jets could follow the enemy plane closely but could not arouse a response from the people they saw through the windows. Hart faced the question first, and he blundered. Unaccustomed to the dangers of gut fighting, he failed to see when to step back and stay out. "If the people they looked in and saw had uniforms on," he said, "I would shoot it down. If they were civilians, I would just let it keep on going." Morally, Hart may have been on solid ground. In practical terms he was less surefooted. A moment's thought would have made him realize the unlikelihood of distinguishing military uniforms from miles away through the windows of a swift-moving target. Mondale, quick of ear, grasped how pathetically naive and thoughtless Hart had sounded. When Chancellor put the same question to him, he laughed and said, "I think that's a wonderful hypothetical thing and it's ridiculous." Glenn jumped in a moment later to lambaste Hart for his "fundamental lack of understanding" of simple mechanical realities. Once more, Hart botched his self-defense.

When the discussion shifted to the economy, Hart renewed his call for a revival of America's entrepreneurial spirit — a bugbear to the competition-shy union leaders who were backing Mondale. Thus the moment seemed ripe for the riposte that Mondale had been rehearsing all weekend. Grinning broadly, seeming to stretch and relax like a sly country lawyer about to spring a trap, Mondale poured charm into his nasal midwestern drawl and said, "When I hear about your 'new ideas,' I'm reminded of that ad, 'Where's the beef?' " The reference was one almost no one in the audience could miss, and its aim was deadly. The line had been popularized by a frog-voiced little old lady, Clara Peller, in a TV commercial for the Wendy's hamburger chain. The target of her wrath, a mythical rival chain, cheated consumers by selling hamburgers that were nearly all bun and no meat. Peller's indignant demand and foghorn delivery had just recently caught the nation's fancy as no other commercial had in years; she became a TV celebrity, and the ad campaign prompted feature coverage in the *New York Times* and on network TV. Her catchphrase carried overtones of a commonsensical citizen outraged at humbuggery. It was, in a sense, an updated version of the child's announcement that the emperor has no clothes. As used by Mondale, it conveyed the message that Hart was some fly-by-night fraud. Hart had no comeback beyond a nervous snicker and an unpersuasive attempt at a casual shrug. Still untutored at the arts of national candidacy, Hart had given scant thought to the way the debate would be reduced to brief snippets in TV news reports. He had prepared no one-liners, no terse summations of his pitch, no spontaneous-seeming moments of human drama for the cameras to record. Thus Mondale won the battle of the "sound bite," and the sound bites were heard by millions more people than watched the debate. The impact might not be felt soon enough to save Mondale in the voting two days later. But he had found a low road to follow, if by chance he did survive.

———✦———

When the results were in from the five primaries and four caucuses, a reporter asked Mondale's campaign manager, Robert Beckel, what would have happened if his man had lost Georgia. Beckel hefted an imaginary golf club and said, "Boca Raton, two hundred ninety yards, par four."

Instead, Mondale emerged from Super Tuesday relegitimized and rejuvenated. Although he finished behind Hart in three of five primaries and three of four caucus states, Mondale and his aides manipulated the news media into presenting Super Tuesday as a draw; by any genuinely objective measure, Mondale had failed utterly to halt Hart's onslaught. Hart was running without much money or organization, or endorsements or identifiable constituencies, against a candidate who had smugly declared himself the best-endowed of all time. Hart won states in virtually every region of the country, representing virtually every kind of economy and ethnicity. No modern Democrat before Hart had ever won contested fights in both the Massachusetts and Florida Democratic primaries, which reflect polar extremes of opinion; Hart won them both on the same day. He prevailed by a landslide in unionized, "ethnic" Rhode Island, a natural Mondale territory, and also in rural Oklahoma and desert-barren Nevada. He beat Mondale in Washington, one of the front-runner's strongest states organizationally, by 53 to 33 percent in caucus voting. Hart even managed a symbolic victory in Hawaii, which he did not contest but which gave 64 percent of its vote to "uncommitted" slates rather than to Mondale. Against all that, Mondale managed victories only in two neighboring Southeast states: Alabama, where his margin was solid, and Georgia, where his plurality over Hart was just 3 percent.

The process by which these wildly uneven results were transmuted into a "tie" began with the persistent propensity of reporters to play the expectations game. On Super Tuesday night, ABC's Peter Jennings made two references to expectations in his opening paragraph of commentary.

So did CBS's Dan Rather and NBC's Tom Brokaw, and NBC commentator Roger Mudd followed with a whole string of them. Most of the commentators apparently "expected" that Hart would win everything in sight, as he had for the previous two weeks. Thus any glimmer of good news for Mondale would, by their standards, merit attention beyond all proportion. The Mondale staff had adroitly played upon this inclination by deliberately exaggerating their desperation, and by defining the Georgia outcome as the measure of whether their man could continue. In this, Mondale's aides showed special cunning and finesse. To be sure, a defeat in the home state of Jimmy Carter, who had made Mondale his vice-president and who had campaigned for him publicly the weekend before the vote, probably should have been enough to drive Mondale from the race. But the inverse was not necessarily true: scraping by in a state where he had so many advantages did not by itself constitute a revival of Mondale's effort. Yet this was how virtually all the correspondents assigned to Mondale's entourage played it. They described the supposed buoyancy and relief of Mondale's aides, and in effect ignored the eight other races that day to make Georgia the yardstick. Brit Hume of ABC, who was perhaps the shrewdest TV reporter on the race, was as readily persuaded as the rest by the Mondale stratagem. He explained off-camera that night, "I wanted to be able to go on the air and report what the Mondale people thought it all meant."

Hart was further shortchanged by deadline problems for the networks and leading newspapers. The five Super Tuesday primaries all took place in the eastern time zone. The four caucuses, where Mondale managed not even one outright victory, were spread across the more westerly parts of the country, and did not yield definitive results until the *New York Times*, *Washington Post*, and major networks had completed their coverage for that night. Thus Hart's caucus victories, which were, in context, even more impressive than his primary triumphs, received almost no play. David Broder of the *Washington Post*, the most influential print analyst, surveyed the early evening tallies and wrote that Hart "kept his bandwagon rolling as the music continued to fade for his rivals." A few paragraphs later, he spoke of Mondale's "crippled campaign." But after Mondale squeaked by in Georgia, and with the caucus outcomes not yet known, Broder dropped the stinging references to Mondale and other fading rivals, and redefined Hart's bandwagon as being limited to New England. The paper's eventual page one headline read, "Hart Wins 3, Mondale 2." A frustrated Hart took a copy of the paper, crossed out "3," wrote in "6½," and tossed it to his press secretary, Kathy Bushkin, saying "Show this to [*Post* reporter Martin] Schram."

To add to Hart's problems, he faced outright bullying and scorn from some TV commentators, notably on NBC. Anchor Tom Brokaw, who proclaimed Mondale "alive and well tonight in this race," airily dismissed Hart as almost a fad, "this season's hit rock-'n'-roll single." Roger Mudd then interviewed Hart live, and belittled his victories. Bafflingly, he proclaimed Florida "not a true southern state" and announced that Hart, despite his cumulative campaign total of ten victories in five different time zones, was "not a national candidate yet." Mudd also asked snidely, "Why do you imitate John Kennedy so much?," thereby hammering home Mondale's theme that Hart was somehow inauthentic, and closed with an insistent invitation to Hart to "do your Teddy Kennedy imitation." Mudd seemed to bear Hart some personal animus, perhaps in part because his candidacy had made fools of the Washington insiders, of whom Mudd may be the most relentless. Although the interview prompted 240 telephone calls, mostly of protest, to NBC in New York alone, Mudd remained unrepentant. "People have gotten so used to soft and pappy questions in interviews," he said, "that when they hear firm and brisk questions, they do not know what to make of it."

Only Rather seemed sure that Hart had won the night. Using a convoluted train metaphor, he opened his report by asserting that Hart's candidacy "keeps moving like a fast freight," adding that Mondale's "is off the side rails and is moving forward again." In his interview with Hart, he asked, "In your heart of hearts, you now believe you have the Democratic nomination, don't you?" Hart answered, "No." To Mondale, Rather said, "If your candidacy is still alive, it's hanging on the ropes?" Mondale, too, answered, "No." By the next evening, CBS had fallen into line with the conventional wisdom. Its newscast showed scenes of Hart and Mondale each arriving in Illinois for the next major primary. For *both* men, the voice-over wording was identical: "The big Super Tuesday winner came to Chicago today."

Super Tuesday also brought a dignified end to McGovern's campaign. He finished third in Massachusetts and dropped out as pledged, but he drew more than 21 percent of the vote there and for a time it looked as though he would edge in ahead of Mondale. For Glenn, the night provided a final humiliation. Desperate to rally last-minute support, and persuaded by polls that the voters least motivated to turn out were most likely to vote for him if they got there, he granted highly unusual live interviews during the network evening newscasts of ABC and NBC. Both Peter Jennings and Tom Brokaw wrecked his gambit by announcing, on the basis of exit polls, that he had no chance to win and had come to the end of the road. An anguished Glenn said, "When you people make projections like that, it discourages an awful lot of good folks from going to the polls." As it turned out, Glenn placed a distant third or fourth everywhere, except in Alabama, where he and Hart ended in a virtual tie for second, well behind Mondale. But Glenn and his aides were determined not to be hounded out by the media, and announced that his campaign would continue. At least one weary member of the Glenn press entourage, ABC's Lynn Sherr, started shouting at the Glenn staff that they had to quit, that enough was enough. "I had visions of us going on for months, a sort of Flying Dutchman on the campaign trail," she recalled. "But of course they had run out of money and only wanted to wait until they got back to Washington to get out, just for the sake of Glenn's pride."

Thus the race narrowed to two candidates — plus one more who had no chance to win the nomination but who carried potent symbolic value. The third big Super Tuesday winner was Jackson. In Alabama, he drew almost 20 percent of the vote and ran virtually even with Hart and Glenn. In Florida, he drew more than 12 percent, substantially ahead of Glenn. And in Georgia, where Andrew Young and the King dynasty had repudiated him, he won the hearts of the plain people as overwhelmingly as he had at Ebenezer Baptist Church. He captured 21 percent of the vote (behind Mondale and Hart, but well ahead of Glenn) and, more important to him, nearly two-thirds of the black vote. Moreover, in state after state his candidacy had boosted black turnout. In Alabama, blacks were only 22.5 percent of the registered voters, but blacks made up 35 percent of the Super Tuesday electorate. In Georgia, they were 20.6 percent of voters and 34 percent of the Super Tuesday turnout. They explained their motive simply. *Time* quoted a mechanic, thirty-year-old James Powell: "I didn't want to miss the opportunity of voting for a black man for President."

Mondale's survival on Super Tuesday, even by the margin of a few thousand votes in Georgia, meant that he would almost certainly reemerge as the front-runner in the days ahead. When he was drafting the schedule to provide for a roundhouse blow to rivals on Super Tuesday, he planned for the knockout punch to follow on Super Saturday, March 17. Four states held caucuses that day. By far the biggest was Michigan, where unions dominated the Democratic machinery. Some precincts actually met in United Auto Workers halls. A union member who wanted to support Hart or Jackson might well find himself doing so under the watchful eyes of his shop steward. In fact, union officials did far more than stand attentively by. Lane Kirkland and his AFL–CIO troops were little short of panicky that their endorsement of Mondale would be interpreted as the kiss of death for his campaign, which would make them pariahs in the nominating process in the future. So unions poured resources blatantly, perhaps illegally, into the resuscitation of Mondale's campaign. Hart never expected to have a chance in Michigan, and he was tempted to boycott the caucuses outright. But as a result of the media analysis of Super Tuesday — colored, probably, by reporters' professional desire to sustain the campaign as knockdown, drag-out news — Hart now faced a prolonged struggle for the nomination. Both sides had begun to refer to the contest as a marathon. Hart could not afford to pass up whatever delegates he might garner in the nation's eighth-biggest state. He settled for 32 percent to Mondale's 50 percent, and, despite the predictability of Mondale's margin, the press promptly debited Hart with a sizable defeat. Mondale also won, more narrowly, in Arkansas, but was topped by uncommitted slates in Mississippi, and finished fourth, behind "uncommitted," Jackson, and Hart, in South Carolina. In the days just before Super Saturday, Hart won a landslide in Alaska's caucuses and Mondale a runaway in Delaware's. The day after Super Saturday, Hart won North Dakota's caucuses, while Mondale scored 99.2 percent of the vote in a Puerto Rico primary that other candidates bypassed as fixed. The apparent standoff amounted to a big comeback for Mondale. And the scrunched-up schedule worked to his advantage in two ways. Not only did it put a premium on organization and money, to make up for a candidate's increasing inability to cover all fronts; it also brought in new results day after day, in numbing confusion, and further pushed to the back of voters' memories the succession of Hart sweeps and especially his underappreciated triumph on Super Tuesday.

<hr>

In politics, half or more of everything is timing. An event, a disclosure, an error, a mishap becomes crucial, not because of what it is, but because of when it happens. So it went with unquestionably the most influential, perhaps historic news story of 1984, which appeared two days after Super Tuesday and which made itself felt over the next couple of weeks. Jim Perry of the *Wall Street Journal*, a dean of presidential campaign coverage, had been assigned to write a candidate profile of Gary Hart, the sort of obligatory piece that every major publication works up about every major candidate. Perry, however, took the time to do what few of his peers had bothered to: he visited Hart's hometown, Ottawa, Kansas, to learn what people remembered of the young man who moved away to glory. What he discovered yielded a sympathetic, at times poignant portrait. But it also suggested a dark, neurotic underside to the buoyant, boyish hero of the hustings. The child Hart came across as religiously obsessed, racked by the clash between good and evil. The adolescent Hart, it was implied, had once cheated on a test at school and had also felt compelled to sneak off with friends to the local airstrip to dance to rock music that came in on a surreptitiously tuned car radio. Hart's mother emerged as strange, almost crazy. Perry described her as moving house compulsively, repeatedly, on occasion uprooting the family between the time young Gary left for school in the morning and when he returned home at night. Hart took deep personal offense at this depiction of his mother, who he insisted had been kind, stable, and supportive. Yet the basic facts in the story were never consequentially challenged.

Perry's piece was revealing enough, but its most significant effect was to legitimize for other major media the whole realm of probing, psychoanalytic criticism of Hart. Much investigative news, especially about political matters, sifts upward into public view by a curious media process of deference and imitation. A fact may be known, or readily discernible, for weeks or months or even years, but it may not be considered worthy of notice. It may not have much obvious weight, except for how it could be interpreted as symbolic or implicative. Then some perceived change in circumstances may induce one of the smaller news organizations to bring the instance to light. That story in turn may trigger a comparable or more extensive story by a news medium of the first rank — ABC, NBC, and CBS, *Time* and *Newsweek* and perhaps *U.S. News & World Report*, the *New York Times* and *Washington Post* and *Los Angeles Times* and *Wall Street Journal*. And once the story has broken in that close-knit inner circle, most or all of the other leading media organizations may conclude that they are missing out on big news, and the chase is truly on. One classic example is Senator Edward Kennedy's involvement in a fatal automobile accident on Chappaquiddick near Martha's Vineyard. The case was exhaustively covered by the press, and investigated by criminal authorities, when it happened in 1969. The truths it suggests about Kennedy's character — which vary with the beholder — are long since established. If his behavior casts doubt on his judgment, candor, or moral fitness, then surely the subject ought to be the focus of an ongoing media outcry for as long as he holds office. Instead, Chappaquiddick becomes an issue for the major media only if Kennedy unbalances the equilibrium by preparing to run for President.

Hart's boyhood yearnings and lapses were plainly old news, at best. So were the troubled state of his marriage and his purported interests in other women. Above all, that was true of three trivial facts that journalists made serve as suggestion, if not proof, of Hart's utter inauthenticity: he had been mildly understating his age for years, now describing himself as forty-six rather than forty-seven; as a young adult, he had shortened his name legally from Hartpence, which had been too easily contorted into smirky nicknames throughout his youth; and he had twice changed his signature. None of these facts had fundamentally altered Hart. None, except perhaps the deterioration of his marriage — hardly an uncommon event — indicated the least vulnerability to the pressures of public life. None had anything to do with the validity of his political message or the acuity of his analysis. But Perry's story, and the sequels it triggered, communicated to the public that journalists regarded Hart as a fraud.

The focus of these pieces, on matters of personal character, could not have been more damaging. The euphoric electorate awakened from its dreams to the disquieting word that Hart was not the man he seemed to be — and worse, that he had a lifelong habit of remaking himself in what could be construed as confidence trickery. The peculiar nature of Hart's quirky fibs suggested, moreover, that he might be more unstable than trustworthy. And this perception in turn tied into Mondale's essential strategy for combating Hart: the charge that he was too unfamiliar, too murky a figure, to be trusted with the fate of the free world. Inexperience was a predictable charge, and one for which Hart had a ready answer: that he, at least, bore no responsibility for the disasters of the past. Hart seemed unready for the cruel precision of Mondale's actual assault. The two men had been friends and colleagues. Hart was sure that Mondale considered him able, sane, competent to be President. He expected that Mondale might claim to be better suited. But he was dumbfounded when a rejected and desperate Mondale decided to claim, not that he himself was more worthy, but that Hart was some dark pretender, not to be trusted at all.

Thus, almost before it started to blossom, the public's love affair with Hart was blighted. He was undone in part by the natural wave of doubt that sets in after any infatuation. But he suffered also from the arrogant exercise of conscience by the news media, who dared to presume that they had created Hart and so were obliged to challenge him. Perhaps Hart's biggest enemy, however, was his own passivity. Confronted with trouble, he demonstrated that in a sense Mondale was right, that the perceived "Gary Hart" was not the real Gary Hart. In a subtle way, the charge of inauthenticity rang true: the supposedly bold, conquering candidate could not slay the dragon attacking him — indeed, he could not even bring himself to try. And the purportedly intuitive master of political rhythm failed to grasp one of the most basic and immutable facts of campaign life. Once the public has given itself to a previously unknown candidate, whether Jimmy Carter in 1976 or George Bush in 1980 or Gary Hart in 1984, it wants to know who the candidate *really* is. As in puppy love, adoration comes first, true attachment after. Carter understood, and he had answered with candor and insight. Bush, who had been answering questions about himself with ballyhoo aimed at building name recognition, never moved on to the next stage of revealing his heart and soul. Had Hart been more like Carter, more willing to risk letting the people come to know his inner self, he might have controlled the damage better and ended it sooner. He succumbed, instead, to the immediate foolhardy impulse of a politician at the peak of popularity — the determination not to offend for fear of losing someone, at the unrecognized risk of disappointing everyone.

Once the Mondale campaign had persuaded the press it was surely in the race to stay, the battle for the hearts and minds of reporters shifted to the meaning behind the numbers. Hart wanted to keep the emphasis on electability, on who could beat Reagan. Polls generally showed him stronger, despite the surge of negative coverage. Exit polls of voters in primary states only reinforced his claim; most Mondale voters were loyal Democrats who would back the party nominee in any case, but many Hart voters were independents, and they threatened to vote for Reagan in November if their man was not nominated. This information did not much help Hart with partisan Democrats. To hell with the independents, they tended to say, we'll win without them. But in fact the swing vote in presidential elections is independent, generally more educated and suburban than the norm, and inclined to favor nominees who campaign on the basis of a personal program rather than a party platform. Thus Hart's assertion of electability rang true to a lot of reporters.

Mondale's countermessage was that Hart was not a true Democrat. Increasingly, his attack centered on social class. Hart had shown an ability to appeal across the board to whites — in some states he even managed a plurality of white union households — but he had little or no following among blacks and Hispanics, in part because those groups tend to vote for time-tested allies. Moreover, Hart had centered his pitch on the Baby Boom generation, addressing them in terms of age and formative social experiences. Mondale's aides cannily strove to diminish Hart's appeal by restating it as one of class, and helped persuade the press to adopt a shorthand term for a previously unrecognized group, the Yuppies. These Young Urban Professionals (or Young Upwardly mobile Professionals) were categorized by the Mondale team as being really closet Republicans. Because they were of the generation in which almost everyone went on to some form of higher education, and because they lived for the most part in two-income households, the Yuppies were affluent citizens who needed no help from government. They were often the children of, but were collectively much mistrusted by, the elderly and blue-collar families who depended on government aid and protection. From noting the existence of Yuppies it was only a short step to linking them to the 1980 candidacy of John Anderson, a liberal Republican whose strongest appeal had been to the suburban, independent upper middle class. Democrats had reviled Anderson voters with shorthand references to life-style — the Volvo crowd, or the Brie and Perrier crew. The terms reflected both the presumed (and envied) affluence of this group, and its suspect preference for funny-sounding, imported goods, some of which, like foreign cars, come at the expense of American union jobs. The shorthand for holders of those imperiled jobs was "lunchbucket" Democrats.

Mondale shrewdly found a way to sum up the antagonism between these two major Democratic groups — and to put Hart on the wrong side of the aisle — by campaigning anew in favor of a years-old bailout of Chrysler Corporation, the auto manufacturing company. Hart had opposed the federal loan to Chrysler on the reasonable but somewhat abstract, unemotional grounds that government ought to favor the development of new technology, not prop up weak competitors in dying or troubled industries. Mondale had supported the bailout because it saved American jobs. Hart's position was prototypical for reformers, who value above all else the intellectual purity of the process of government. Mondale's position typified the preference of liberals for results over principles.

The new emphasis on class antagonism served Mondale's needs particularly well in the next pivotal campaign event, the Illinois primary. Illinois has produced a succession of scholarly, magisterial Democrats, from Adlai Stevenson and the late Senator Paul Douglas to Senator Paul Simon and ex-Representative, now federal judge, Abner Mikva. But its characteristic Democratic politics is the raw, combative, conniving gutter war of Chicago, a metropolis so ghettoized ethnically and economically that it has become a sort of Beirut of the Midwest. More than any other American city, Chicago had epitomized the effort of each successive wave of immigrants to wrest power from the last, and then to suppress the ambitions of the next. Anglo-Saxons had given way to the Irish, who then battled the Italians, the eastern Europeans, the Jews, and last those native "immigrants," southern-born blacks. Less than a year before the presidential pri-

mary, and with more than customary bitterness, Chicago had fought perhaps the most dramatic of its Armageddons of displacement, the mayoral
election that installed Harold Washington as Chicago's first black chief
executive. Washington won office, but he did not win power. White al-
dermen and the white-run Democratic machinery had frustrated most of
his initiatives, and had in turn aroused him and his supporters to a near-
fury of resentment. Thus Chicago lay ahead, a minefield for even the
most deft and experienced politician: to win the support of one side was,
all but automatically, to alienate the other.

For Hart, Chicago posed special problems. Reformers rarely inspire
much enthusiasm among urban voters, who tend cheerfully to regard lar-
ceny and preferment as the perquisites of office. High-tech schemes for
economic redevelopment seem impossibly remote from the lives of the
permanently unemployed. "New ideas" do not matter much to people
seeking old-fashioned empowerment. And when Hart deplored "special
interests" and the politics of making promises, he was attacking the very
way — for most Chicagoans, the only conceivable way — that the city
did business. In the Chicago of March 1984, the one overriding issue was
not arms control or budget deficits or military readiness, but whether you
were with the mayor or with the leader of the white opposition, Alderman
Edward Vrdolyak.

Mondale: now, there was a candidate whom Chicagoans could understand. He was a Democrat's Democrat, blackguarding the rich while living himself in a suburban mansion in Minnesota and a stately home in
Washington. His hypocrisy was just the kind that Chicago's plutocrat
populists had accustomed the voters to. Mondale professed to be a friend
of blacks, but during the mayoral primary the year before he had endorsed
and campaigned for one of Washington's white opponents, the son of the
late Mayor Richard Daley. Mondale accepted Vrdolyak's support, but not
too warmly: everyone knew that the ultraconservative Vrdolyak would
prefer Reagan to almost any Democrat. Mondale tugged his forelock in
the presence of labor leaders. He appeared to endorse the all but divine
right of public employees to extract high wages. He admired Chicago's
system, or seemed to. Above all, he was palpably square. Nothing in his
manner suggested trendiness or casual achievement or ease. He seemed
like a man whose earnest accomplishments came from hard work. Unlike
Hart, with his good looks and grace, Mondale could win without giving
city-mired everymen the feeling that the rich bastards from the suburbs
were commuting in to take over once again. The truth, of course, was that
Hart had grown up with far fewer privileges than Mondale, had depended
less on the patronage of highly placed men, had probably sweated harder.
Yet in the state of Lincoln, Mondale looked more like a son of toil.

Given the inhospitability of Chicago, Hart might reasonably have expected defeat from the outset. And indeed, in his original plan for a slower build toward the nomination, he had envisioned winning his first primary a week later than Illinois', in Connecticut. But the same magic wand that had touched him in Vermont, in Wyoming, in Florida seemed at first to be working in Illinois. Polls taken just after Super Tuesday showed him ahead. Those polls may have been misleading. They reflected the electorate's initial impulse, before it focused closely on political coverage in the final days of the primary fight, and before it had been exposed to a wave of anti-Hart reporting. But two stupid mistakes wrecked Hart's chances. Once again, he undid himself in a crisis; once more, he did not live up to the image people had of him. Far from being bold and decisive, he dithered. Far from being upbeat and affirmative, he complained. He squandered his appearance of unstudied virility. And because the press and public still felt they knew so little about him as a national candidate, the coverage of his two big gaffes immediately magnified their importance.

The first error came in equal measure from the haste imposed by the compressed campaign schedule, Hart's tiny staff's inadequacy to its suddenly prominent role, and the candidate's own imprudence. One of Hart's aides heard that Mondale planned to run a commercial attacking Hart explicitly for having changed his name and misstated his age. Panicky staffers alerted Hart, and within hours, apparently by the very next campaign stop, he condemned Mondale's as yet unseen ad. The alleged commercial never actually aired, and Hart immediately found himself forced to apologize to Mondale. Instead of being the aggrieved party, Hart had made himself the offender. Some aspects of the affair remained unclear. They led to a Chinese puzzle-box of speculation. Hart's aide may have overreacted to a rumor, and the rumor in turn may have been entirely false, or it may have had a core of truth — that is, Mondale's staff may have contemplated such a commercial without preparing one. But according to some versions of the story, Hart's aide had either seen the ad footage, or had heard its audiotape, or at least had been read the text of it. If that were so, the ad still could have been readied without Mondale's foreknowledge or approval. But alternately, it could have been withdrawn and deep-sixed by Mondale in an alert response to Hart's impulsive lament. Or indeed the whole episode could have been a setup; the ad could have been created only to gull Hart's aide, unnerve the rival candidate, and if possible induce him into just the misstep that Hart took. That would have been a dirty trick, but no worse than the savagely personal campaign that Mondale was already running against his erstwhile friend.

Whoever bore ultimate responsibility for the flare-up over the phantom commercial, Hart alone took the blame for the second and worse boner, involving an actual commercial that decried Vrdolyak personally as a "boss" attempting to dictate his presidential choice to voters. Ostensibly the ad would gratify suburban and independent voters who disliked the shopworn, often corrupt Chicago Democratic machine. But Hart already appealed to many of those voters, and in any case they were not by themselves a large enough group to enable him to win. His deeper need was to cut into Mondale's white vote in Chicago. Hart had little hope of capturing strong support among blacks or among the metropolitan area's half-million Hispanics. But then, Mondale himself would doubtless be more vulnerable to Jackson in Chicago, the firebrand's hometown, than he had been in Georgia and Alabama. If Hart could hold his own with Mondale among Chicago's whites, he would squeak by. Attacking Vrdolyak, it should have been apparent, was the least likely way to endear himself to them. To slam Vrdolyak was perforce to help Mayor Washington, and therefore to be on the side of the blacks, not the whites. For suburbanites who professed racial tolerance, to defend Washington was nonetheless to endorse incompetence, political stalemate, and governmental turmoil. And, apart from its ill-advised impact in Chicago's polarized politics, the attack by a national figure on a strictly local one inflamed many of the Second City's most parochial fealties, or at the very least offended voters' sense of proportion. Vrdolyak could attack Hart, of course. But except to defend himself, Hart had no right to treat small fry like Vrdolyak as fair game.

The ad was bad, but Hart's handling of it was worse. When Vrdolyak and Mondale, predictably, lambasted the commercial, Hart did not hang tough with it and thereby look brave, if pigheaded. Instead, he managed to offend even those who agreed with him by apologizing and pledging to withdraw it. Thus he further shredded his own reputation for credibility, sincerity, and candor. And he opened himself to another cheap shot by Mondale. Although Hart announced his revocation of the commercial on the Friday before the primary, it was still airing two days later. TV stations do not particularly welcome political advertising, which they are obliged to sell at discount rates, and managers were unwilling to drop everything to replace Hart's scheduled spots, especially on a weekend. Mondale knew all that. But he gleefully wondered in public how a man could hope to lead the free world when he could not even manage his own TV advertising schedule.

In the end, the actual tally in Illinois was close. Mondale got just over 40 percent, Hart just over 35 percent, and Jackson 21 percent. But after the polls had closed, the election-night commentary damaged Hart, almost devastatingly. Illinois, the network pundits said, is America in microcosm. If Hart could not carry such a state, his claims of electability became highly suspect. And the analysts discounted the closeness of the margin. If Jackson had not run, they said — adding that Jackson was *not* really in the race for the nomination — then, according to exit polls, Mondale would have won a landslide.

On the same night that he won in Illinois, Mondale unsurprisingly took nearly two-thirds of the vote in caucuses in his home state, Minnesota. A few days later, Mondale embarrassed Hart in his native state, Kansas, by edging him there. Virginia gave roughly equal percentages of the caucus vote to Mondale, Jackson, and uncommitted slates. Hart recouped by carrying Montana's caucuses and, by a two-to-one landslide, the Connecticut primary that he had expected to take all along. Despite the relative evenness of the results, the overall nomination race was in no sense a fair fight. Mondale continued to receive substantial, covert, and potentially illegal help from labor. He enjoyed the favoritism of the party's national organization and many state chairmen. Because he had splurged early, he was now bumping against federal campaign spending limits. So he concocted a subterfuge whereby additional money could be channeled to supposedly independent committees created to help elect his pledged delegates, rather than elect him directly. This scheme, too, was illegal. But if it enabled him to win the nomination, he knew the Federal Election Commission would at most slap his wrist.

The caucuses, even when they operated according to the rules, often had little to do with the genuine expression of individual sentiment. At a Saturday caucus in one of the more upscale state senate districts in Wichita, for example, Mondale workers and some supporters arrived in buses and vans. Organizers wearing Mondale badges tried to close the doors a few minutes early, knowing that stragglers were more likely to be supporting one of the opponents than their man. Many of those who gathered on Mondale's side of the room sported union insignia and sat together. The nominally neutral chairwoman of the meeting operated a political consulting business; her partner was the paid coordinator of Mondale's local campaign. Both said they saw no hint of any conflict of interest in this arrangement.

Mondale won this caucus handily. Once the turnout for each candidate had been counted to determine his delegate entitlement for the next round of caucuses (at the congressional district level), each camp had to decide who those delegates would be. The Hart supporters acted organically. They nominated people, heard little speeches from them, asked questions, debated pros and cons. The process went on for more than an hour. The Mondale people were presented with a preselected slate of the party faithful, dutifully ratified it, and went home far sooner, even though their total numbers were much larger. The Jackson supporters in the district, finding that they were too few to qualify for delegates on their own, approached the Mondale group to trade support for delegate seats. Before the voting had even started, they were told that all the Mondale delegates had been selected. So they joined up with the Hart group, where they had a chance to win some seats.

The geography of each presidential campaign is unique. Issues, events, rules, and circumstances that seem like enduring landmarks in one election crumble into dust in the next. Matters that were barely glimpsed on the horizon four years before loom up like mountain ranges. The crucial turning places in the road may shift without warning. Often it cannot be seen that a turn was crucial until long after.

In 1960, West Virginia, among the most backward of states, gave the presidential nomination to John Kennedy. The decision-makers reasoned that if a Catholic could win among those miners and fundamentalists and hillbillies, then he must be a force too potent to be denied. In six subsequent presidential elections, West Virginia never mattered again.

In 1976, Jimmy Carter started toward the nomination by carrying the previously unknown Iowa caucuses, in a state he did not take in November. He lost in New York, the biggest state that Democrats have a chance to carry in general elections, but it did not matter. In 1980, Carter lost in New York again, and once more it did not matter. In 1984, New York was the crucial turning in the road, and perhaps none of the candidates realized it until the struggle there was over.

The New York debate on March 28, anchored by Dan Rather and televised in prime time by CBS, became probably the most viewed and most influential debate in the campaign. TV commercials aired in New York became perhaps the most significant TV ads. The factional struggle among Democrats, divided by race, class, economics, and ethnicity, reached its flash point in New York. And to almost everyone's astonishment, the actual vote count in New York provided the most decisive, one-sided outcome of the nomination struggle. Primaries continued for another two months after New York's vote on April 3, and the scratching for delegates lasted six weeks beyond that. But in retrospect, it was evident that the landscape had been charted by the Empire State.

Hart had to win in New York. Not "had to" in the sense of some journalist's imposed expectations, but "had to" numerically. Mondale had pulled far ahead in the delegate count, and he seemed assured of continuing to draw a disproportionate share of the "superdelegates" chosen from among party hierarchs and elected officials. In caucuses, Mondale enjoyed the upper hand except in the sparsely populated West, where Hart was winning almost every jurisdiction but the delegate pickings were slim. Mondale could lose nearly every remaining primary to Hart and still lead in delegate count. And if by some chance Mondale were held short of a first-ballot victory on his own, he seemed better positioned, because he was drawing significant black and Hispanic support, to bargain for Jackson's endorsement. Hart's only chance was to beat Mondale often enough in primaries, in enough different kinds of states, to discredit him whatever his numerical advantages.

The discrediting would have to be accomplished through the press, and the emerging conventional wisdom of reporters rated New York as rocky, testing terrain for Hart. He had fared best in "open" primaries, in which independents could participate; New York's was "closed" to all but Democrats. He appealed in areas where incomes ranked above the national average and unemployment below it; New York combined extremes of suburban, mostly Republican affluence and sprawling urban decay. Above all, Hart had fashioned his persona as a leader by stressing his lack of ties to encumbering special interests. In New York, where Democrats perhaps invented and surely perfected the technique of the balanced ticket, special interests made up the bulk of the party, and they all wanted to be sure they owned a piece of the nominee. Independence was mistrusted, not prized, in a candidate campaigning in New York. Indeed, in every contested presidential primary the state had held, it had preferred the Democratic candidate who paid the most attention to labor unions and the Jews.

Hart had burned his bridges with the unions. But he could, and did, decide to truckle to other constituencies, rather than play New York's politics his own way and assume that a reputation for consistency and integrity was a greater asset than any marginal gain in votes. His first major strategic decision was to endorse a plan, put forward by New York's senior U.S. senator, Daniel Patrick Moynihan, to move the American embassy in Israel from Tel Aviv to Jerusalem. Most foreign policy experts in both parties thought the idea was dangerous. It would inflame Arab countries, which regarded Jerusalem as occupied territory. It would further the image of the United States as a submissive endorser of anything Israel chose to do. And it would therefore weaken the Americans' effectiveness as peacemakers in the region, all for no practical gain. Jews, however, by and large loved Moynihan's idea, in part because it affirmed Israel's right to Jerusalem, the emotional center of the Hebrew faith, but even more for the very reason that others objected to it: the move would force the

United States to cast its lot with Israel alone, more unequivocally than ever. Hart had always been contemptuous of campaigners who in his view prostrated, even prostituted, themselves to win votes. He had also warned his aides that such moves often backfire. Yet he urged the embassy transfer, and when Mondale predictably characterized him as a latecomer to the issue, Hart plunged into an unedifying, hairsplitting attempt to prove how long he had been a believer.

Hart's second fundamental choice was to try to run to the left of Mondale, at least on foreign policy. This change of tack seemed at least as expedient and shortsighted as his posture about the embassy: New York's Democrats were among the most liberal in the country, and the antiwar movement remained strong there, but the consensus in the nation as a whole was shifting toward more interventionism and military assertiveness. Even if Hart's feint to the left helped him win the primary battle, it could make it harder for him to win the nomination and general election wars. And it might well entail some further loss of credibility. Nonetheless, Hart prepared a TV commercial urging that the United States stay out of Central America, in which he in effect accused Mondale of wanting to make American soldiers the bodyguards or hostages of unspecified dictators. He linked Mondale's marginally more interventionist position on Central America to Reagan's out-and-out covert war there, and tied them both to the mistakes of the Vietnam era. Hart's ad infuriated Mondale, just as Hart had intended. Hart had been growing steadily angrier for weeks at Mondale's tactics. He had been especially unsettled by a commercial known throughout the political world as "red phone." That ad featured a ringing telephone rigged up to look like the popular notion of the "hot line" linking the White House and the Kremlin. The voice-over narration characterized Hart as inexperienced and potentially unsteady, and suggested that he could, through ineptitude, start World War III. "Red phone" had apparently blemished Hart when it aired in Georgia just before Super Tuesday; it had been an unqualified bull's-eye in Illinois, and it was alarming voters in New York. Ostensibly the ad simply underscored Mondale's superior experience. Subconsciously, it was meant to play on voters' sense that they did not know Hart well enough, and to suggest that he might be a touch loco. More than once during the campaign, when asked what the public needed to know about its candidates, Mondale answered, "Whether they're sane."

Bitterness between rivals for the presidency may be unavoidable. But in most elections, the main contenders manage to preserve at least a core of civility and respect toward each other. In 1980, however, the Democrats had been riven by the open hatred between Jimmy Carter and Edward Kennedy, and by the final days before New York's primary on April 3 it looked as though 1984 would yield equally implacable antagonism. Tempers flared so high that it seemed time for someone to sit the candidates down around a table to talk.

As it turned out, that was just what CBS did in staging the New York debate. The format was unexpectedly intimate. Group debates are usually conducted with long tables of candidates facing the audience; in one-on-one debates, the candidates stand at podiums on opposite sides of the stage. In either case, the speaking style and body language of the candidates almost automatically become formal, and they almost always talk to the live audience instead of each other. But CBS News politics producer Joan Richman placed Dan Rather and the three candidates around a small circular table, so that they were as unaware as possible of the hundreds of people crowded into Columbia University's Low Library to watch them: instead, they needed only to nod left or right, or lean slightly into the table, to be talking intensely to each other.

For Mondale, the experience seemed to be liberating. He showed a personality that the public had almost never seen. He broke through his reserve, his pomposity, and for once sounded like a compassionate yet practical man instead of an impersonal compendium of slogans and party history. His stentorian manner eased appealingly into the commonsense ways of a family father in his shirt sleeves, talking things over around the kitchen table. He was tough but not shrill. Even his piercing, nasal voice took on a deeper, more resonant, less querulous tone. He radiated quiet, confident authority.

Hart, who had seemed to be possessed of such grace and ease when things were going well, continued to squirm when things were going badly. He was taut, withdrawn, almost frail-looking, and he could not manage a smile or laugh other than his too-familiar nervous grin and whinny. More than knowledge, more than competence, more than quickness of learning and of wit, the American public examines its presidential candidates for resilience, for the capacity to lead even when all seems lost. Fair-weather leaders are many; foul-weather leaders are few, and are remembered for greatness. Hart had the haunted look of a man unprepared even for the mild storms that had already washed over him. In conversation, several CBS News executives and reporters remarked on how uncomfortable with himself he seemed, how unprepossessing. He did not look ready, they noted, to sit down and bargain with, say, Soviet Foreign Minister Andrei Gromyko.

Hart's passivity seemed doubly baneful to such dispassionate political professionals as David Sawyer, Glenn's erstwhile media adviser, because the Hart seen in the debate contradicted so completely the bold, combative Hart portrayed in his own commercials. Thus, instead of helping the public to get to know Hart and therefore trust him, his dual exposure in "free" and "paid" media served only to suggest dissonance, inconstancy, and to heighten the sense that Hart was in some fundamental way inauthentic.

Jackson had the greatest natural ease and assurance of any Democratic candidate. He had an almost intuitive gift for making exactly the right adjustments of manner and intonation to fit any circumstance. For this encounter, half debate, half conversation, he had to shed the sweeping gestures, the organlike cadences, and most of the alliterative jargon of his sermonlike stump speeches. He did so, and more: he demonstrated by the aptness of his bearing that he had a legitimate right to be sitting at the same table with his rivals. The New York debate was his first sustained exposure to much of the public as a presidential candidate, rather than a celebrity newsmaker. He needed to prove to voters, black and white, that he had made it into the finals of the Democratic contest, not merely because of his race, but because he knew what he was talking about and if elected could capably serve. Still, the debate belonged chiefly to Mondale and Hart. They had to be careful not to patronize Jackson, but they conveyed in their every skirmish that they accorded him no real chance to win. Perhaps the clearest sign of their dismissal of him as almost irrelevant was their politeness. They scarcely bothered to attack him, only each other. If Jackson had been a more conventional politician, he might have sat back and enjoyed watching his rivals bicker. But he recognized that their condescending benignity toward him gave him the opening to take an active role, to play peacemaker in reply. He spoke to them almost like a schoolmaster counseling bright but ructious boys, reminding them that they had an urgent, constructive message to deliver to the electorate. By their behavior, he said, they were ensuring that the media story of the debate would not be their shared values, but instead the petty "rat-tat-tat" between them. They were letting ambition get in the way of vision. Jackson reaped a significant subsidiary benefit from this posture: reporters, and a larger audience of white liberals who had been put off by the "Hymie" episode, found themselves admiring Jackson, and some resolved to vote for him.

The issues in the debate were not significantly different from what the candidates had been talking about for the previous few weeks. Therefore, as Jackson had guessed, reporters decided they were bored with the candidates' conflicting visions of America, even though millions of newly attentive voters might not be; hence, the national news media afterward focused on the cut and thrust of personal rivalry. But what the candidates talked about was nonetheless rich in substance. Mondale continued to tick off the liberal "wish list," and to portray Hart as at best a belated convert to the one true faith. Hart continued to point out, to Mondale's genuine indignation, that coalition building inevitably led to intellectual incoherence; the policies of the party amounted to nothing more than the accumulated desires of whatever voting blocs agreed to come on board. The New Deal approach, as practiced by modern imitators, afforded no opportunity to develop a genuine, fully integrated set of principles around which people as individuals might rally.

Jackson, greatly excluded from center stage during this argument, continued to bring up most of his plausible, populist notions for rearranging national priorities. We should save money abroad, he contended, not by shortchanging the Third World, but by putting greater pressure on our prosperous allies in Europe and Japan for them to make trade concessions and to pay for more of their self-defense. We should stop the outflow of entry-level, modest-wage manufacturing jobs by changing tax laws to make it unattractive for American companies to transfer operations abroad. We should develop a foreign policy that would be secure enough, yet accommodationist enough, that we would not have to spend so much money on the Pentagon. And we should proceed immediately to ensuring full participation for every group in our society, ending poverty and unemployment in years rather than generations.

The most memorable clash, however, or at least the one that television executives found easiest to reduce to a few vivid seconds of footage, was a painful exchange between Hart and Mondale on the matter of their integrity. Mondale wheeled on Hart and asked, seemingly man to man rather than rival to rival, in a way almost embarrassingly sincere and private, why his opponent had put ads on television accusing Mondale of wanting to sacrifice the lives of young U.S. soldiers in Central America. Hart, looking justifiably ashamed of his commercials, asked with equal hurt and bewilderment why Mondale had been going around telling people that Hart had a bad record on civil rights. "You know that's not true," Hart implored. For a moment it seemed possible that they would decide, in the full glare of the cameras, to mute the savagery of what should be a collegial campaign on behalf of their party. Then the moment passed. When the debate ended, Jackson lingered to shake hands and mill with the crowd, as best he could under Secret Service scrutiny, basking in the glow of acceptance, while Mondale issued merely perfunctory greetings on his way out, and Hart skulked off without much of a word to anyone.

In some ways, New York was much like Illinois, or at least Chicago. New York politics *was* special interests. New York had great ethnic diversity, including huge Hispanic and black populations. New York had no city machine like Chicago's, or rather, it had several that were usually in a state of armed readiness if not outright war with each other. But it had suburbs that were comparably suspicious of and disaffected from city politics. Ethnic New York favored Mondale, the preferred candidate of Jews, and Jackson, the preferred candidate of blacks, more than Hart, the candidate of no ethnic group in particular. But New York was also the first major state in the campaign where Hart, the telegenic candidate, had enough of a war chest to outspend Mondale substantially on TV ads; Jackson, who was if anything even more effective than Hart on television, had no money for TV commercials and could not buy even thirty seconds of airtime.

The outcome on election day, April 3, decisively ended the Gary Hart phenomenon: he might remain a candidate, but he was clearly no longer a wonder. Mondale drew almost 45 percent of the vote, to just over 27 percent for Hart and 25.5 percent for Jackson. Thus Hart came close to finishing third. Even worse, he lost the allegiance of his core supporters. Mondale did not have to depend on New York City voters — he ran barely even with Jackson there — because he beat Hart soundly in the suburbs, among independents, among the college-educated and affluent, and even, according to some polls, among voters under forty. Hart still ran stronger among those groups than with the rest of the population. But for them, too, he had fallen to second choice.

The week also brought yet another reminder of how thoroughly Mondale had stacked the deck in his favor. On the night of the New York primary, Hart won Wisconsin's nonbinding primary over Mondale, 46 to 42 percent; but the following Saturday, the caucuses overruled the will of the voters in favor of Mondale, by 58 to 30 percent.

———

From New York onward, Mondale resumed a strategy of attrition. By selling himself as an inevitability, he expected once again to scare or dishearten Hart's supporters and, especially, contributors. By concentrating on caucuses, he would build up a delegate total high enough to ensure a first-ballot victory, or at worst a total so close that he could stampede a few dozen uncommitted delegates into joining him. He began stockpiling delegates, supposedly uncommitted but in fact privately pledged to him, who would throw their support his way at strategically opportune moments.

Meanwhile, now that Hart no longer looked like a sure thing, he found his money drying up. He had counted on Mondale's being short of funds, too, until Mondale devised the subterfuge of channeling funds through his delegate committees. When Hart protested this injustice, reporters at first dismissed him as a sorehead. Gradually, however, they came to view the mechanism as violating the spirit and perhaps the letter of campaign finance laws, and peppered Mondale with questions about it. The front-runner reluctantly bowed to pressure: he agreed to shut down the committees and give back the money they had collected. In fact, he did neither. The committees went right on operating, and when the Maryland unit was asked the date on which it would fulfill Mondale's promise to quit, a spokesman replied, "May eighth" — the date, of course, of Maryland's primary.

May 8 would, in fact, be a sort of second Super Tuesday, with primaries in four sizable states, Maryland, North Carolina, Indiana, and Ohio. But Mondale hoped not to have to wait that long to knock Hart out of the race for good. The Pennsylvania primary on April 10, just a week after New York, looked like the place where he could settle the contest. Like Illinois, Pennsylvania was a big state that substantially mirrored the nation in its demographics. In 1976, it had decided the nomination: when Jimmy Carter defeated Scoop Jackson there, the most formidable, if undeclared, Democratic rival to Carter, Hubert Humphrey, ruled out any chance of his entering the race. In 1984, there was no opponent waiting in the wings. Another defeat for Hart would presumably reduce him to the level of ephemera.

Mondale, hoping once again to appear "presidential" and above the fray, campaigned a little less brutally in Pennsylvania than in New York. Hart continued to disdain fighting back. Jackson savored the dignity that came with his stance as peacemaker, and sensed that unless he somehow upset the balance, he would continue to draw as much as 80 percent of black votes and enough scattered support from whites to survive to the end of the primaries. The major media event, another televised debate a week after New York's, turned out to be almost devoid of fireworks. The moderator, Elizabeth Drew of the *New Yorker*, admonished the candidates that she would not tolerate any bickering and the candidates only too willingly complied.

The outcome was similar to that in New York: Mondale captured 47 percent of the vote, Hart a stronger but still distant 35 percent, Jackson 17 percent. Mondale aides started to tell reporters that the nomination fight was really over. A downcast but indefatigable Hart refused to agree. He sensed that Mondale remained vulnerable and that the right combination of circumstances might still thrust a newcomer back into the lead.

During the four weeks between the Pennsylvania primary and the second Super Tuesday in Maryland et al., the momentum seesawed. Hart won Arizona's caucuses, Mondale swept Missouri's. Hart won caucuses in Vermont, although by a far narrower margin than his landslide in the nonbinding March primary there, and he clobbered Mondale in Utah's caucuses. But Mondale comfortably won Tennessee's primary. In the District of Columbia, the predominantly black electorate gave Jackson 67 percent of the vote, Mondale 26 percent, and Hart an embarrassing 7 percent. No serious contender for the Democratic nomination in recent memory had had so hard a time attracting blacks as Hart. In Louisiana's primary, Jackson took nearly half the vote with virtually unanimous support from blacks; Hart, who placed second by a slight margin, and Mondale divided the other half. In Texas, a pivotal state in any conceivable Democratic plan for victory in November, Mondale captured an even 50 percent of the caucus vote to Hart's humbling 27 percent. Hart's home state of Colorado caucused for him by an even wider margin than Minnesota had given Mondale. Despite Hart's gritty persistence, the plan of attrition was working: Mondale maintained a wide lead in delegate support.

As May 8 approached, the conventional wisdom had Mondale the sure winner in all four states to be contested. If Hart had a chance anywhere, the thinking ran, it would be in prosperous Maryland and North Carolina, where the population contained higher percentages of the mobile, affluent suburbanites he seemed to attract. But Maryland and North Carolina had closed primaries, limited to Democrats, which meant Hart's independent supporters could not participate. So Mondale won in North Carolina, by a modest 36 to 30 percent, with Jackson capturing 25 percent. In Maryland, Mondale had something approaching a landslide, with 43 percent to Jackson's 27 and Hart's 25. All Mondale needed to do now was capture two unionized, industrial midwestern states to knock Hart out of the running altogether.

But Democratic voters resist agreement. In 1972, the battle for the nomination continued until the convention. In 1976 and 1980, as soon as Jimmy Carter had assured himself the nomination, late spring primary voters gave state after state to other contenders. And in 1984, the independents and stubborn-minded Democrats of Indiana and Ohio kept Gary Hart in the race. Both primaries were open to non-Democratic voters. Both ended in photo finishes: Hart won by 42 to 40 percent in Ohio, by 42 to 41 percent in Indiana. The split result on Super Tuesday II ensured that once again, for the sixth straight election, the Democrats would still be squabbling as they reached the primary season's final day, in California and New Jersey on June 5. And in the minds of some, though not all, party professionals and pundits, the outcome that day could still make Hart the winner.

Politicians normally spend a decade or two in the public eye before they presume to run for President. Yet in the few months' duration of a campaign, their political personas can emerge, transform, cloud over, and emerge yet again. Jackson, the arrogant self-promoter of January, the loose-tongued bigot of February, the Great Black Hope of the South in March, had become through April and May a kind of statesman, inspiriting his neglected people. Hart, the bold new leader of February and March, the empty bubble of April, had metamorphosed by late May into the gallant underdog. Mondale, the arrogant overlord of January and February, the stunned victim of March, the admirably manly Fighting Fritz of April, had reverted by May to the would-be king who claimed his throne by divine right rather than conquest. Even among his constituents, many disdained him and few felt much enthusiasm. At most his presence reassured them that the old-fashioned, paternal Democratic party was still alive and holy. Hart inspired genuine passions, both of zealotry and of disgust.

Among the most attractive things about Hart was his sober sense of responsibility to the people. In a dark moment, he confided to a *Time* reporter that he was burdened, almost frightened, by the exuberant response of crowds to his candidacy. He knew that sooner or later he was bound to disappoint them. Defeat had in a way liberated him. As his chances for capturing the nomination narrowed, he spent more time mingling with reporters, going out for dinner, clowning at sports, "skating" on slippery pieces of plastic from the nose to the tail of his campaign plane as it tilted upward during takeoff. He shook off all appearance of the unwholesome power-obsession that had plagued Richard Nixon and Jimmy Carter, and that seemed to bedevil the latter-day Walter Mondale. Hart appeared to grasp that life could be meaningful without political office. He began to expose, to the press and the public, the thoughtful, questing side of himself, the part of him that had journeyed from a small, fundamentalist town in Kansas to the Yale Divinity School, thence to Yale Law School and the McGovern campaign. After the weeks when his elusive behavior only reinforced Mondale's charges of inauthenticity, Hart began to put himself across as a substantial man.

Jackson remained a nightmare for reporters to cover, because his campaign was so chaotic. The people running it had little or no experience in national politics. There was never enough money to plan very far ahead. Frequently the staff had no idea what city the candidate would be in on what day of next week, let alone what he would be doing, by what conveyance he and his entourage would travel, and when a journalist might be able to attend to little necessities like filing a story or just telephoning the newsroom. Yet Jackson seemed to be growing in stature, to be taking more seriously the full historic significance of what he was doing. His ego remained boundless, and he still paid foremost attention to his status within black America. But he also responded increasingly to the genuine desire of many whites for racial harmony — for cooperation rather than confrontation. The anger and outrage that had marked Jackson's speeches in the early primaries, his harping on the "misery index" of the unheeded poor, had been muted. More and more, he focused on urging blacks to celebrate the fact of their own power. Rather than using his candidacy and votes to extort a legislative agenda, he seemed to want most of all to serve as a role model, a wellspring of hope for the young, a beacon of conscience for the forgotten.

Mondale, meanwhile, seemed to become ever more the prisoner of his constituencies. As Jackson captured more of the black vote, black leaders upped the price they would extract for their support. As Mondale neared the nomination, women lobbied ever louder for a big share of cabinet jobs, and perhaps the vice-presidential slot on the ticket. Labor leaders came out from their discreet silence to proclaim Mondale's candidacy their creation. Through it all, Mondale continued to offer himself as the tribune for the Democratic party that had been, and not as a thinker about the party that could be. Mondale was fairly widely disliked by the entourage of reporters, the people outside his staff who spent the most time with him. Some of their complaints were tactical: Mondale had held himself generally unavailable in the early days, then had opened up when he needed help. Indeed, when he appeared on one of the network morning news shows for the first time in months, and was asked why he had agreed, after many previous rejections, to grant an interview, he answered candidly that he was there only because he had to be: he was in trouble. Once his lot improved, he withdrew again, and reporters felt manipulated. But they sensed deeper problems in Mondale: a lack of leadership; an inability to direct his staff; a shortage of sound intellects around him, and an unwillingness among even them to challenge the boss; a preoccupation with short-term strategic advantage rather than a long view. Moreover, despite Mondale's sometimes smug claims of humanity and charity, some felt he had run an ugly, mean campaign. And among the not inconsiderable number of partisan Democrats in the press corps, there was a general fear that Mondale could never beat Reagan, because he had no insight into how to articulate a salable rationale for his candidacy.

Still, politics was a game of numbers more than sentiment, and the numbers favored Mondale. He had boasted that he would have enough pledged delegates for a first-ballot nomination by noon of the day after the final primaries. According to the public counts of major news organizations — in 1984, United Press International's came to be trusted as the most reliable — Mondale was right. Only one scenario seemed likely to short-circuit him: if he lost both major events on June 5, in California and New Jersey.

California's politics was an amalgam of the old-style, interest-group voting favored by Mondale with the new-style, nonideological reformism represented by Hart. The heavy concentration of blacks and, especially, Hispanics ought to have worked to Mondale's advantage. Mondale, however, made a clumsy, ultimately unsuccessful play for Hispanic votes by appearing to oppose a controversial bill restricting immigration, while prevailing on House Speaker Tip O'Neill to delay a vote on various alternatives to the bill until the California primary was safely past. Meanwhile, the state's large population of affluent, technologically oriented workers, many of them migrants from other regions of the country, leaned toward Hart. Perhaps the chief factor in his favor, however, was that he was a fellow Westerner at a time of increasing regional consciousness. While Easterners tended to see Hart in terms of the Republican reform tradition, Westerners preferred to claim him as a western progressive in the tradition of such California governors as Hiram Johnson, Earl Warren, and the two Edmund Browns.

New Jersey, on the other hand, clearly belonged to Mondale. Its Democratic primary was open to independents, but the state had long been dominated by tightly run, frequently corrupt urban party machines. Mondale had made his peace with New Jersey's bosses, and they would work on his behalf. Still, some optimists in Hart's camp saw a chance for an upset. New Jersey had in recent years broken free of the cycle of decline that beset most Northeast industrial states, in large part because it had emerged as a center of high-tech investment. If Hart sold himself shrewdly enough, linking his appeal to New Jersey's economic comeback, he might be able to pull off a surprise.

Mondale sensed that possibility, and to avert it, sank to his lowest moral level in the campaign. To alarm crime-sensitive New Jersey residents, he saturated the TV airwaves with an ad depicting a revolver on a turntable, spinning toward the viewer; the text reminded listeners that Hart opposed federal gun control, and implied that he was directly responsible for giving handguns to hoodlums. Once again, the TV commercial served a dual purpose for Mondale: it delivered his message, and it infuriated Hart and consequently threw him off balance.

[155]

Hart continued to advertise the positive qualities of his own leadership. For the West Coast, he offered an ad combining a graphic that looked like an engineer's chart paper; a state-of-the-art video image of pages turning; a rhythmic, pulsing sound (hence the commercial's in-house name, Heartbeat), and romantic images of the candidate, including a glimpse of him walking by the ocean in a fashion more than faintly reminiscent of a famous photograph of John Kennedy. For New Jersey, Hart prepared a more traditional, less symbolic ad that had him talking to people with unmistakably local accents while standing at the site of a major renewal project. He told them on-camera about his belief in New Jersey; they told him about their disgruntlement with Walter Mondale.

Once more, however, Hart showed his penchant for the ill-timed remark. In the hubbub of campaigning one day, he remarked that his wife had the good fortune to be representing him in California, while he was stuck in New Jersey. The insult would have caused him difficulties anyplace. In New Jersey, where people are defensive, if not explosive, about the state's well-deserved reputation for ugly highways, urban crowding, spreading slums, and an oversufficiency of uncontrolled toxic-waste dumps, Hart's offhand slur proved unforgivable. The more ads he ran hailing New Jersey's reclamation, the more people remembered his unfunny joke and dismissed him as a fraud who thought they were fools. Hart apologized but it did no good. New Jerseyites were sure he had meant what he said, because in their heart of hearts they, too, believed their state a wasteland.

Overshadowing both Mondale's and Hart's ads during the final two weeks of the primary season was a far costlier media buy by President Reagan, who had to burn off some of the fourteen-million-dollar remainder of his primary spending allocation. His commercials, all but indistinguishable from the feel-good advertising used to sell hamburgers and soft drinks and long-distance telephoning, intoned to viewers that a new day was dawning in America. That new day was made up of smiling grandmothers, families moving into new homes, boys lugging fishbowls, workmen restoring the Statue of Liberty. The text barely mentioned government or spending, and said nothing at all about nuclear arms or Mideast peacekeeping missions or even the invasion of Grenada. In a slick yet subtle way, the commercials revived the ever-popular message that the goodness of the country sprang full-blown from its people. Reagan was hardly a presence in these commercials. He, like government, was made to disappear, or at least diminish to the equivalent of a benign wave from a distant hill. The ads reminded practical politicians that Reagan had managed to corner that most precious of commodities, optimism. Hart supporters thought that the obvious success of Reagan's ads only proved the need for a candidate like Hart; he spoke of optimism, too. Mondale's supporters lashed back that the country was in far worse shape than Reagan admitted, and insisted that they could expose Reagan as a gasbag, not unlike Oz the Magnificent.

As the June 5 finale approached, six facts shaped the thinking about who ought to be the nominee. First, Mondale had so many delegates that it would be almost impossible to stop him. Second, his defeat would enrage and alienate the labor movement. Third, Hart's stronger showing against Reagan in polls, his chief asset, had lately dwindled to a virtual dead heat. Fourth, Hart's valid claims that the delegate allocation system had cheated him would apply in even greater force to the campaign of Jesse Jackson, who had won about 19 percent of the popular vote but only 9 percent of the delegates. Thus any movement to take delegates away from Mondale would not necessarily place them in Hart's camp. Fifth, Hart's strength came predominantly in states where Reagan was already so far ahead that Hart's appeal to independents would not matter. Sixth, many believed that Hart remained chiefly a receptacle for anti-Mondale votes, not a force on his own.

The only way to change that calculus to Hart's advantage would be for him to win decisively on the primary season's final day. He had to be able to claim that the voters had spoken for him. Then he could pursue, right up to the convention, his claim that hundreds of Mondale delegates should be disallowed because they had been elected with the help of the illegal delegate committees, in what he called a "tainted" process.

On June 5, Hart carried two more states in the West, New Mexico and South Dakota. Predictably, he lost troubled, blue-collar West Virginia to Mondale. In California, Hart won a landslide: he carried 32 of the state's 45 congressional districts, to 9 for Mondale and 4 for Jackson. Of the state's delegates, Hart won 205 to Mondale's 72 and Jackson's 29. But in New Jersey, where the vote was also tallied by congressional districts, and delegates were allotted on a winner-take-all basis, Mondale captured 103 of the 107 delegates. Jackson had 4. Hart had none. The wipeout in New Jersey for Hart was yet another consequence of the skill and ruthlessness with which Mondale had rigged matters in his favor.

Hart and Jackson announced that they would carry their fights to the convention floor. Jackson simply wanted concessions and respect. Hart believed that Mondale's support was squishy-soft, and he hoped for some thunderbolt that would let him win. In fact, Mondale's own count after the final primaries showed him at least two dozen delegates shy of certain victory. By the next day, he had done enough wheedling, cajoling, and threatening to go over the top, and every major news medium in the country affirmed him as the nominee. He declared victory sooner than that, however. With the vote still coming in from California on the night of Super Tuesday III, he shrugged off the rejection there. His voice cracked with exhaustion and delight as he told supporters in Saint Paul, "Three months ago, I said this would be a marathon. Now, as you know, marathons are long and hard. Every one of them has a finish line and a winner. Well, this is it. And here I am."

V

A Midsummer Day's Dream

THE Fourth of July parade in Andover, New Hampshire, comes up the hill along Main Street every year, past the motel cabins and Proctor Academy and Town Hall, to the reviewing stand where the emcee knows everyone by name and shouts out teasing comments to the marchers and passersby. Franklin, a city of fully 7900 people some miles away, always shows off its old fire-station pumper, and Alan Thompson, the insurance agent, always brings his stagecoach. The annual highlight, though, is Leapin' Lena, a car that rears up into the air at a tilt of nearly forty-five degrees, like a bucking horse. Some people display a lovingly restored Ford Model A or a 1950s Thunderbird, some a pickup truck garlanded with crepe paper. There are floats or motorcades or marching drills by the Grange and the Masons and the rescue squads, the Little League and scout troops and snowmobile clubs. People gather from Tilton and Boscawen and Warner. From East Andover, which makes a point of demonstrating it too is a sovereign town. From Salisbury, where just up the road Daniel Webster's birthplace still stands. (So does the one-room schoolhouse he went to, which this writer's wife attended through the fourth grade.) When the parade is over and the pie contests have been judged and the hot-dog stands have run out, everyone gets into the year's only traffic jam to go home until the fireworks display starts after nightfall. Not much ever changes in the ritual. Nobody seems to want it to.

For more years than she can remember, Gladys Manyan, author, columnist for the *Concord Monitor*, part-time fruit and vegetable saleswoman, matriarch and mother-in-law, has gathered her clan and her friends to her farmland in Salisbury, New Hampshire, every Fourth of July. The Fourths merge together in memory into one continuous, endlessly repeated day. Everyone in the family always goes to the Andover

[161]

parade in the morning. Everyone eats a big lunch out in the sun by the barn — in New England, heat and summer sun are commodities too rare to be wasted — and gets a little tipsy. Toward the end of the afternoon, what Gladys calls "the riffraff" (the term covers anyone not actually related by blood or marriage) begin to arrive, and everyone eats again.

The guests, in 1984 as always, included state legislators, local officials, political activists, newspaper and broadcast journalists, and a sprinkling of more private people. They gloried in the ease of a weekday at leisure, they grumbled about the overcast skies and cooling winds that came late in the afternoon, they chatted about the Boston Red Sox and movies and television. They did not talk about politics — except for Eugene Daniell, a white-maned old radical who ran for President as some sort of socialist in the 1930s and who, ever since, in an expression of New Hampshire's reverence for eccentrics, has successfully held every conceivable office in the nearby city of Franklin. Gene expressed the common opinion at the party: "Reagan is going to win by a mile, and I'm not going to like it at all." His trained, resonant speaker's voice penetrated the hum of chitchat around the makeshift bar in the barn, and several people looked up to nod in agreement. But even normally passionate liberals did not find Mondale inspiring enough, nor times hard enough, for them to want to join actively in the lament.

Politics is, the philosophers say, the noblest pursuit of a free people. But for many, perhaps most, Americans, the ultimate freedom is a freedom from politics. Oftentimes their ancestors came to get away from turmoil, and they chose a nation that has almost always favored stability over excitement. Every American election takes place in a distinct social and cultural context. When the country is happiest and working best, the context is something akin to indifference. In a poem of the 1930s, that decade of jangled nerves, the Anglo-American W. H. Auden wrote about

> How, when the aged are reverently, passionately waiting
> For the miraculous birth, there must always be
> Children who did not specially want it to happen, skating
> On a pond at the edge of the wood.

In the most turbulent of times, the music of the spheres for mankind is still the harmonious hum of the ordinary. The grand opera of public life, even the spectacle of hundreds of millions of people agreeing peaceably on the bestowal of power, can command the attention of workaday audiences for only a few days or at most weeks at a time. They live for job and home and family and gossip, for friends and clubs and recreation and community. And when they are ready to heed some all-embracing story, the election of a President must compete with the narrative of a TV series, the measured unfolding of a baseball season, the glorious emergence of some brilliant rookie in some arena of endeavor whose promise can give rise to that most persistent of hopes, that the best is yet to be.

———

The Fourth of July is a sunny day of picnics, a *Walpurgisnacht* of cherry bombs. It used to be called Independence Day, and was marked by patriotic speeches and reminders of a little colony's bold bid for freedom. Over the years the United States increasingly found itself embarrassed by its opposition to the bold bids of other little colonies to attain their independence, and so the day gradually altered from a spiritual affirmation to a suntanning and beer-drinking festival. It retains nonetheless one traditional significance: it marks the midpoint of the baseball season, the time to take the All-Star break.

If Americans were looking for optimism in 1984, no aspect of life offered greater reason to trust in the triumph of justice than the standings in the American and National Leagues. The Detroit Tigers, standard-bearers of a grim urban ghetto as depressed as the auto industry on which it depends, had leaped ahead of all rivals with the winningest start in major league history. The Chicago Cubs, a team so purist they still played only day games at home — and seemed genuinely to believe the sportsman's dictum that it matters not whether you win or (mostly) lose — were on the way to a division championship, their closest approach to a league pennant in more than forty years. The most electrifying player on any team was a black teenager, Dwight Gooden of the New York Mets, who pitched without complaint for a forty-thousand-dollar salary and outperformed veterans earning millions. In the All-Star Game, Gooden helped break a strikeout record that had stood for fifty years, since Carl Hubbell had faced an American League starting lineup made up entirely of Hall of Fame players and mowed down five in a row. In a sport where every game, however thrilling, is subordinate to the pleasurable continuity of legend, all things suddenly seemed possible for Gooden, all manner of adulation, just thirty-six years after Jackie Robinson became the very first black to break the racial ban in the majors. Justice might come slowly, for any man or team, but in 1984 there was reason aplenty in baseball to believe justice would always, someday, come.

For those who seek pleasure indoors in the dark, luxuriating in the bounty of sunshine by squandering it spending afternoons watching movies, the days just before and after July 4 bring the year's biggest would-be blockbusters, the epics of slapstick and terror. In 1984, three were hugely, instantly popular. *Indiana Jones and the Temple of Doom* sent a whip-cracking, woman-scorning macho man against an Evil Empire. *Gremlins* warned that even the cutest, furriest, and sweetest-faced strangers were not to be trusted. The Ghostbusters who conquered the malicious spirits of the otherworld were unprincipled vigilantes for hire, and the movie's ad campaign featured a slogan that befitted the bygone image of, say, the Marines: "They're here to save the world." Gone, along with the economic hard times and liberal resurgence of 1982, were the sweet tolerance of ET, the passive resistance of Gandhi. Americans wanted heroes who would kick ass and take names — if there were any enemies of America left breathing to gasp out their names at all. Virile Clint Eastwood in 1984 released three successful movies: *Sudden Impact,* in which he blasted what the police call "perpetrators"; *Tightrope,* in which he explored sadomasochistic sex while on the trail of a killer; and, later in the year, *City Heat,* in which beating after beating was meant to have comic effect.

On television, the nation admired the profit-taking vigilantes of "The A-Team," who were a group of Vietnam war veterans, and of "Riptide," who were a trio of all-American, danger-loving boys. The most popular news program, as had been true for several years, was "60 Minutes," in which vigilante reporters, also operating for profit, ambushed malefactors with perhaps the most satisfying weapon short of a six-shooter — the camera, used as a means of humiliation. The quartet of beloved nighttime soap operas, "Dallas," "Dynasty," "Falcon Crest," and "Knot's Landing," featured wealthy, vulgar, despicable people whose chief pleasure in money seemed to consist in not having to be polite. If these plutocrats were surrogates for viewers engaged in fantasy, then seemingly the American people yearned, not only for vast wealth and conspicuous consumption, but also for the wherewithal to crush enemies and exact revenge even from siblings. Compassion had its place, but only if those to be pitied were white and middle class, or elderly, or female, or in childhood, or sick. The prevailing mood in entertainment seemed to be anger, surging to the surface and ready to erupt.

Thoughts of the Apocalypse seemed not to have quelled the combative urge. Although more than 100 million Americans had watched ABC's three-hour depiction of the consequences of a nuclear attack, *The Day After,* in November 1983, there was scant sign of its intended residual effect. The film had, if anything, rather than discouraged hawkish people from wanting to make war, stimulated them to want to ensure that America's weapons were better. Or bigger.

In popular literature, publishers continued to do brisk business with books about every sort of future shock — impending financial panic, adaptation (or resistance) to technology, the remaking of business theory or even the restructuring of American corporate life, the emergence of whole new ways of categorizing information as in the best-selling *Megatrends*. If Americans were bullish about the future, they nonetheless feared they would have to protect their turf and were eager to sharpen their horns for combat. In fiction, the year began with a million-copy rush to buy George Orwell's apocalyptic 1984, a vision of a passive, suppressive, spiritless Communist society. Thereafter, horror and the supernatural competed with success sagas for pride of place.

Humor, in the traditional sense of wry wit or amiable anecdotes, was supplanted by the proliferation of unabashedly titled books of "gross" and "tasteless" jokes, most of them shaped to insult the ethnic, racial, and sexual-preference subgroups whose dignity had become sacrosanct in official conversation. Newspapers in sophisticated Atlanta and Dallas had discovered an audience for similar humor in pseudoredneck columns, supposedly written as parodies of bigotry but enjoyed by many readers, it seemed, as straightforward assertions of home truth. Something ungiving, downright mean, seemed to have slipped loose from the darker corners of the nation's soul. If indeed 1984 was as fearful a time as George Orwell had envisioned, then the nation was not reacting with contemplation like his postwar gloom, nor with the bathetic yet heartening affection of the more affirmative art of the populist 1930s, but with rugged, roughshod individualism.

In popular music, the most applauded woman newcomer was a shrieking, gutter-accented, deliberately uglified harridan called Cyndi Lauper, whose message was that "girls just want to have fun," not respect, and whose video performances incorporated pointlessly violent histrionics by professional wrestlers. The anthem by the best-liked veteran woman performer, Tina Turner, sneered spitefully the sort of words that macho men had uttered for decades: "What's love got to do with it . . . what's love but a secondhand emotion." The two most popular male singers, Michael Jackson and Prince, were androgynous blacks who radiated sexual availability and submission and an utter unwillingness to challenge white men. Except in smugly pious country music, which seemed more concerned with dictating rules than urging kindness, there was scant hint of charity or brotherhood or romance. In music, as in every art form, the vision of America seemed to be one of self-assertion and mistrust.

———

A parade like Andover's celebrates the small world the people know around them, not the larger world they see in the media. The meaning of life is not something that the people at the parade would ordinarily talk about, but if the parade speaks for them, they must think life's meaning lies in the ordinary, the repetitive, the familiar, the everyday. Pilgrims and pioneers and cowboys show up in some groups' displays, in part because the claim to a place in America's early history may be the chief pride of people in the ever less powerful region of New England. Space exploration may merit a float now and then, put together by some dreamy-eyed, would-be rocket jockey looking for yet another terrain on which to wave the flag. Military exploits are honored in diorama, too, if only because so many middle-aged men here knew of nothing more obvious than soldiering to do in their youth, and because so many of their sons still sign up to go. In 1984, one further American outlet for patriotism inspired several dozen costumed celebrants: the Olympic Games that would start later that month in Los Angeles. To the founders, the games may have meant to honor individual accomplishment. To the cheering throng in Andover, the contests looked more than ever like a chance for Americans as a nation to win.

————✧————

Who could deny there was equal opportunity in America? What could the scoldings of Jesse Jackson mean? Rafer Johnson, who looked godlike as he ran up the steps of the Los Angeles Coliseum, a few weeks after Independence Day, to ignite the Olympic torch there, was a black American champion from 1960. The woman who handed him the torch was a granddaughter of Jesse Owens, a black American champion in 1936. Edwin Moses, who spoke the Olympic oath on behalf of athletes from all nations, was a black American champion from 1976 who would be a champion again in 1984. The most-watched performer of the games in Los Angeles, the one from whom the most was expected, was Carl Lewis, who would become, four times over, a black American champion in 1984. And as if that were not enough, the most loved and admired performer of the games would be a woman, or rather a tough, chunky little girl aged sixteen. A child of backward West Virginia, Mary Lou Retton vaulted, in the literal gymnastic sense, to money and glory and the ultimate American validation of athletic heroism, a Wheaties cereal contract; in her TV commercials, to exuberant music she ran and spun and then, kittenish and feminist, warned: "Watch out, big boys." For the lucky, the gritty, the magnificent few, who could deny equal opportunity in America?

ABC brought America's Olympics to the world. And as the world's athletes, gathered in Los Angeles, experienced the games the only way they could, through the medium of American television, they found it infuriatingly apparent how very American these Olympics seemed to the

United States. Although far more than a hundred hours of competition aired, a sport would be slighted if no Americans were contenders. If strong American competitors faced equally serious rivals, the rivals were short-changed. If Americans won, the broadcast "journalists" gloated. If Americans lost, the "journalists" made excuses or belittled the officiating. ABC's cameras were transmitting to the world a far more inclusive and objective "feed" than to the American viewing public. In their home countries, no athletes were cheated of honor. But in America, the athletes saw American television, and they protested. The International Olympic Committee protested to the organizers in Los Angeles, who passed along the complaint to ABC. No matter. The joyous cheerleading went on.

In fact, half the world's great athletes were absent. The Soviet Union, East Germany, and more than a dozen other satellite nations had stayed away, purportedly because they feared for their competitors' safety at the hands of terrorists or some ravening mob. In fact, Americans assured themselves, the Soviet bloc feared defections, or humiliation through massive failures of drug tests, or the simple ignominy of defeat by superior opponents. Or perhaps the absenteeism was all in childish retaliation for the American-led boycott of the Moscow Olympics in 1980. In any case, ABC repeatedly hinted at what so many Americans said out loud: who cared if the Russians stayed away? It only meant more medals for *us*.

In the end, Americans won exactly as many gold medals in Los Angeles as Soviets had won in Moscow. They won most of what they were supposed to win, and much that they were supposed to lose. They dominated in the modern American national game, basketball, and lost an exhibition contest in the traditional American national game, baseball. They provided heartwarming human interest — the tearfully grateful wrestler who had recovered from cancer; the brave, methodical woman marathoner who had undergone perilously recent knee surgery; the woman basketball player who did not make the team but who sat in the stands to cheer on her twin sister who did — and they became national heroes beyond anyone's anticipation. When all was over, America did not want it to be over. The athletes were entreated, urged, implored to crisscross the country for parades and celebrations, reverence and gifts. There was momentary sympathy for losers. Love and honor went to those who won.

———*———

Their nation may have been, in 1984, a country suited to a warrior king. But the people parading and the people watching in Andover rarely think of themselves as belonging to Ronald Reagan's America, or the Republicans' or Democrats' America, or anyone else's America. They think of it, in a way Reagan would find congenial, as *their* America, and they unself-consciously assert their right to join in it. They honor the mythology of the nation, and they expand the myths, gently, to fit the needs of changing times. In 1984, two of the floats in Andover's jubilant celebration of a nation at peace honored the same glorious memory of victory in war, the raising of the flag by the Marines at Iwo Jima. Both of the floats featured people in uniform, poised in tableaux as much as possible like the famous photograph of the magnificent teamwork of America's fighting men. On both of the floats, at least some of the soldiers in khakis and helmets were women. They did not pretend to be men. They did not wear makeup or otherwise demonstrate that they were women. They just were there, taking part. In small towns, in traditional rituals, in time-honored male duties, women were finding and assuming their place.

VI

A Choice...

At the moment when Walter Mondale announced the one venture of his life that, win or lose, would guarantee him a place in history, he hardly seemed to grasp the full, cathartic emotional significance of what he was about to do. He was white, and male, and Protestant, and of more or less Anglo-Saxon ancestry. No door of opportunity had ever been closed to him the instant he showed his face or spoke his name. So as he droned the words, "This is an exciting choice," he did not wait for applause or approval, let alone the happy clatter that in fact erupted. He dropped his eyes to his written speech and started his next sentence: "I want to build a future. . . ." Only then did he sense the joy welling up around him, the pride and fealty he had just inspired. He turned to the woman at his right, the *woman*, the *first* woman ever to be chosen by any major presidential candidate as his running mate, and, as if seeing her for the first time, or perhaps himself, he grinned and joined in the fervor of the moment. "Let me say that again," he nearly shouted. "This is an exciting choice!"

And so it was. All across America, women had gathered in front of television sets to watch Walter Mondale's announcement, and many were brushing tears of rapture from their eyes. For days to come, they would talk of what had just happened, perhaps with their families or sweethearts or friends or coworkers, above all with each other. Walter Mondale had thrilled them. The battle for participation was far from over, but the grandest victory had been won. Housewives and hardened professionals alike felt a new dignity, a new belief that the system could work for them, too. The mantle of honor would rest on just one woman. But every woman in America who had spoken up for equality could feel that her effort in some way had helped.

White men were almost all as unready as Mondale for the surging sentiment. They saw only a political ploy, a calculation, a desperate measure to shore up sagging ramparts and to rally new troops for a seemingly hopeless war. They saw a presidential candidate at risk of losing control of his convention, a man almost certainly fated to be humbled in November, grabbing at whatever device might slash the bonds of prevalent assumption and allow him to start anew. The white men of the television networks were the first to be caught unawares. They said ho and hum and be done with it, the candidate of interest blocs has found yet another group to truckle to. Only when their women reporters came onto the air, late if at all during the first reports, a little more visibly by nightfall, did the supposed shapers of America's imagery begin to catch up with reality already throbbing like a Wagnerian crescendo in the pulses of many, many millions.

Walter Mondale went about selecting a vice-presidential candidate the way he went about everything in his campaign: he made up a lot of lists, ordered a lot of staff work, undertook a protracted if futile effort to please pretty much everybody, and kept his options open as long as possible. The outcome may have been bold, but the process brought back to mind that telling description, "He dares to be cautious."

Although Mondale had come out of the marathon of primaries the all but universally acknowledged winner, Jesse Jackson vowed to hold his delegates until doomsday unless he received some concessions — not so much to accomplish any particular goal as to certify his position as leader of black America. That genuflection of respect was just what Mondale could not give, not without enraging the Jews and the unions, or those black leaders who had risked so much to support Mondale.

Gary Hart would hold out until the convention, too, and there was no way for Mondale to please him, short of withdrawing his own candidacy. Hart sensed, correctly, that much of Mondale's support was expedient rather than enthusiastic, and that the right set of circumstances, whatever they might be, could still unhorse him as the nominee.

When Jackson and Hart pleaded to the news media that all was not settled, that the stories should reflect caution and doubt, reporters only laughed. Jerry Brown had tried the same tactic for a few ineffectual days in 1976. Edward Kennedy had made a similar plea, to scarcely more persuasible audiences, in 1980. No convention of either party had gone to so much as a second nominating ballot since 1952.

Still, Mondale could suffer some embarrassing if meaningless setback on a tactical point, a rules change, a minor platform matter: almost any rebuff would satisfy the wounded pride of his opponents. Moreover, even if he held down or overcame every potential challenge from the floor, it would scarcely be helpful to have to preside over a sullen or dispirited convention.

So Mondale began to ponder the advantages of naming his vice-presidential choice beforehand. His selection, if misguided, could aggravate the discontent among delegates; even, in extremis, make Hart's unyielding challenge look more plausible. But if he guessed the delegates' mood aright, Mondale could bring his party out of the doldrums and inspire the will to win.

He borrowed from Jimmy Carter the attention-getting, suspense-building device of inviting his most likely choices to confer with him at his estate in North Oaks, Minnesota. As his conspicuously balanced list emerged, candidate by candidate, it became apparent that Mondale was really choosing as much among strategies as among people. He had, as he saw it, six basic options.

Option one was a northern white male, moderate to liberal in outlook, someone who would neither add any new element to the ticket nor, conversely, alarm any of Mondale's core constituencies. The notion of compatibility between running mates was a relatively new concern for the major parties, a by-blow of their transformation from all-embracing, anti-ideological groupings to more distinct and philosophically coherent units. The change had focused attention on sobering questions: If a vice-president comes from a faction too conspicuously different from that of the man who chooses him, what happens if the President dies? Utter discontinuity in policy? Would the shift frustrate the will of the people? The concern was real: half the Presidents in the twentieth century had died, resigned, or been gravely incapacitated while in office. The Northeast liberal option offered Mondale perhaps the longest list of would-be partners, but it soon narrowed to two. New York Governor Mario Cuomo had won his office just two years before and insisted he felt honor-bound to complete his term in Albany; Massachusetts Governor Michael Dukakis, attractive, articulate, and indisputably scandal-free, had been in office six years and would cheerfully move up.

Option two was a white male Southerner, neither a racist nor a closet Reagan enthusiast, but someone whose accent and voting record, especially on defense, would reassure macho men that Mondale was no pussy-footer. This sort of ticket balancing would not necessarily bring to Mondale any voters who actively opposed him. But it might retain some doubtful Democrats. The respected Ernest Hollings would normally have been the obvious choice, but he had endorsed Gary Hart, not Mondale, when he withdrew from the race, and he furthermore displayed scant interest in joining what he openly regarded as Mondale's futile crusade. So the attention shifted to Sam Nunn of Georgia, perhaps the Senate's foremost expert on defense; he preferred to run for reelection. To Dale Bumpers of Arkansas; he balanced the exposure he would gain against the likely proportions of what he, too, judged to be Mondale's impending Waterloo, and bowed out. The last Southerner standing was shrewd but austere and colorless Lloyd Bentsen, a Texas senator and, briefly, 1976 presidential candidate; Mondale aides feared that Bentsen's family real estate fortunes might not withstand the frequently anti-entrepreneurial scrutiny of the national press. And although the conservative Bentsen might help Mondale carry Texas, he seemed scarcely enough of a good ole boy to help in the Southeast.

Option three was a black, and there was only one plausible candidate: Mayor Thomas Bradley of Los Angeles. Like Mondale, Bradley was a solid but unexciting leader who inspired few passions pro or con. Elected mayor after working his way dutifully up through the ranks during two decades as a policeman, he had managed Los Angeles capably; he had largely avoided the appearance of catering chiefly to minorities — a customary pitfall for minority politicians; and he was about to bask in the glow of the Olympics. In traditional vote-gathering terms, Bradley offered perhaps the broadest conceivable gains of any potential running mate. He would appeal to blacks in the Northeast and Midwest industrial states that have to be at the heart of any Democratic plan for capturing a majority of the electoral vote. He would enhance, perhaps enable, Mondale's effective appeal to black voters throughout the South. And he would substantially improve Mondale's chances of capturing California, which by itself would provide a seventh of the electoral tally needed to win. Bradley's shortcomings, however, were equally weighty: he was sixty-seven, far too old if the Democrats were to make an issue, however subtly, of Reagan's age; he had lost a race for governor of California two years before, and thus would give the party a ticket made up entirely of recent losers, running against a President who had skillfully associated himself and his party with winning; in that gubernatorial race, Bradley had slipped precipitately in polls during the final days, reinforcing the widespread belief that Americans were reluctant to empower any black, even a former cop.

Option four was a Hispanic, and again only one candidate surfaced. New Mexico Governor Toney Anaya would have liked to be considered, but in campaigning to make himself the leading Hispanic spokesman in America he had annoyed Anglos in his home state. Instead, Mondale turned to San Antonio Mayor Henry Cisneros, a smooth, articulate, Harvard-educated administrator who combined patrician looks and manner with an earthy effectiveness and street smarts. Of all the vice-presidential prospects, Cisneros was the least credible: at thirty-seven, he was much too young, and after just three years in office he was far too inexperienced; he had no claim to knowledge of national issues, and his city's problems were for the most part the specialized concerns of border towns. Moreover, although Hispanics of Mexican descent might be a factor in the voting in California and Texas, they would not count in most other jurisdictions. Even in Florida, where Cubans have become a major force, and in New York, where Puerto Ricans have been reaching for power, there was no clear sign that a Latin of wholly different descent would command any special loyalty. And blacks, who viewed themselves as having waited in line far longer, would actively resent seeing a Hispanic nominated first.

Option five was Gary Hart. Selecting him would substantially unify the convention and might placate the Baby Boomers who threatened to vote for Reagan. Hart had displayed at least occasional gifts as a campaigner and a consistent regional popularity throughout the West. Balanced against those advantages, however, were reasons for misgivings. Hart did not seem particularly to want the job, and he certainly did not want it enough to abandon his quest for the presidential nomination well in advance of the convention; Mondale had no intention of appearing to choose a partner out of helplessness or vulnerability. Worse, Mondale and his aides feared that the ticket might prove much less than the sum of its parts. The acrid exchanges of the spring would doubtless be brought up time and again in the fall, just as Bush's derisive reference to Reagan's "voodoo economics" had haunted the Republican ticket in 1980. Hart clearly did have a constituency of his own, but it was unclear how much of it would abide with him at the price of swallowing Mondale. Indeed, the New Deal faction of the Democrats saw Hart as primarily a vehicle for anti-Mondale votes, and not effectively pro-anything. To the extent that Hart had actually emerged as a substantial ideological figure, he had done so by envisioning a future in sharp contradistinction to almost everything that Mondale's sort of Democrat admired about the party's past. Compounding all these calculations was a deep residual ill will between the two erstwhile front-runners. Senator Edward Kennedy was eventually able to broker a meeting between them, but not an *entente cordiale.*

The last option was a woman. The argument for that unprecedented choice rested on two known truths: that women were already a majority of the electorate, and that women were measurably more likely than men to mistrust Reagan as a potential war-maker and to view the Democrats as a party of compassion. The disadvantages of selecting a woman were, worryingly for the methodical Mondale, all but impossible to calculate: there was simply no meaningful precedent to consider. A woman might help everywhere, but she would not necessarily add to the chances of winning the electoral votes of even one state. There were, on the other hand, several large and identifiable groups who might well vote against any woman. In the Democratic strongholds, the ethnic blue-collar areas of the Midwest and Northeast, the women's movement had consistently been greeted with something less than enthusiasm. In the conservative South, the choice of a woman running mate might irritate white traditionalists — and exacerbate their doubts about Mondale's mastery and virility — without ensuring any greater support from blacks. The progressive states of the Far West might take kindly to the choice of a woman, but Mondale was so far behind throughout the West that it probably would make little difference.

The value of putting a woman on the ticket had first been promoted by Jesse Jackson, who had explicitly promised to do so and had pressured his rivals to pledge the same. At the time, Mondale and all the other white candidates equivocated: they said that women would be considered seriously, but would not be accorded any guarantees or special preferences. That modest formulation seemed to satisfy all but the most militant feminists throughout the spring. By the end of the "marathon," most women activists had reconciled themselves to a Mondale-Hart ticket, as a gesture toward party unity.

But then it became apparent that Mondale wanted no part of Hart, at least not under terms and conditions that Hart would find acceptable. As time passed without decisive action on a running mate by Mondale, militant feminist sentiment began to spread to moderate women; soon, not even the choice of Hart or Bradley would have deflected their insistence on the selection of a female running mate. Indeed, a caucus of women Democrats, many of them committed Mondale supporters and practicing politicians themselves, vowed to put up a woman against any man Mondale designated. Their first choice was Congresswoman Geraldine Ferraro of New York City, and Ferraro said she would not try to stop them from placing her name in nomination. In fact, she had been lobbying for the designation for months, with the help and guidance of her mentor, Mondale's friend, House Speaker Tip O'Neill. Mondale resented, and at first resisted, the pressure. But he remained ever the pragmatist, and recognized that he could ill afford to rile women on the eve of the convention. If Ferraro had built herself a constituency, she deserved serious consideration. Still, from the beginning he allowed himself alternatives: he toyed with the notion of nominating Kentucky's Governor Martha Layne Collins, the party's highest-ranking woman elected official, but set her aside because she had been in office only a few months; he invited San Francisco Mayor Diane Feinstein to visit him at North Oaks, well ahead of Ferraro. The roster could have been longer, but not by much. Women had come into public life so infrequently until the mid-1970s that there was still only a handful of even moderately seasoned officeholders. There would be no possibility of claiming that a woman running mate had been chosen solely on her qualifications. Rather, Mondale would have to contend that a woman vice-presidential nominee's inevitably modest qualifications did not fully reflect her ability.

———✦———

Choosing a vice-presidential candidate has frequently been an offhand affair: Harry Truman was more or less stampeded into taking Alben Barkley of Kentucky after Barkley delivered a rousing keynote address in 1948; Adlai Stevenson threw the whole matter open to a convention floor fight in 1956; Richard Nixon gave at least the appearance of casualness, uncharacteristic for him, in settling on Spiro Agnew in 1968. But in 1972, the Thomas Eagleton fiasco taught both parties to be more cautious.

When George McGovern, casting about for a Roman Catholic moderate, settled on the Missouri senator almost haphazardly during the Democratic convention, he asked whether Eagleton had any secret defect that would disqualify him from candidacy. Eagleton said no. In truth, Eagleton had been hospitalized repeatedly for depression and had required electroshock therapy to snap him out of postelection blues. Neither the condition nor the treatment reflected a deep, disabling instability; but in the ignorant layman's mind, electroshock was associated with the horror-movie image of Frankenstein's monster, and thus Eagleton's medical history was an absolute bar. Surprisingly, Eagleton had managed to keep his problem a secret during campaigns in Missouri; no Republican nurse or doctor had revealed his background, and he seemingly presumed none would during a national race. But the scrutiny of the national news media is immeasurably more intense than what faces a senatorial candidate in even the biggest states. And as it happened, the efficient and ruthless Nixon administration swiftly dug up the story of Eagleton's problems: days before the news broke into print, an aide to Charles Colson described to this writer exactly what would be coming out. The ensuing mess killed whatever small chance McGovern had of victory. His bad judgment in choosing Eagleton, and his carelessness or ineptitude in failing to uncover Eagleton's fatal flaw, persuaded undecided voters that McGovern lacked the toughness and discernment to be President.

Ever since, nominees of both parties had deemed it wise to narrow their field of potential running mates well before the party convention, and thereby be able to undertake with each one a formal investigation into health, wealth, and personal and business history. In 1976, Howard Baker and other also-rans for Gerald Ford's choice as vice-president each willingly spent thousands of dollars on accounting and legal services to supply information to Ford's campaign. The shortcoming of this procedure is that it offers scant safeguard against the very problem McGovern faced with Eagleton: a running mate who is not candid, either because he is deliberately lying or because he has a blind spot about his potential vulnerability. Examining medical and financial records could help, but without extensive time and resources — commodities that a candidate on the eve of a convention generally lacks — an investigation is unlikely to pinpoint subtle problems. And if the probe becomes too sweeping, too assertive, it could risk souring relations between the presidential candidate and someone who should soon become either his future running mate or an important ally.

Mondale trusted only a handful of senior aides to investigate his potential partners, and he refused to narrow the list prematurely. The week before the party convention, less than three days before he announced his choice, his top staffers were spread out among Boston, New York, and San Francisco, trying to check out Dukakis, Ferraro, and Feinstein — and their spouses, all of whom had careers of their own. There was hardly enough time to spot even glaring deficiencies: aides to Mondale spent about fourteen hours surveying the financial records of Feinstein's husband, Richard Blum, and apparently rather less time with the Ferraro and Dukakis households. The two women offered particular challenges: like many "self-made" wives in politics, they had been greatly helped by their husbands. Although as public officials the wives had faced close examination, the husbands had not, and both men were multimillionaire investors who had complex business involvements. Ultimately, Mondale had to presume, without certainty, that all his potential running mates knew enough about the family finances and were dealing in good faith.

———✦———

In the end, the choice came down to mythology. As he sat drafting his convention acceptance speech, the week before the hubbub in San Francisco, Mondale longed to seize back from Reagan and the Republicans the right to invoke the American dream. And he could find no better example than the immigrant Italian woman, a widow, a seamstress, working long hours crocheting beads on dresses to send her daughter to a fancy girl's school and equally fancy college, so that the daughter in turn could work her way through law school and rise to high elected office. The story was the true history of Geraldine Ferraro Zaccaro. Her family's efforts had been rewarded, with money, with glory, with acceptance in the inner circles of power. She had become a prosecutor, then a congresswoman, and she prided herself on toughness. She reflected, on a grander scale, the life cycles of many ethnic Democrats who had prospered with the help of the party, and had then moved on to vote for the party of prosperity, the Republicans. But Geraldine Ferraro remained a loyal, passionate Democrat. She alone, of all Mondale's choices, could by word and deed tell the former Democratic majority to come back home.

Having decided on the Wednesday night of the week before the convention, Mondale telephoned Feinstein in San Francisco and Dukakis in Massachusetts and the other runners-up. He telephoned Ferraro, who was also in San Francisco, site of the party convention, where she had loyally been doing Mondale's bidding as the nominally neutral chairman of the platform committee. He summoned her to Minnesota, under cover of as much secrecy as possible, to be introduced to the nation the next day from the state capitol in Saint Paul.

He chose her in part because she was an Italian-American, a member of the most Republican of all Catholic ethnic groups, and might therefore add more votes from among her kinsmen. He chose her because she spoke in the unmistakable accents of the urban Northeast, where he was welcome but an outsider. He chose her because she was trusted by Mario Cuomo and Tip O'Neill, politicians he trusted himself. He chose her because she had been married only once (Feinstein's husband was her third) and had remained a devoted wife and attentive mother throughout her career. She had attractive, exuberant children about the age of Mondale's own, and her selfless old mother was still alive, still quotable. Ferraro reflected in every way the family values of Middle America. And unlike Mondale, she was glib and funny and blond and warm. She made her life seem all the more like the fulfillment of the American dream because she was so likable. His intuitions were correct: America fell in love with her within hours, long before getting to know her. Geraldine Ferraro was indeed an exciting choice. But there remained much that she, and Mondale, and America had painfully to learn.

San Francisco, perhaps the most congenial of all American cities, had last been the site of a national party convention in 1964, when the fratricidal Republicans had nominated Goldwater and jeered Rockefeller. The Democrats had hesitated before agreeing to go there, because in the intervening time the city had become a mecca for homosexuals. They constituted a majority of the city's unmarried adult men; they lived openly,

sometimes flagrantly; they often delighted in defiling mainstream convention; and some of their leaders had a genius for generating publicity. A
man who dressed as a nun and campaigned under the name Sister Boom
Boom had drawn 23,000 votes for city council in the last election. More
sober-minded homosexual backing had gone to Feinstein, who openly so-
licited gay support. Latterly, homosexuals had grown disaffected from her
over an issue that could not remotely have affected the politics of any
other major American city. To the consternation of gay militants, Feinstein refused to accord the legitimization of "marriage benefits" to the
unwed lovers, of whatever sex and preference, of city employees; the homosexuals contended that, because marriage was legally closed to them,
they should be able to designate partners who would qualify for health,
pension, and funeral coverage. If homosexual community leaders decided
to use the Democratic convention as a vehicle for attracting national attention, particularly from the sensation-hungry television networks, the
Democrats might be inseparably linked with abnormality in the minds of
down-home Americans.

Along with the homosexual activists, San Francisco had its share and
more of religious extremists, Zen Buddhist communitarians, left-fringe organizers, vegetarian ideologues, and lobbies representing every conceivable ethnic bloc. It had been the home base for the church that the
Reverend Jim Jones led into exile and, later, mass suicide at Jonestown in
Guyana. Drugs were sold openly on downtown street corners. Although it
could scarcely compete with New York City, the site of the 1976 and
1980 Democratic conventions, as a modern Sodom or Gomorrah, San
Francisco at its most flavorful was truly the sort of community that the
Democrats could not afford to embrace.

It also offered perhaps the least convenient of all major convention
halls in America. The new Moscone Center, a virtually windowless un-
derground bunker, had been built to house trade shows. As delegates discovered on arrival, the ceilings were low, the configuration more like that
of a bowling alley than an auditorium, the passageways and entrances
hopelessly few for so large a crowd, especially one that had to pass
through metal detectors for security reasons whenever entering the building. The heat inside, as people milled around hour after hour, grew almost
intolerable despite San Francisco's outdoor mildness. And any West
Coast convention imposes a further discomfort: in order to be on television during prime time in the East and Midwest — which was, after all,
the major reason the large-scale gathering still took place — delegates
would have to assemble in midafternoon and work well through the normal dinner hour.

Against all these disadvantages, San Francisco offered one incomparable asset that had won it the convention bid. It brought the Democrats out to the West, a region where they had almost entirely lost credibility in presidential balloting; to the West's most populous state; and to the metropolis in that state that was most hospitable to Democrats. The other realistic option in California would have been Los Angeles, and that was Ronald Reagan's loyal hometown.

—————

Mondale had announced his choice of Ferraro the day before delegates started streaming into San Francisco, in part to establish in the minds of his remaining rivals and their adherents that he was the boss. He and his aides then looked around for other news they could make. They happened onto a "healing" gesture of coalition building and compromise that proved to be among the gravest miscalculations of the campaign. Just as delegates and journalists assembling for the convention were praising Mondale for his perspicacity in choosing an appealing woman running mate, word came that Mondale was rudely ousting Democratic National Chairman Charles Manatt, on the eve of a convention in his home state, and was replacing him with the slippery southern banker Bert Lance. The motives for the choice were sound: to thank Lance for past favors, to recruit a canny adviser, and above all to reassure white Southerners who were put off by Ferraro because she was an Italian, a Catholic, a New Yorker, and a woman. Privately and in print, however, the choice was uniformly and instantly pronounced disastrous. Lance had been forced out as Jimmy Carter's budget director after a prolonged, complex controversy over his business history, personal finances, and involvement with Carter's campaign, which many people still suspected Lance of having improperly underwritten. He had indisputably shown a pattern of extending questionable loans — some to relatives — with the funds of banks he ran. Once out of office he had grown unbecomingly close to Arab investors; in one deal with them, he had had to enter a consent decree after he had been accused of violating securities laws. He had even been indicted for fraud. Although he had won acquittal or a hung jury on some charges, and the rest had been thrown out by the judge or dropped, he was widely perceived as less than innocent. His physical appearance did not help: bug-eyed, triple-chinned, oily-skinned, he was so much a stereotype of the southern wheeler-dealer that he could have been a stand-in for the venal Boss Hogg on the TV series "The Dukes of Hazzard."

Only one move could have been more ill-considered than selecting Lance, and that was the step Mondale took next: stunned by the depth of public and media hostility to the choice, he backed down. Manatt could stay, he said, and Lance would instead take on an ill-defined role as a national campaign counselor. He owed Lance that much consideration: bound to Mondale through their mutual loyalty to Carter, Lance had poured himself into the last-ditch effort to rescue Mondale's primary candidacy in Georgia on Super Tuesday. Only Atlanta Mayor Andrew Young and Montgomery, Alabama, Mayor Richard Arrington could claim anything like comparable credit for having salvaged Mondale's campaign during the Hart attack. The counselor title was a mere fig leaf, of course: neither Mondale nor Lance wanted to endure a spotlight focused on Lance's business dealings, and after an interval just long enough to salve his pride, it was understood, Lance would withdraw from the campaign.

But the damage had been done. Mondale had managed to remind everyone of his fealty to his unlamented mentor, Carter. And he had saddled himself with a lame-duck national chairman who could only bear him ill will. The gambit would have been a failure, perhaps a disaster, at any point during the campaign. But when Mondale unveiled it, some ten thousand or so journalists, everybody who was anybody in the business, were all in San Francisco talking to each other, magnifying the significance of the moment, exciting each other into outrage at Mondale's stupidity. He had set the tone for coverage of his convention, his candidacy; the tone would be skeptical and often snide from now on.

Before the brouhaha over Lance had died down, Mondale faced a delicate diplomatic problem involving Carter himself. Unlike other disgraced leaders — Lyndon Johnson in 1968, Richard Nixon and Spiro Agnew in 1976 and the years following — Carter was determined to show himself at his party's convention. He wanted to speak. And he wanted to do so in prime time on live national TV. That could hardly prove helpful to Mondale's chances. Carter had in his four short years supplanted Herbert Hoover as the verbal shorthand for presidential ineptitude. The gentler light of recollection had done nothing to soften the public's disregard. So convention schedulers, operating under a guise of independence but in fact answerable to Mondale for every detail, had booked Carter to appear outside the two-hour "window" of prearranged network TV coverage. While he was to be speaking, the networks would be carrying entertainment shows. Carter, however, was having none of it. He forcefully reminded Mondale that had it not been for Carter — choosing him and keeping him as running mate, stumping for him during the dark days just before Super Tuesday — someone else would be accepting the presidential nomination on the convention's final night. The attempt to keep Carter out of the eyes of the people was shabby, and Mondale knew it. As with Lance, as with so much of everything, he once more backed down. The speech in the end proved innocuous, and was quickly forgotten by an electorate that seemed to want to forget everything about Jimmy Carter.

—————

Delegates to conventions represent, but only partially reflect, the makeup of their parties. The median Republican delegate is far more likely than the median Democrat to be white, Protestant, and employed in private business. Few Republican delegates, but many Democrats, are union members. Democratic delegates tend to be younger than Republican delegates, they are far more often attending their first convention, and they are more typically chosen because of their commitment to a particular candidate than because they have been ardent devotees of the party as an institution. Democrats tend to carouse more, and sometimes more venturesomely. San Francisco permitted an unofficial hookers' ball, with a stiff admission fee. Streetwalkers plied their trade openly, and complained to newspaper reporters that the Democrats were eager customers but cheap. At the Republican convention in Dallas, by contrast, all would be circumspect. Well before the Republicans arrived, the police were closing down "escort services" and other fronts for prostitution.

Despite these differences, delegates to both parties' conventions tend to be alike in one regard: they are members of the privileged elite. Republicans are a little richer, but the Democrats are rich enough. The majority of the convention delegates in San Francisco had gone to college. The majority had household incomes nearly double the national norm. Even Jackson's campaign for the dispossessed was represented primarily by delegates with good jobs and, often, advanced degrees. Many of the delegates were arrestingly ugly, astonishingly fat, garishly dressed; some had the manner of lifelong misfits who had channeled their frustrations into political activism. Some played up their natural conspicuousness by wearing bizarre hats, eccentric clothes, cascades of badges and buttons; they looked as though they had come to an esoteric religious festival or blood-letting athletic contest, not a forum for philosophical debate. For the most part, however, the Democratic convention was a cross section of upper Middle America. If times were as bad as their party said, for most of the delegates that knowledge would have to be an article of faith, based at most on childhood memory, not the result of direct personal experience. But then, the same was true for the party's impending nominees.

—————

In earlier times conventions used to select presidential candidates. Now they merely ratify foreordained results and serve as public-relations exercises. Convention schedules, accordingly, are carefully stage-managed. A candidate chosen without serious opposition, most likely an incumbent, normally will want to make the convention a celebration of his career. Speakers and events will be selected to point up his strengths; all other egos in the party will be subordinated to his. A candidate who survives a divided contest, by contrast, will likely want to mollify and unify the rival factions by hailing the diversity of the party, allowing each major figure his moment in the sun. This diffusion of attention may make the nominee look a little less godlike, but it diminishes the likelihood that any major group within the party will feel excluded and sit out the general election.

Mondale reconciled himself early to having to share center stage, indeed to accepting the distinct possibility that he would be overshadowed by one or more of the convention's other speakers. In a characteristic effort to make a virtue of necessity, he found a theme for the convention that would require a display of varied leadership. His chosen theme also would allow the party to move toward the mainstream, to recast its compassion in terms more congenial to the prosperous majority. He envisioned the Democrats, and all of America, as a "family." The theme was not original — but then, competent execution, not original thought, had always been Mondale's forte; he lifted it outright from New York Governor Mario Cuomo, whose touchstone in campaigning and governance had been "the family of New York." Following Cuomo's lead, Mondale described the nation in family terms: some members were rich and others poor, some blessed and others handicapped by circumstance, some did not even like each other very much, but all were bound together by a sense of common heritage, turf, and purpose. This rhetorical device was meant to counter the increasing fragmentation of the country by region, race, and class. It was meant to reassert for the Democrats the right to invoke self-directed values — family, hard work, belief in the American dream — without abandoning the parallel other-directed traditions of community service and compassion. It was meant to explain, or at least paper over, the apparent discontinuity among Gary Hart, Walter Mondale, and Jesse Jackson, each articulating a competing vision of what America ought to be. Cuomo, presiding over perhaps the most diverse and complex state in the nation, had succeeded beyond all expectation by articulating this unifying metaphor. And so it was to Cuomo that Mondale turned for the convention's keynote speech.

Cuomo proved the most rousing party keynoter in decades. Hardened, skeptical journalists such as David Brinkley of ABC and John Chancellor of NBC pronounced his speech perhaps the most effectively delivered political address they had ever heard. Overnight, it made him a presidential contender, and caused more than a few Democrats to wish he were the nominee for 1984.

Mayor Bradley of Los Angeles introduced Cuomo as having come to "beat up on Ronald Reagan." But Cuomo shrewdly offered a lament, not an attack. He meant to portray the President as unseeing, out of touch, not heartless or cruel. Time and again Cuomo addressed him in the speech, and always called him "Mr. President." Cuomo showed respect for the office, and deference to the man. Language that might have seemed nasty on the page was softened by Cuomo's modulations of tone, his apparent sincerity, his flashes of pained and righteous indignation.

Cuomo's argument moved gracefully from first person to third, from family reminiscence to encapsulated history, from patriotic celebration to pointed social criticism. He recalled his immigrant father's long labor and physical suffering; he preached that the implication of the memory was not that the laborer's son was therefore entitled to peaceful enjoyment of middle-class pleasures, but that he, and America, had an obligation to ease the struggles of the next group seeking to rise.

He invoked his Catholic heritage, quoting Thomas Aquinas; but the central image in his speech came from the Puritan founding father John Winthrop, who spoke of his dream for America as a "shining city on a hill." To Cuomo, Reagan represented the mistaken belief that Winthrop's dream already had come to pass for all Americans. Democrats, he said, saw more broadly: "This nation is more a tale of two cities than it is just a shining city on a hill." Cuomo implied that Reagan was blind to the poor, to the newly arrived, to everyone but the comfortable. "A shining city," he said, "is perhaps all the President sees from the portico of the White House and the veranda of his ranch, where everyone seems to be doing well. . . . There is despair, Mr. President, in the faces that you don't see, in the places that you don't visit in your shining city."

It was the classic New Deal argument, movingly spoken. But Cuomo took it too far. He began to envision the unemployed, the dispossessed, the homeless sleeping on city streets. As he talked, he evoked a nation reminiscent of fifty years before, at the height of the Depression, an America remembered from his own childhood. The scenes he described were distant from the lives of ordinary suburban Americans of 1984. The deprivation he so piteously depicted seemed all but impossible in a modern, prosperous welfare state. And indeed, many of the people whose griefs he most graphically described were the victims, not of Reagan's policies, but of their own mental illness, and ironically of the liberal push in the 1970s to get such people out of institutions in favor of the purported panacea of "community-based release." They wandered unwashed in

[185]

their overcoats in midsummer, stood on street corners shouting at unseen phantoms, sought winter warmth above subway grates, because they were unable to cope with life. No party, no program, no philosophy would heal their psychic wounds.

Once again, Cuomo and all the Democrats were affirming that the central concern of government was ministering to life's losers. But the Democrats seemed out of step with reality in assessing the actual numbers of the needy, in defining the extent of the help that they required, and in judging the degree to which government could afford to neglect society's winners. The vast productive economic engine of America was to Cuomo not a delicate and sophisticated nexus of machinery, but a sturdy, self-sufficient cash cow. Chancellor, who hailed the speech's fireworks, remarked on air that it nonetheless seemed not to be about the America he knew. Brinkley, who at first had expressed no such reservations, came to a similar morning-after wisdom: for all Mondale's hopes of outreach, Cuomo had preached only to the already converted.

There was more to Cuomo's speech, to be sure. He condemned "the utter insanity of nuclear proliferation." He said acidly, "We give monies to Latin American governments that murder nuns and then lie about it," a telling shot at Reagan's support of the repressive right wing in El Salvador. He charged that Reagan appeared trigger-happy and lacked a clear-cut foreign policy, especially in the Middle East. He warned of the dangers of Republican flirtations with the religious right, of the possibility of intolerance enacted in the name of piety. In all, he sketched out the lines of a campaign based on peace and pluralism. But for Cuomo, and for the party, the crucial, overstated, all-or-nothing issue was fairness. "We believe in a single fundamental idea . . . the idea of family. Mutuality. The sharing of benefits and burdens." Americans had to realize that they were a family. And having been put in touch with needy cousins they had never heard of before, the members of the family of America were supposed to reach into their wallets and help. In an age when the family is increasingly nuclear, when even the dotage of grandma and grandpa has become a federal responsibility, this notion of duty and kinship was bound to be hard to sell.

———————

The featured performer the second night of the convention was Jesse Jackson. But the day's real action, manipulated by Mondale to take place out of prime time, was debate on the party platform. This was the last stand for Mondale's rivals, the last opportunity to extract some attainment, however trivial, to reassure themselves that the long effort had not been in vain. There was essentially no chance of stopping Mondale's nomination; even a threatened first-round abstention by Hispanics (to protest the bipartisan Simpson-Mazzoli bill to restrict immigration) appeared all but certain to be offset by Mondale's raiding of delegates from Jackson and Hart. The Colorado senator, recently the political phenomenon of the century, now seemed a lonely, passive, almost pathetic figure. David Brinkley of ABC remarked in conversation: "They rigged the system so that, even though he got as many votes in the primaries as Mondale, he got little more than half the delegates. And now they are taking away what he did earn, bit by bit."

Despite the seeming inevitability of Mondale's nomination, syndicated columnist George Will and other observers wondered whether, if Hart had been the daring, venturesome leader he once seemed, he might have been able to use Ferraro to win. The convention seemed euphoric about her. Little else about Mondale seemed to inspire much exuberance; even his labor supporters showed only grim determination. Suppose, the theory ran, Hart had gotten to Ferraro first, and had announced her as his running mate: might that gesture have turned the tide? Ferraro had been a de facto Mondale backer, to be sure, even during her tenure as chairman of the platform committee. But four days before he announced her as his choice, Mondale had seemed to repudiate her. The *New York Times* reported, based on a leak from a high Mondale aide who apparently preferred Feinstein, that Ferraro had made a poor impression during her visit to Minnesota and had pretty much dropped out of the running. Ferraro was furious. She had been humiliated in her hometown. She had been lofted into the elect of potential running mates, only to be insulted; the anonymous words could leave a lasting stain. Mondale promptly telephoned to apologize and to reassure her. But more than a few Democrats insisted that she had been angry enough that Hart might well have persuaded her to sign up. And if Hart had opted for a woman, Mondale would most likely have countered by announcing as his choice exactly the opposite sort of running mate, a low-profile liberal such as Dukakis, or a Southerner, probably Bentsen. The comparison could only have made Mondale look stodgier and might well have caused enough slippage to have forestalled his nomination on the first ballot. If that had happened, Hart might have won.

As it was, Hart took no such bold step to change the political equilibrium. He forlornly continued to insist, on no discernible evidence, that he would be the party's choice. Yet he showed no will to put up any sort of fight. His only quibble with the platform — a document of record length, specificity, complexity, and internal contradiction — was his desire for a pledge against the use of U.S. troops, particularly in the Middle East, until after all negotiations had failed, and even then only when U.S. national security was endangered. The plank was of questionable intellectual value. No President commits troops lightly, and the designation "national security" is broad and vague enough to embrace almost anything that a President wishes it to cover. But as an expression of principle, as a response to a feeling that the United States was too rapidly taking on the dangerous role of world policeman, the plank might have had a chance of appealing to delegates on the floor. Rather than go for broke in an effort to embarrasss Mondale and perhaps regain some support for the nomination, however, Hart hammered out a compromise, and in return promised not to back the most important of Jackson's platform insurrections. The final incentive for Hart, apparently, was the assurance that he would indeed be allowed to speak as scheduled during prime television time the next night, just before the nominating ballot.

Jackson held to his plans for a floor fight, even though the debate on his planks delayed the convention considerably and at one point threatened to push his own speech out of East Coast prime time. He demanded that the United States renounce the first use of nuclear weapons; cut rather than raise defense spending; and eliminate runoff primaries when no candidate gets a majority — a device that he claimed had been used to hold back black candidates in the South. On all three measures he lost, but in each case he attracted between double and triple the number of votes he would eventually get on the nominating ballot. He compromised only on affirmative action. He wanted the party to favor retention of "quotas" in hiring and promotion; Mondale wanted to avoid the incendiary code word, and they settled on an endorsement of "verifiable measurements," an inspired neologism. The argument over Jackson's proposals painfully divided blacks. When Atlanta Mayor Andrew Young opposed the ban on runoff primaries, on behalf of his candidate, Walter Mondale, Jackson supporters screamed and booed.

Jackson's speech had not remotely been the most eagerly awaited moment of the convention, but it proved by far the most memorable. Based on the text alone, the networks hyped it for its conciliatory message, incantatory fervor, and potential for roof-raising theatrics. Dan Rather of CBS urged viewer households to gather all the clan, even to "get grandma in" to watch. The written speech was long, rambling, repetitive. It seemed to build to a peak too early. But when Jackson delivered it, he aroused an uninterrupted, all-consuming burst of kinetic excitement, as sensual and exhilarating as a Reagan speech was soothing.

He began with a soft-spoken, almost plaintive confession, a plea for forgiveness from Jews and others who had been offended by Jackson's excesses: "If in my low moments, in word, deed, or attitude, through some error of temper, taste, or tone, I have caused anyone discomfort, created pain, or revived someone's fears, that was not my truest self." He moved through rocket bursts of partisan crowd-rousing, sometimes lauding the party's past, sometimes flaying opponents: "I would rather have Roosevelt in a wheelchair than Reagan on a horse." He ended, in climax upon crashing climax, with an affirmation that for American blacks there need no longer be a dream deferred; the glory days were now. "Our time has come!" he cried, again and again, and it was as much a statement of mutual acceptance between blacks and white America as it was a personal jubilation. "Our time has come! Our faith, hope, and dreams have prevailed. Our time has come!" The night ended with the singing of a hymn, while delegates, black and white, joined hands and shared the warmth of what Jackson, too, had called "the human family."

After Jackson, anything would have seemed an anticlimax. Alas for Walter Mondale, the next formal item on the convention schedule, the following night, was his designation as the party's choice. In a week of big-league oratory, the customary nominating and seconding speeches were so little valued that they barely were carried on television. The one showcase speech before the official roll call came from the loneliest of long-distance runners, Gary Hart. His was a cool, detached, in some ways ungenerous speech, and like Hart the man, the address provoked controversy. Some canny observers thought it among the best political oratory they had ever heard, some ranked it among the worst. Some regarded it as a substantive elucidation of the better road that the party had not taken, others found it empty and petulant. The division paralleled the deep uncertainty about Hart's prospects for the future. CBS's Dan Rather plainly regarded Hart as a flash in the pan. His colleague and predecessor Walter Cronkite openly predicted that Hart would be recognized as a prophet, undeservedly without honor, and could become the man to beat for 1988.

Hart deplored the preoccupation in both parties with restaging old debates. He implicitly condemned the Democrats' outworn reliance on the mythic power of Franklin Roosevelt and the New Deal. "We have failed when we became cautious and complacent," he said. He attacked the unthinking affection for "the policies of the past that do not answer the challenges of tomorrow." He invoked issues of technology and of the environment that Mondale and his labor-union lunchbucket Democrats either ignored or actively willed away, because they saw change not as progress but as a threat to jobs.

But Hart also hailed Mondale for "unsurpassed grit, perseverance, and determination." He pledged he would "devote every waking hour and every ounce of energy to the defeat of Ronald Reagan." And he reassured his supporters that he would be back, that his generation and his "generational" theme would prevail, if not now, then eventually. More catchily, he said, "This is one Hart you will not leave in San Francisco." His partisans cheered as loudly as Ted Kennedy's followers had cheered in 1980 when their candidate vowed, "The dream shall never die." But of course Kennedy had not run the next time. Hart, too, offered only a placation, not a promise.

Then the Democrats held their roll call. Mondale drew 2,191 votes, 224 more than he needed. Hart drew 1200, Jackson 465. The marathon was truly over, and the front-runner had won.

Mondale broke with tradition and appeared on the convention floor some minutes later to express his gratitude and confirm the obvious, that he would formally accept nomination the next night. His appearance was an effort to give him a little more television exposure, as his party's choice and therefore a winner, and also to show him as a man of unfailing humility and politeness. The gambit may not have worked. Anchor David Hartman of ABC's "Good Morning, America," who was working around the clock to keep to East Coast time in the morning and to gratify his hobby as a photographer at night, looked up at Mondale from the convention floor and judged that the candidate had doomed himself "with his first six words." They were, "Thank you, thank you, thank you," which Hartman delivered in a deadly parody of Mondale's high, nasal voice and awkward, arms-thrust-out, Nixonian posture. And indeed, the happy warrior looked more relieved and wrung-out than triumphant.

―――⌐―――

The next night, virtually every network TV reporter who spoke of the formal nomination of Geraldine Ferraro described it as a "historic" moment. But neither ABC nor NBC nor CBS carried the roll call live. The networks had wearied of the static spectacle of conventions. They were talking of cutting back coverage even further for the Republican gathering in Dallas, and they were predicting that no future party convention would ever again merit even the 1984 allotment of two hours per day for four consecutive days in prime time. They wanted suspense, unpredictability, not precisely scripted ritual. The balloting on Ferraro seemed especially likely to lack drama. While the networks were off the air, however, a skirmish broke out, minor in itself, that foreshadowed much bigger battles to come. A handful of delegates, mostly from Mondale's home state of Minnesota, had protested both Mondale's and Ferraro's support of abortion rights by withholding their votes from him the previous night. Now they said they would vote against her too. To head off a repeat of this protest during the balloting for Ferraro, the Mondale forces moved almost immediately to nominate her by acclamation.

This little outburst of defiance made no difference in the immediate outcome. But it reminded Democratic optimists that even on Ferraro, there was something less than unity. And it at least hinted of a problem the Democrats would soon have to face squarely: despite the century-long association between the party and the Catholic church, the relationship remained a business deal more than a marriage, and the clerical partners were in the process of jacking up their price for continuing the collaboration.

Ferraro nonetheless was the star of the night, less for what she said than for the vitality and glee she radiated. To most delegates, indeed most Americans, she was still only a symbol — the two-fisted liberal lady from the fictional Archie Bunker's actual district in Queens. A more balanced examination of her was bound to follow. But this was not the time for caution. She emerged to accept the nomination, in her first official appearance at the convention, dressed in virgin's white that accented her blondness, her healthy glow, the demure pearl necklace at her throat — in short, her femininity. She had been coached to strike a balance between womanly sweetness and manly vigor. She must seem strong enough to lead, but not forceful enough to intimidate men, including her running mate. She reminded her audience that she was a mother — and a prosecutor. She linked her struggle, women's struggle, to other social movements, other adventures undertaken by the country: "Change is in the air, just as surely as when John Kennedy beckoned America to a New Frontier; when Sally Ride rocketed into space, and when Reverend Jesse Jackson ran for the office of President of the United States." In keeping with the traditional role of running mate as tough cop (so that the presidential nominee can play the statesman), she lambasted Ronald Reagan. She had already clashed with Reagan once, a day after Mondale chose her, saying, "The President walks around calling himself a good Christian, but I don't for one minute believe it because the policies are so terribly unfair." That line had been universally judged too harsh, and Ferraro had apologized for it. But she took on the national grandfather again in her acceptance speech; addressing him in absentia, she said, "You fit the classic definition of a cynic — you know the price of everything, but the value of nothing."

When she was speaking, Ferraro did not sound much different from any other Democratic politician. But when her running mate joined her on the podium, audiences were reminded again of how new her position was: the body language between her and Mondale was studied, stylized, and awkward. As Maureen Dowd reported in a much-copied story in the *New York Times*, Ferraro and Mondale decided they could not do anything that would make them seem like a romantic couple. They could not kiss, or hold hands, or hug; indeed, they could hardly touch. For all Ferraro's warmth, Mondale had to treat her as unapproachable. They had few models to follow: the closest parallels were male-and-female teams of local TV news anchors.

Ferraro's prominence resulted in another, unanticipated event: it thrust Joan Mondale, the candidate's wife, into the shadows. Ferraro, not Mrs. Mondale, was now the first lady of the party. If the Democrats were elected, Ferraro, not Mrs. Mondale, would be in a sense the First Lady of the country. Joan Mondale had been one of the most adept of political wives: discreet, loyal, well-groomed but not flashy, dedicated to the uncontroversial pursuits of education and the arts. She had combined the traditional roles of spouse and mother with a steady, respectful presence by her husband's side on the campaign trail. Unlike Rosalyn Carter, she seemed not to harbor any political ambitions of her own. Unlike Nancy Reagan, she did not let it be known that she was her husband's most trusted and intimate adviser. And she was secure enough in her background role that she had lobbied, quietly but insistently, for him to choose a woman as his running mate.

———

Walter Mondale had said all along that his acceptance speech would have to be the best public performance of his life. He knew that the moment would be both his first and very nearly his last chance to persuade the American people to follow him.

It was his first chance, despite his having been a figure in national life for nearly two decades, because the fact of being nominated as a major-party candidate for President always prompts the public to look at a man afresh. The acceptance speech is his opportunity to define himself, to express the ways that personal experience and spiritual belief have led him to a vision of the country. Far more than in a televised debate, in which he must confront an opponent, the acceptance speech is a candidate's moment to communicate with the voters one by one, to establish a shared faith.

It was also nearly the last chance for Mondale, because polls already showed him trailing Reagan by up to twenty percentage points. If his performance on the convention's final night did not change the public's view of him, he would have scant meaningful opportunity until a debate with Reagan, two or three months away, and by then it would likely be too late.

Mondale had three goals this night: to explain why he was a Democrat; to persuade voters to abandon a likable man, Ronald Reagan, for an abstract and seemingly shopworn idea, the party of the New Deal; and to depict himself as he was, a man of common sense and compromise, a believer in practical rather than radical solutions. He held stubbornly to the idea that the Democrats were the natural majority party, and he was sure that the American people could be persuaded to recognize Reagan as a radical, and therefore to reject him. Underlying Mondale's strategy was a conviction that, although things appeared on the surface to be just fine in Reagan's America, they were about to go gravely wrong, and that the people knew it. Mondale tried to concede as much good as possible to Reagan's first four years in office, but the praise did not come naturally. When his feelings broke through the protective layer of polite rhetoric, it was plain that what Mondale really wanted was for the American people to admit that in 1980 they had made a big mistake.

The personal, reflective quality of the acceptance speech was the crucial one for Mondale, and it failed. He came across as two-dimensional. He sounded as though he rarely pondered the meaning of life, his own or anyone's, as though he rarely wrestled with values. The preacher's son had taken a lifelong posture of righteousness; that may have been different from self-righteousness, but it looked and felt the same. His deep convictions about justice were almost impossible to distinguish from pigheadedness. Perhaps the overriding problem was that Mondale's life apparently included no moment of revelation, nothing like what befell the saint-to-be Paul on his way to Damascus. Mondale's sermons carried the dull thud of certitude, not the urgent poetry of zeal. He had not been moved by inner yearnings like Richard Nixon's or Jimmy Carter's for a broader and better life, nor had he been shaken out of decades-long affiliations by disquieting experience like Ronald Reagan. Or if he had, he could not communicate the emotional quality of what he had undergone. Mondale tried after a fashion to answer the voters' most basic and most intimate question: Who is he? But none of it really came through.

The closest Mondale reached toward an admission of doubt was an oblique reference to his decision, in 1981, to spend a year reconsidering his philosophy. In truth, that venture had not discernibly changed Mondale or his agenda. But after the adverse landslide of 1980, he had needed to indicate he felt chastened. He still did. So in his speech he said, to the Democrats who had turned away from Carter that year, "I heard you.

And our party heard you." The lessons he claimed to have learned from the 1980 election were that America needs a strong defense and "must have a sober view of the Soviets," that "government must be as well managed as it is well meaning," and that "a healthy, growing private economy is the key to the future." Those phrases acknowledged the new conservatism of the electorate. But they did not commit Mondale or his party to changing anything in the real world of budgets, legislation, diplomacy, and war. And indeed there seemed to be no social program of consequence that Mondale had once favored yet would now be willing to give up. Instead, he wanted to spend more money than ever for a "renaissance in education, in science and learning," so that America might have "a season of excellence." He wanted to continue the protective welfare state. He pledged to veto needless spending, but his only target appeared to be the Pentagon.

He spoke of peace. Challenging the Republicans on nuclear arms control, he said, his hoarse voice rising in evident anger, "Why can't they understand the cry of human beings for sense and sanity in control of these god-awful weapons? Why can't we meet in summit conferences with the Soviet Union at least once a year? Why can't we reach agreements to save the earth? The truth is, we can."

He spoke of pluralism: "I do not envy the drowsy harmony of the Republican party. . . . They are a portrait of privilege, and we are a mirror of America."

But he played up fairness: "To the corporations and the freeloaders who play the loopholes and pay no taxes, my message is, your free ride is over." As he had done increasingly in the later primaries, he concentrated on two warning signals in the economy, the budget deficit and the imbalance of trade. His implicit warning was that the pie of American prosperity would soon be shrinking, as these numbers purportedly proved, and that the common man would be better off with Democrats, not Republicans, reapportioning the shares. In both budget and trade policy, he said, America was living on borrowed time.

To underscore this theme of inevitable austerity, Mondale took the boldest gamble any candidate had attempted in an acceptance speech since Harry Truman, in 1948, announced he would call a special session of the adjourned "do-nothing Eightieth Congress." Mondale pledged to cut the budget deficit by two-thirds during his first term, not by pie-in-the-sky promises of discarding "fat" and "waste," but the old-fashioned way: by taxation. No candidate for any office wants to associate himself with the likelihood of higher taxes. The most common reaction to bad news has always been to kill the messenger. But the taxation pledge was especially hazardous for Mondale and his party, who had been labeled, not only by the Republicans but by the public, as reckless spenders and obsessive redistributors of property and income to the poor. The positive side of Mondale's high-stakes venture was that it would label him a man of integrity and at the same time unnerve his opponents. If Reagan admitted that he, too, would have to raise taxes, he would lose much of his constituency and tacitly concede that Reaganomics was a failure. If he denied that he would raise taxes, people might consider him out of touch, or suspect that he was harboring some secret plan to tax them without owning up to it. And if he waffled, in characteristic Reagan fashion, it would reinforce Mondale's suggestion that the President was old, out of touch, not in charge, letting the country drift.

Knowing that what he was about to do was either one of the cleverest, or one of the stupidest, undertakings of his life, Mondale said, "Mr. Reagan will raise taxes. And so will I.

"He won't tell you. I just did."

VII

…And an Echo

Mondale and the Democrats came away from San Francisco buoyed by optimism. The gambit of admitting that higher taxes were inevitable had caught the Reagan administration off balance, just as Mondale had hoped: the President's lieutenants stumbled over each other making contradictory statements until even Vice-President George Bush appeared to admit that Mondale was fundamentally right. By the time Reagan insisted in his own voice, not just through spokesmen, that new taxes would not even be considered, his words sounded more like a willful denial of reality than a pronouncement of doughty conservatism. Persuading the electorate to abandon so popular a President would be an uphill task. But if Mondale's strategic cunning enabled him to continue to set the campaign agenda, it was just possible that he could intimidate Reagan and show him up as not in full control of his White House.

Opinion polls indicated the Democrats were enjoying the customary postconvention upswing accorded almost any nominee, but not much more, contrary to inflated initial claims by Mondale's top aide, James Johnson. Despite the sensation caused by Geraldine Ferraro, her presence on the ticket did not seem to have transformed the public perception of the man who chose her, at least not yet. For one thing, a substantial number of poll respondents thought Mondale had acted under pressure, to please yet another strident interest group, rather than out of deep conviction or daring. For another, people rarely vote for a presidential candidate because of his choice of running mate — although they may well vote *against* his choice, as they did in 1976 when Gerald Ford chose Robert Dole. Mondale's people nonetheless found cause for great optimism in the seemingly inconclusive results. They reasoned that any innovation takes time for people to accept. If the choice of Ferraro had not resulted in a big drop in Mondale's standing, that amounted to good news: voters were not rejecting out of hand the idea of a woman in high office. If Ferraro proved as fresh, natural, plainspoken, and appealing as the Democrats hoped, and if she continued to receive the volume of publicity that the party had gambled on her getting, people would in time warm to her and to the idea of women in power.

This cheery scenario lasted little more than a couple of weeks. Ferraro had been handling herself well, although with the predictable awkwardness and occasional irritability of a newcomer to high-visibility national politics. Then, almost casually, she announced one day that she had overpromised in pledging full disclosure of her family finances. She was willing to tell all about her own income, which consisted chiefly of her congressional salary, and about her taxes. But her husband, who considered himself a separate business entity, and who had therefore filed a separate rather than joint tax return for every year Ferraro had been in Congress, refused to join her. He contended that releasing his personal and corporate tax returns, a net worth statement, and other basic financial information could only help his competitors in New York City's lucrative, cutthroat real-estate business. His argument was reasonable. But ever since the ouster of Spiro Agnew for taking bribes while vice-president, and of Richard Nixon for offenses that included tax dodging, abuse of public funds, and an inrush of illegal corporate cash to his campaign, substantial disclosure had been an absolute legal, or at least practical, necessity for virtually all major elected officials. To hold out was to invite unceasing, even harassing press inquiry in pursuit of one's presumed dirty secret. For a national party nominee, especially a running mate chosen in defiance of conventional rules, the alternatives amounted to disclosure or disqualification.

Ferraro tried to put a brave face on matters. She joked that any of her listeners who had been married to Italian men could understand the stone wall of husbandly resistance she had encountered. But she seemed to sense almost immediately that she had little room to maneuver. During her six years in the House, Ferraro had claimed that her detachment from the family businesses entitled her to an exemption from the chamber's rules requiring disclosure of virtually all assets and their approximate values. The House had accepted her assertion without demur. But that history only made her problems worse. Reporters began to question whether she had really met the House's strict rules. The possibility that she might have violated a formal ethical standard gave journalists an added incentive to pry into her affairs. Mondale suddenly found himself faced with exactly the trouble that had wrecked McGovern in 1972: deep doubt about whether his choice for vice-president was fit to serve. During the buoyant days for the Democrats, case-hardened journalists and politi-

cians had speculated with each other about how long it would take for reporters to start covering Ferraro as just another office-seeker. The answer
became clear: only as long as it took for people to suspect that she or her
husband might be unsavory, perhaps crooked.

From the moment Ferraro was named, rumors and idle speculation had
linked her or her husband to organized crime: on the very day of Mondale's announcement in Saint Paul, reporters from at least three of the
nation's foremost news organizations asked each other, only half joking,
whether it was true that John Zaccaro was "mobbed up." Beyond his ethnic surname, Zaccaro was suspect because he and his father before him
had owned or managed property in Manhattan's Little Italy, traditionally
the Kremlin or Red Square of the American Mafia. Once Zaccaro declined to open his private records, journalists began to assume the worst:
that he must have disgraceful holdings, or scandalous partners, or a dou-
ble-booking system set up to cheat the Internal Revenue Service. Over-
zealous investigative reporters dug up, among Zaccaro's myriad residential
tenants, a couple of malcontents who groused about the inadequacy of
heat or repairs, and then implied he was a slumlord. Much was made of
his having rented space to a business that turned out to be a pornography
distributor, although there was no evidence that Zaccaro even knew
what was going on. He was impugned on still more tortuous, tenuous
grounds: he had managed a building owned by a rabbi who was convicted
of swindling a federal food program; a reputed mobster rented an apart-
ment in a building that he had inherited from his father thirteen years before and promptly sold. Even wise and seasoned reporters joined the hunt.
Syndicated columnist George Will predicted, on ABC News's weekly
Sunday roundtable discussion with David Brinkley, that Zaccaro would
turn out to have taken advantage of loopholes — real estate affords plenty
of them — and thus not to have paid much in taxes. For Democrats running a campaign based on "fairness," the failure to have paid a fair share
of taxes could be devastating; in 1982 the party's extremely appealing
woman candidate for governor in Iowa, Roxanne Conlin, had blown a
seemingly insurmountable lead and lost her race after it was revealed that
she and her husband had taken advantage of loopholes to pay virtually no
income taxes despite millions of dollars in assets. Mondale, well aware of
that spectacular decline, must have been unnerved: his bold stroke to salvage a weak campaign seemed to be turning into the hammer-blow that
might destroy it instead. He was doubtless further estranged because Ferraro had discussed her problem for days with numerous others, including
Democrats in the Texas congressional delegation, before coming to him.
Yet Mondale did not try to strongarm Ferraro or her husband, partly be-

cause he had seen their tax returns and knew that they would cause little scandal unless they turned out to be materially untrue.

As the media onslaught continued, Zaccaro began to grasp that he had no winning options; either he would reveal his finances voluntarily, or, by refusing, he would force his wife off the ticket. And her resignation would not bring peace and privacy. Instead, that historic setback for women would turn his business involvements, however innocuous, into a continuing target for prize-hunting investigative reporters. The time for Zaccaro to demand his privacy had come and gone: he had had his chance during the dickering before Ferraro accepted the nomination. Having been silent then, he had to yield now. So long as Ferraro's fate hung in the balance, nothing else that she or Mondale discussed, no campaign venture they undertook, would attract much coverage or be accorded much meaning. The Democratic candidacy had come to a halt. Zaccaro slowly yielded, though not all the way. He would release his own tax return, but not those of all his various corporations and partnerships. Thus, while analysts could trace the disposition of money that flowed through to the household, they would gain little insight into the rest of the Zaccaro empire's complex, chaotic asset management. Whatever secrets he was keeping, dark or benign, they would remain secret a while longer.

Ferraro chose to accompany the release of her financial papers with a press conference. She meant to face all comers and wear them down with candor. No relevant questions would be barred, no time limit for discussion would be imposed, and even fringe publications — for example, the *Washington Times*, published by the Reverend Sun Myung Moon — would be allowed to attend. Some observers likened her risky undertaking to Richard Nixon's speech in 1952, when he defended his use of a secret political slush fund primarily by diverting attention to his wife's "plain Republican cloth coat" (which he implicitly contrasted with the furs some Democrats had been accused of extracting as bribes) and to his children's acceptance of a gift puppy called Checkers. The Nixon speech was a landmark of political self-rehabilitation; but unlike Ferraro he faced only the camera and told only his side of the story. She would confront reporters who would probe the weaknesses or omissions in her self-defense. Ferraro, moreover, was responding to the more intrusive ethos of 1984, and was expected to reveal far more information.

The press conference coincided, by happenstance, with the second day of the Republican convention in Dallas. Indeed, although the Grand Old Party wambled on with its script that day, almost everyone who mattered in the party or in Reagan's White House entourage was watching Ferraro. If she survived the press conference, she would stay on the ticket, and the questions about her ethics would retreat to the background, balanced by the considerably greater "sleaze factor" among Reagan's Republicans. If she did not acquit herself well, her candidacy, and in all likelihood Mondale's as well, was finished. Like Nixon in 1952, Ferraro above all had to create the impression of innocence. If she projected confidence and certitude, if she took command and answered questions comfortably, if she appeared to have the facts at her fingertips and to be able to deflect unwelcome questions, then so long as the facts were anything less than devastating, she would win the battle of appearances. But she would also need to provide tenable answers to three basic questions: Were she and her husband honest, law-abiding taxpayers? Were their business practices proper and fair? Was she entitled to the "spousal" exemption from disclosure that she had claimed in the House of Representatives, and if not, had her claim been deceitful and had it produced significant consequences?

The press conference began badly. First, the release of Ferraro's disclosure statements had been delayed by hours; the reason, according to Ferraro, was their complexity, but suspicious reporters thought she was trying to get the confrontation behind her before journalists had had an adequate opportunity to survey her records and prepare knowing questions. Thus even some of the previously sympathetic reporters who were regulars in Ferraro's entourage came to the conference with a hostile attitude. When Ferraro showed up, the sound system did not work properly, and she insisted on waiting until it was fixed. Another problem was beyond redemption: the dress Ferraro was wearing, a becoming purplish blue with a Paisley-style pattern of red amoebas, blended indistinguishably into the identically purplish blue curtain hung behind her. She appeared to be an almost disembodied mouth and hands. Ferraro was not at her most photogenic, and in many shots she looked arrogant or combative or walleyed and downright ugly.

The chief news was good. She and her husband had paid more than average taxes for their income, and had used no obviously questionable deductions or shelters. Admittedly, the returns were less than complete. It seemed likely that substantial amounts of cash income might have been retained, perfectly legally, by Zaccaro's various corporate shells; although he and Ferraro reported a joint net worth of nearly four million dollars, the return on that sum was modest. His gross income before adjustments had been barely $200,000 in 1983, and as little as $41,000 in 1981. As it turned out, the family consistently paid plenty of taxes on the income it did receive: the bill was more than $120,000 in 1983.

There were, however, four substantial embarrassments to be gotten over. Ferraro had a down-to-earth explanation for each. First, Ferraro's own records showed prima facie evidence that she had not qualified for the House exemption on disclosure, which required essentially separate financial lives: her husband had paid the property taxes on their three homes (a large Tudor house in Forest Hills, Queens, a summer place on trendy Fire Island, a winter condominium in the U.S. Virgin Islands). He had paid for family vacations, for schools and other expenses for their children. When such facts were pointed out to her in questions from reporters, she replied that she had reviewed the House regulations repeatedly and had concluded that no reasonable person would read them literally, because they effectively nullified the very exemption they supposedly created. To follow the House rules to the letter, Ferraro said, she and her husband would have to have maintained "two separate refrigerators." They probably would: the House rules required that a member claiming the exemption must get no benefit from a spouse's wealth, nor even have "the possibility of an inheritance" of the spouse's business interests.

Second, Ferraro was plainly more involved in her husband's enterprises, at least technically, than she had admitted to Congress or in other disclosures. She depicted herself, oddly for a feminist, as almost totally unaware of how the family's principal income was earned. She sounded at times almost like a helpless widow in the making. But she was an officer of P. Zaccaro, the family holding company created by her father-in-law, and other subsidiary companies, and she had often been the attorney of record on Zaccaro transactions. She explained that she had obtained a real-estate license long before entering public office, after her husband's father and brother died in quick succession of cancer in 1971, as a protective step urged by her husband "in case something happens to me." Her motive was "to keep the business going and, you know, take care of our kids." The business itself was run in slipshod, even questionable fashion. The same week as Ferraro's press conference, her husband had to go to court to explain why he had broken the law and lent himself money for one of his projects by borrowing from an estate he managed as conservator. The loan had been repaid, at considerably higher interest than the best bank deposit rate, but the transaction was unquestionably against the law. Zaccaro claimed not to have known, and he was not significantly punished.

Third, Ferraro's first campaign for Congress, in 1978, had plainly violated Federal Election Commission laws. She had borrowed some $134,000 from trust funds set up for the benefit of four family members, far over the legal loan limit of $1,000 per person, and had paid a fine of $750 for the technical error. That much was public record. But to repay the trusts, Ferraro had sold off her part ownership in a New York City building to one of her husband's business partners — who had in turn sold it back to her husband once the election was over. Ferraro said she had only recently learned of the incestuous nature of the transaction, and had confronted her husband to criticize him about it. She conceded to reporters: "It doesn't look so hot. But you know, what can I tell you? The point is that it was legal." She noted, "I can give you a speech about how hard it is for women to raise money to run for office."

Fourth, the family had misreported the profit from the sale of the building that financed her campaign, and thus had underpaid its taxes by $29,709 and owed another $23,750 in interest. Ferraro blamed the lapse on her accountant and noted that there was no attempt to deceive — the erroneous calculations had all been plainly included in the tax form, as the IRS had acknowledged in choosing not to impose any penalty for fraud. Ferraro's new accountants claimed they had discovered a similar error, this time an overpayment, but in a year too far back for the family to claim a refund by filing an amended return.

Through it all, facing more than two hundred reporters for one hundred minutes, until no one had anything left to ask, Ferraro showed almost flawless instincts for public relations. When a journalist started a question with a premise that she disputed, she interrupted him, politely but forcefully, before he got any further. She was frequently wry and self-deprecating. Speaking of her being listed as variously vice-president, secretary, or treasurer of Zaccaro properties, she said, "It's sloppy, I'll grant you that." Asked about the impact of the disclosure episode on the Democrats' campaign, she smiled ruefully. "Let me put it this way: it has not been a positive thing." But she waved away any thought that she might resign from the ticket as Republican "wishful thinking." She demonstrated detailed command of the intricacies of her family's finances, but she did not hesitate to call on the lawyers and accountants accompanying her. When one started to whisper a protracted explanation into her ear, she broke away and said, "Irwin, why don't *you* tell them?" Above all, she presented herself once again as a beneficiary of the American dream. She did not claim to be a modest Queens housewife. (In fact, when a press photographer had wanted to snap her in the kitchen, Ferraro's daughter jokingly wondered whether her mother even knew where the kitchen was.) But she rejected any suggestion that she and her husband were self-indulgent or frivolous in the fashion that Democrats had attributed to Nancy Reagan. "You are seeing people who work very hard. We are not flashy. We buy property and maintain it and it appreciates. That is what America is all about."

Most journalists were deferential to her. One conspicuously was not.

Ferraro opened her press conference by saying, "I released more than anybody has released in the history of this country." That somewhat grandilo-
quent assertion was pounced on by Gregory Fossedal, a writer and editor
for the *Wall Street Journal*'s rightist and occasionally loony editorial page.
He asked her about the 425 members of the House of Representatives
who complied with the disclosure requirements when only Ferraro and 9
others claimed exemptions. Had not the 425, he demanded, disclosed
more than she had? Ferraro hesitated, and Fossedal, with the impetuous
indignation of youth, shouted, "Answer it!" He was booed by many of his
fellow journalists — not, as he and other conservatives later contended,
because reporters preferred the Democrats, but more because arrogance
and rudeness by any reporter abruptly diminishes the credibility and effectiveness of the whole craft.

When the conference was over, Ferraro still looked fresh and cool and
unshaken. Mondale, who had watched her in his living room in North
Oaks, praised her "superb performance" and said, "I am even more confident that I made the right choice. There has been a clear demonstration
here of leadership, of strength, of candor, of values that the American
people will respond to favorably." Mondale made no mention of facts, of
truth, of innocence. He dealt in imagery. And he was not alone. Ferraro's
confessional discussion was reviewed by every major news organization as
though it had been a theatrical entertainment. Daniel Schorr said on
Cable News Network, "In media terms, it was a sort of colossal success
for her. She came across as a very sincere, very gutsy lady." Dan Rather
appraised her on CBS as "cool, collected, professional." ABC's Lynn
Sherr said, "She seems to have gotten back some of her original spunk.
Geraldine Ferraro seems to have been on top of the situation today." Almost everyone agreed she had made an unacceptably weak case for her
entitlement to the House disclosure exemption, and that her other behavior had been at best untidy, but no one seemed to care. *USA Today*, the
national daily newspaper that had zoomed to the nation's third largest
circulation primarily by shrewd packaging, calibrated the morning-after
news just right: its review of Ferraro's mood and style was the biggest story
on page one, while the serious concessions she had been forced to make
about her behavior were put in a small hole on the bottom of page three.
Still, the ordeal had been harrowing, and Ferraro suspected it was far from
over. In an interview at her Queens home with correspondents from
Time, just after the press conference, Ferraro said, "I didn't know I was
going to subject my husband to all this. I just never thought it." She was
asked if she would have accepted the nomination, knowing what would
follow. She said, "I don't know."

VIII

The City of Money

For the Republicans, the presidential campaign of 1984 had never really started, and they hoped it never would. They had come into the year proclaiming Ronald Reagan's reelection an inevitability, and they wanted it to remain that way. In a sense, Reagan as incumbent had done exactly what Mondale had done as challenger: he denied the very existence of a contest. His allies seemed to see him as some great, immovable mountain around which his rivals rain-danced, hoping by some flurried burst of activity to cause the solid earth to move. Part of this imagery was mere cunning, of course: invoking the mystique of Reagan's patriarchal appeal helped to perpetuate it. Yet among even the most hardened of Reagan's subordinates, the professional henchmen who in 1976 and 1980 had shifted from candidate to candidate, at least some of the awe and reverence they voiced was real. Reagan apparently had the gift of making people feel good about the country — and the even greater gift of making people feel good about the rich. He dispelled class resentments; he eased the pangs of conscience among those who have toward those who have not; he reconciled his countrymen to inequality, and absolved the prosperous of any hint of shame at making gaudy display of their riches. His party had become increasingly a meeting place for fundamentalist preachers, and of them all Reagan still preached the basic sermon best: God has blessed America with riches; seek, and ye, too, shall find. Reagan had other messages, of course, and resonated with America in other ways. But in August, as the Republican party's ruling elite gathered in Dallas for the convention, Reagan's benign certitude of the sacred rights of money was foremost on the party's mind.

Dallas is a city where avarice will never be the love that dare not speak its name. It is a city made of money: its chief industry is buying and selling. Houston and Midland and Odessa are the oil-money towns of Texas. Fort Worth is the cattle town. Dallas is the Wall Street. Its city center is a shimmery fortress-state of mirrored skyscrapers, vertiginous atria, profligate waterfalls in a land of dust. The posh neighborhoods are full of mansions, side by side with small, externally modest and breathtakingly expensive houses that are crammed with every conceivable ornamentation, embellishment, and gadget. Buildings are traded — "flipped" in the local parlance — with dizzying frequency. By the time the paperwork is completed on a transaction, the property often has been sold again, and again, so that the transfer eventually resembles the toppling of a long row of pinstripe-suited dominos. People get rich quick in Dallas, but they often get poor again, too. It is a city where a man could go bust three times before he is thirty-five, and still end as a billionaire. Dallas believes everything can be bought, even sophistication, and it is prepared to pay the price. When the city fathers wanted a new artistic director for the theater, they went not to New York but to Providence, and hired someone very talented with a predilection for plays about homosexuality, transvestism, and prison. He riled the locals, but he stayed. Dallas, like the Republicans, like *nouveaux riches* everywhere, wanted style at any cost.

Dallas is known to the rest of the world mainly for two things: the television series that bears its name, and the fact that John Fitzgerald Kennedy was assassinated there, a stigma the city has been trying to live down for more than twenty years. The TV show, an international hit, has been warmly embraced by much of Dallas because it idealizes what the city sees in itself: raw power, shrewdly handled by braying country boys who can outfox any old international financier. The women are beautiful and strong, the men are virile and stronger. They all exude the aphrodisiac scent of money. The characters in "Dallas" are perpetually in combat; no empire is secure from predators except through vigilance. The politics of "Dallas" is the foreign policy of the Republican party, often fratricidal within the family, but absolutely paranoid toward outsiders. "Dallas" was Dallas was the Republican party was America. It was a neat syllogism that the convention delegates did not necessarily articulate, but that — as some of them journeyed out to the show's ranch setting at "South Fork" — they could not help but feel.

The assassination was far more ambiguously bound up with the city's identity. In the days and months after John Kennedy's murder in 1963, intellectuals in and outside the city pondered how Dallas had come to breed an assassin, sought for the elements in the city's character that made it the place where John Kennedy had to die. They blamed the tradition of venomous right-wing politics, although Lee Harvey Oswald was a Communist; they blamed the free use of guns and the lingering cowboy tradition, although Oswald was trained in sharpshooting during military service and obtained the fatal rifle by mail order; they blamed the police, the city government, the people themselves. In time, as assassination grew all too common, Dallas was relieved of its unique burden of guilt. But its citizens, still abashed and resentful, could never make up their minds whether to create a major historical shrine at the site of Kennedy's death, or to ignore it altogether and if possible redevelop the landscape to help obliterate sad memories. The eventual compromise was a small, unobtrusive museum. Even so, Kennedy's death had made Dallas, in truth one of the most Republican of cities, renowned as a mecca for Democratic pilgrimage. The Republicans symbolically reclaimed the city by gathering in convention in 1984 to renominate Reagan, the man who in 1960, as a Democrat, had described John Kennedy as a disciple of Karl Marx. During the week when the Republicans were assembled, a fire broke out in the Kennedy museum, seemingly without political cause or connection; priceless Kennedy memorabilia burned.

———✦———

Just as the Democrats liked to talk of themselves as the instrument of social change, yet hearkened whenever possible to the homilies of fifty years before, so the Republicans liked to talk of themselves as representing stability and tradition, yet were the most altered institution in American political life. The party that had nominated Thomas E. Dewey and Dwight D. Eisenhower was no more. That party had favored an equal rights amendment for women, steady if measured progress toward civil rights, and the outlines, at least, of the welfare state. Even Robert Taft, the trademark conservative of the forties and fifties, urged public housing as a basic right of the poor. The party of Taft's time was newly converted to bipartisan internationalism, and leaned to foreign aid rather than military intervention. It was capitalist but enlightened; it was corporate more than entrepreneurial; above all, it valued the Ivy League look and manner and way of doing things, and it overtly mistrusted populist movers and shakers. Its motto might have been *"Noblesse oblige,"* and its ideal candidates were loftily born progressives who had masses of gilt-edged securities and scintillas of egalitarian guilt. Nelson Rockefeller was the prototype of that era's Republican, and Richard Nixon, sweaty, smarmy, and risen from nowhere, was exactly the sort of jumped-up salesman who seemed in many ways better suited by origins to be a Democrat. The Republican party of that era had been the ally of the Wall Street bankers, and the protector of the nascent multinational corporations. The Rockefeller family bank, Chase Manhattan, led the post–World War II march of American capital to governments and enterprises throughout what were then known as backward or undeveloped nations, not yet dignified by the ideological nomenclature Third World. Republicanism was in short the antithesis of western populism. Adherents to that philosophy, perhaps the most enduring in American history (although its "western" center moved erratically south and westward), had been driven into the Democratic party, in uplifting form in the persons of William Jennings Bryan and Lyndon Johnson, and more mean-spiritedly in the racist southern demagogues Theodore Bilbo and George Corley Wallace.

But by 1960, when Nixon defeated Rockefeller for the presidential nomination before Rocky had formally entered the race, the *noblesse oblige* element in the party was already beginning to decline, and populism in both its moral aspects was becoming a Republican phenomenon. Goldwater in 1964 represented the paradigm of the new kind of populist Republican: a Westerner, an ideologue, a career politician; largely self-made; with a hobbyist's interest in technology, aviation, and space, but far less concern for art and culture; and willfully intemperate in voicing opinions that were normally excluded from polite conversation. He thrilled many in his party who had wearied of the barley-water niceties of Wall Street Republicans when he said that the country would be better off if the entire East Coast were sawed off and floated out to sea. Goldwater defeated Rockefeller and then, when the *noblesse oblige* Republicans made their last stand at the convention, he bested a comparably highborn fill-in for Rockefeller, Pennsylvania Governor William Scranton. Although Goldwater lost the election, his coreligionists savored the fresh taste of power and set about planning the ouster from the party of the liberals, the moderates, the Ivy Leaguers, the elite. Like all true revolutionaries, they had patience. They were willing to risk losing seats to the Democrats in the short run in exchange for electing only their own kind of Republicans in the long run. The right-wingers knocked off Senator Charles Goodell of New York in 1970 and Jacob Javits, the state's other liberal Republican, in 1980; both times the party managed to hold the seat only by embracing the state's formally organized Conservative party. They toppled Clifford Case of New Jersey and damaged Millicent Fenwick, a blue-blood Senate nominee there, in 1982; in both instances the party lost a seat it had held or seemed sure to win. The right-wingers targeted Charles Mathias in Maryland, who nonetheless survived, and Edward Brooke of Massachusetts, who weathered a 1978 primary but went down in the general election. Connecticut Republicans tried, but failed, to destroy Lowell Weicker in 1982. Former Attorney General Elliot Richardson, a Watergate hero, seemed a likely Republican victor for the Senate in Massachusetts in 1984; but the right wing in his state was determined to challenge him because he refused to endorse the convention platform, and the rightists would rather have no Republican than a renegade one. The party had even turned on Gerald Ford, who had been the most conservative President since Calvin Coolidge, yet who ranked as some sort of liberal in the minds of latter-day true believers. He came from an urban center, Grand Rapids, and a state, Michigan, that many considered to be economically part of the East. He had gone to Yale Law School; he favored free choice on abortion and the Equal Rights Amendment; and he remained married to a wife who spoke her mind in public.

Time, in a convention-week analysis, contended that the party consisted of five factions:

- *moderates,* such as Weicker, so designated on the questionable theory that neither he nor any other prominent Republicans qualified as liberals
- *"preppies"* such as Vice-President George Bush, who might be conservative on the issues but who shared with the moderates a business orientation, a flexible approach to problem solving, and an Ivy League personal style
- the so-called *pragmatists* of the party's congressional leadership, who were preoccupied with translating the President's theoretical conservatism into practical, workable policy, and who really represented the old-fashioned values of Taft and Ford — balanced budgets, pre-Keynesian economics, and the general interests of midwestern small-city businessmen and their ilk
- the *populist conservatives,* who from a vantage point safely distant from the corridors of power could advocate pie-in-the-sky policies including "supply side" economics, a return to the gold standard, and tax-abated "enterprise zones" in urban areas (to solve the problem of minority unemployment without inflicting quotas on business or public housing projects on suburbs)
- the *religious right,* who blended almost paranoid anticommunism with dictatorial insistence on marriage and family and sexual fidelity, who urged a ban on abortion and promoted prayer in schools, and who endorsed any and all other Christian pieties except, perhaps, charity

The five groups all were present at the convention, but only the latter two, the most extreme, exerted much influence on the rhetoric of the platform and the speechifying on the convention floor. Although Ronald Reagan appeared to be well to the right of the country on most issues, his record was well to the left of the views uttered at the convention by the activist elite of his party. And although Reagan could be guilty of insensitive, intemperate language — he had caused a ruckus early in his first

term when he demanded to know whether it was really news that someone was unemployed out in "South Succotash" — he was never so coarse
and frankly self-indulgent as were his myrmidons assembled in Dallas. At
a Lucullan feast at the spread of oil billionaire Bunker Hunt, singer Pat
Boone laughed off the scandals of the Interior Department and the Environmental Protection Agency with the one-line crack, "Who says we
don't care about the environment? — just feel that air-conditioning."
Television monologist Joan Rivers assured Republican women that
Nancy Reagan's preoccupation with high-priced coiffure, clothes, and
grooming was only proper for a woman, and sneered at the selection of
Geraldine Ferraro with a particularly derisive reference to the Democratic
hero who had been slain in Dallas: "A woman in the White House. Big
deal. John F. Kennedy had a thousand of them." Gloating at the ascendancy of a party that had put money back into style and had diligently
lowered the taxes of the rich, Rivers told an audience of hundreds, at a
lunch honoring Nancy Reagan, "I don't do housework. That's the fun of
being a Republican. You don't have to do housework." The unspoken
punch line was that the Democrats were the party of cleaning ladies.

The combative stridency of the right was directed at the press just as
inimically as at the Democrats — in the minds of many Republican delegates, the two groups were one and the same. Democratic delegates in San
Francisco had turned to gaze into the network anchor booths and wave to
familiar faces. Republicans in Dallas glowered at network reporters on the
floor, insulted and sometimes shoved them as they hustled around trying
to interview party figures. Delegates from heartland states seemed especially hostile. They admonished reporters that they were "guests at a
party," and scolded them for behaving rudely.

The convention schedule had been arranged to balance militantly self-
congratulatory rhetoric with the traditional bands, marching squadrons,
bland entertainment, and a climactic release of fifty thousand balloons —
with young people climbing along perilous catwalks and batting sticks at
the netting to knock the trapped ones down. This was indeed a party, long
and loud and not a little boozy. But in among the horn-blowing and the
funny hats (one woman wore a skimmer topped by an elephant that was
in turn topped by an Uncle Sam *chapeau* in miniature) was candid self-
definition, cunning media manipulation, serious political talk, and full-tilt
jousting for position in determining the party's, and the country's, future.

The nominal keynote speech on the opening night came from Kath-
erine Davalos Ortega, the treasurer of the United States (a high-sounding
but trivial position usually reserved for a woman or minority member).
She had no known gifts as a speaker, and very little to say. She was chosen

to appear because she was female and Hispanic and would provide a suitably earnest yet quiescent contrast to the electricity of Ferraro. The real highlight of the evening, however, was a speech by another woman (and a lifelong registered Democrat), United Nations Ambassador Jeanne Kirkpatrick. Arrogant, acerbic, unforgiving toward her liberal critics, Kirkpatrick had retained her Democratic registration despite White House pleadings that she shift at the convention; she believed that the social programs of the welfare state were here to stay, and that it was a waste of words to talk about massive tax and budget cuts or a radical restructuring of government's priorities. Her concern instead was with the United States' strength in dealing with the rest of the world, and on that score her ferocity exceeded Reagan's. She bargained with the stern inflexibility and table-pounding assurance of any member of the Soviet Politburo, and believed that only iron will, not accommodation, could induce the Soviets and other enemies of America to behave with reason and restraint. She regarded her own party as hopelessly weak — fearful of force, lacking in resolve, unready to face the sorrowful necessity of shedding blood. She knew that Reagan's belligerence was more talk than action: he had been willing to send troops into Grenada, but not Poland or Afghanistan or Nicaragua or Cuba. She was sure that accommodationists dominated the State Department, that pressure was mounting for an arms-control agreement at whatever price, that heightened military spending meant nothing without the determination to fight. Yet she believed that Reagan offered at least the hope of moving the country in the right direction, and the Democrats did not; and, of course, he had given her a high post, while the Democrats would surely offer her none.

Kirkpatrick unloaded with a stingingly precise history lesson that simultaneously set the hard right to cheering, and the more moderate press corps in the hall to nodding in rueful agreement. Citing example after example, she contended that the United States had for too long blamed itself for problems it did not cause, had cast itself as villain in a world in which it still ranked as a comparative exemplar of virtue. "Jimmy Carter looked for an explanation for all these problems and thought he found it in the American people," she said. "But the people knew better. It wasn't malaise we suffered from. It was Jimmy Carter and Walter Mondale." Reagan, she said, had restored national pride and had reclaimed America's dignity in the company of all nations. He had "silenced talk of inevitable American decline and reminded the world of the advantages of freedom." It had become fashionable among intellectuals to refer to the United States and the Soviet Union jointly as "the superpowers," and to equate their behavior on the world stage as comparably self-interested and thus morally equivalent. No assertion could more inflame the sensibilities of conservative patriots: they were sure that the Soviets sought to enslave where the United States sought to liberate, that the Soviets were deceitful where the United States was candid, that the Soviets gloried in bloodshed where the United States acted more in sorrow than in anger. Kirkpatrick agreed with Reagan that history would judge the United States a noble nation, the Soviets a tyrannical one. Her speech rekindled a rationale beyond self-interest for reasserting the justice and stability of the Pax Americana. The delegates gave her almost riotous applause, and more than a few suggested that if she changed parties, she could have a place on the ticket in 1988.

The second day of the convention was devoted to adoption of the platform. This document was largely without meaning: unlike the platforms of European political parties, the purported statement of principles of an American party exerts essentially no influence over its officeholders. The Democrats had fought over their platform as a means of testing strength among Mondale and his fellow stallions Hart and Jackson, each seeking to be herd leader. But the Republicans were tolerating no challenge to their old bull elephant Reagan, and thus no dissent was voiced, let alone voted on, from the convention floor. The party backed a return to the gold standard, an implausible pipe dream of highly uncertain consequences, promoted by the faction that George Bush had once excoriated for "voodoo economics." The platform endorsed a balanced-budget amendment, despite the inability of the party's own President and Senate to hold the annual deficit much below $200 billion, or nearly $1,000 a year for every man, woman, and child in the country. The party backed "voluntary" school prayer, which many of its members privately acknowledged would be coercive, but which would achieve the rightist faction's tacit goal of making America once more a de facto Christian nation; it endorsed tuition tax credits for private and parochial education, which would starve the public schools that serve the poor (and that employ unionized teachers who are overwhelmingly Democratic); it demanded an anti-abortion amendment to the Constitution, and it renewed its 1980 call for scrutiny of all prospective federal judges to be sure they shared the party view on the undesirability of abortion.

Democrats privately conceded that the Supreme Court decisions legalizing abortion had been judicial lawmaking, based on perceived social necessity rather than the principles of the Constitution, but the Republican proposal went to a frightening opposite extreme: judges were to be vetted specifically to ensure that sooner or later their numbers on the Court would be enough to overturn the prior decision. For more than two decades, as the Earl Warren–led Court had issued decision after decision unsettling to Republicans (including the one-man, one-vote rule that smashed their power in many state legislatures), the right wing of the party had wanted to vitiate the traditional role of the Supreme Court as the final arbiter of the Constitution. In proposing that nomination be limited to judges who shared the party's view of abortion, the Republicans were opening the door to real legislative scrutiny of judicial appointments, perhaps even a constitutional amendment to provide for their election — radical alterations to the traditional senatorial review based strictly on nominees' scholarly qualifications to sit on the bench.

The Republican platform reflected to a considerable extent the agenda of the populist conservatives and the preachers, and on the same day it was adopted, the podium was handed over to their foremost representative, Jack Kemp. He had been discussed as a potential President as early as 1976. He had flirted with a candidacy in 1980. He had toyed with the idea of running for senator or governor in New York. And this convention saw him as Bush's only rival to be front-runner for 1988: delegates waved hundreds of signs supporting him, staging the kind of "spontaneous" rally traditionally reserved for a man actually about to be placed in nomination. Kemp had the same regular-guy virility as Reagan. He also shared Reagan's Johnny-come-lately fascination with ideas, not uncommon for an undereducated man who has achieved success as an entertainer (Kemp's was as a pro football quarterback for the Buffalo Bills) and who longs to turn his fame into something more substantial. Kemp was known in his Buffalo district as an assiduous campaigner, in Congress as a tireless (indeed, wearying) advocate of complex, frequently exotic economic treatises. But at the convention he tried instead to enter the world of imagery in which Reagan was so adept. Kemp referred to Carter, whose name was invoked more often at the convention than Mondale's, as "seeming to grow old before our eyes." Reagan, he said, "actually seems to be getting younger." To a party whose delegates included large numbers of the old and self-righteous and rich, nothing was more seductive than to believe that their principles were the fountain of youth. On behalf of an incumbent whose advancing years were almost the only issue Democrats could exploit, nothing would be more helpful than the claim that he had somehow reversed the aging process by intellectual certitude and inner virtue. Kemp, like Kirkpatrick, belittled the Democrats for a lack of manly vigor in the conduct of foreign affairs. He attacked them for opposing the administration's intervention on behalf of what he claimed were fledgling free societies in Central America, and said, "The leaders of the Democratic party aren't soft on communism; they're soft on democracy."

Although Kemp's appearance was the most celebrated, the convention displayed most of the other would-be successors to Reagan. Senate Majority Leader Howard Baker, who was retiring to become a full-time candidate, spoke Monday. Joining Kemp on Tuesday were Senator Robert Dole of Kansas, who unlike Baker believed he could campaign for the White House from within the confines of Washington, and Dole's wife, Elizabeth, a former Ford administration aide and Reagan's secretary of transportation. Like Kemp, each of them had scheduled a ceaseless round of meetings with delegates, power brokers, and the press; when Baker arrived for a midmorning meeting with *Time*, it was his third breakfast of the day, as he noted while ruefully patting the expanding midsection of his diminutive frame. The Doles joked all week about the felicitous coincidence that their convention hotel room was numbered 1988. In conversation and in formal, televised interviews, all the potential aspirants seemed to accept that Kemp would be the likely choice of the hard-right zealots in the party, and that Baker and the Doles and other seekers of moderate support would be competing with the loyalist-in-waiting, Vice-President Bush.

After the shadow warriors had moved through their rites on Tuesday, the true warrior king arrived in Dallas to an elaborate, triumphal reception, not at the convention, but in the fourteen-story atrium of the newly refurbished Loews Anatole Hotel. He assumed for himself the entrepreneurial spirit of the city, pledging "an opportunity society for every man, woman, and child." But he had come to do battle, not to philosophize. "There's an expression you have down this way that I like," Reagan said. "You don't just score victories. You whomp 'em." After that afternoon extravaganza, Reagan retreated to his hotel for an evening celebration of his wife and of his mentor, Barry Goldwater. Nancy Reagan spoke to the convention, almost embarrassingly blandly, then asked the delegates and the American people to "make it one more for the Gipper" and blew kisses to the crowd. Joined by family, including her journalist son, Ron (who had covered the Democrats for *Playboy* and was commenting from Dallas for newspapers), and her previously estranged stepdaughter, Maureen, Mrs. Reagan watched a film celebrating her life. It depicted her kindness to children, her lobbying against drug abuse, her devotion to her husband, and even her brief film career. The highlight was a tender snippet from the one movie the Reagans had made together, the submarine epic *Hellcats of the Navy*, in which their characters, as lovers, talked of the wholesome lives they hoped to lead once the world was again at peace.

The film was displayed on a giant television screen that hung permanently above the speaker's platform, partly to enhance the delegates' views of events, but also to remind them that they were not engaging in private festivity but were staging a show for the nation. Toward the end of Mrs. Reagan's time in the spotlight, as she sat in the presidential box waving to the crowd, the screen displayed a live closed-circuit hookup from the President's hotel room, where in shirt sleeves he sat watching the convention proceedings. She saw him on the big screen; he saw first himself, mirrored on the hotel TV set, then her watching; she waved at him; he saw the wave on the TV set and waved back, expressing intimate affection for his wife to an audience of tens of millions. The moment was heartwarming but also eerie. It was so staged, its reality so layered. It reminded the public, almost flagrantly, that Reagan was a televised image, distant, serene. Like Big Brother, the leader in Orwell's 1984, Reagan manifested himself chiefly as an electronic impulse, an ionized, ethereal stream. He gave the illusion of closeness, familiarity, and all the while secluded himself.

The Reagans that night played the beloved royal family, almost entirely abstracted from ideology. But this was a convention of avid combatants, and the next major speaker was the sternest old soldier of them all. Twenty years earlier, Barry Goldwater had stood before a Republican convention and proclaimed the words that remained in spirit the right wing's rallying cry: "Extremism in the defense of liberty is no vice. Moderation in the pursuit of freedom is no virtue." Goldwater had led the party to disaster in 1964. But he had also shown the tepid me-tooers from Wall Street the road to future triumph. Reagan's presidency was the direct consequence of Goldwater's crusade. The product was the same. Only the salesman was new and improved.

Goldwater, hobbled by age and illness but more outspokenly cantankerous than ever, offered no calming valedictory, no bemused reflection on how America had changed. He shouted out a war cry — the same one, in fact. "Let me remind you," he said in an echo of his 1964 crusade. "Extremism in the defense of liberty is no vice." Some delegates winced; others cheered. He accused the Democrats of starting every American war of the twentieth century, and presented the Republicans as the party that attained peace through strength. He did not hesitate to blast the very Democrats whom Reagan most often invoked as heroes, Roosevelt and Kennedy. Goldwater in effect told the Republican delegates to give no quarter and to take no prisoners, but to strew the battlefield with enemy dead.

Then Reagan's best friend in elective office, Senator Paul Laxalt of Nevada, nominated him. Laxalt's speech described the President's style as "guts with reason," thereby answering those who thought Reagan too aggressive and impulsive, while reminding the public of the supposed timidity of Carter and Mondale. Laxalt's speech had been carefully screened by Reagan's staff; they had entrusted him with much of the bare-knuckles attack that Reagan, inflamed by watching the Democrats in San Francisco, yearned to undertake himself. Laxalt described the Democratic party as "the home of special interests, the social-welfare complex, the antidefense lobby, and the lighter-than-air liberals." The litany was right; but his flat descriptions lacked Reagan's gift for vernacular scorn. No candidate but Reagan was nominated, and the roll call for President and vice-president was combined, in part to save time and stave off boredom, in part to keep any right-wing zealot from proposing an alternative to Bush, most likely Kemp. Missouri put Reagan over the top, and he joshed, "We've been sweating this out."

Reagan emerged into public the next morning at an "ecumenical prayer breakfast" for seventeen thousand people. He swore his allegiance to most of the agenda of the religious right and concentrated his fire on the opponents to resumption of school prayer: "Isn't the real truth that they are intolerant of religion? They refuse to tolerate its importance in our lives." He added that "religion and politics are necessarily related," thus reaching out beyond the evangelicals to the Roman Catholic church, which had been sharply criticized by many Democrats for adding its institutional weight to the anti-abortion cause.

That night, Reagan was introduced to the convention, not by a human being making a speech, but by a film, a sort of extended commercial, in which he extolled himself. NBC ran the whole display on the theory that it was indeed the equivalent of a nominating speech, but CBS and ABC refused to, on the basis that it amounted to free partisan advertising. The distinction between the movie and the rest of the convention, *all* of which had been free partisan advertising, remained unexplained. The climax showed Reagan choking up as he addressed assembled veterans of the D-day invasion in Normandy. The film proved the truth of what had been a common Washington joke: that Reagan's burst of travel in the spring and summer — to China, to his supposed ancestral village in Ireland, to Europe for the D-day commemoration — had been undertaken, not only to provide pretty pictures for the evening newscasts, but to take his ad campaign on location at public expense.

Reagan's acceptance speech amounted to a collection of Las Vegas–style one-liners. Comparing the Democrats to drunken sailors, he said, "would be unfair to drunken sailors — because the sailors are spending their own money." He noted that the Democrats had never met "a tax they didn't like — or hike." He whipped up the crowd to applause, and seemed to be back once again on the dinner circuit, as he had been during the years of political exile, when his only task was to give his paying audience the catharsis of an angry roar. His text rambled, and so, it seemed, did his mind. When he tried to talk of the future, there was no vision, no goal, barely even an evocation of principle.

When Reagan talked of his administration's accomplishments, he spoke only of having slowed the growth of domestic government and having forestalled the spread of communism — one a basically negative policy, the other a blend of luck and an overblown invasion in which the United States played Goliath, not David. Grenada, most predictable of victories, was made to prop up his whole first term. Reagan described the Republicans as a party of "hope, confidence, and growth." But not of plans. Perhaps he was being cagey, avoiding any unnecessary commitments, any entangling political alliances. Yet it seemed more than ever that his vision of the proper role of government was passive, and that he believed the nation's private enterprises could heal all wounds, solve all problems on their own. So intent was Reagan on defining what government should *not* do that he barely indicated what, if anything, government *should* do. Naturally he scarcely talked about the problems his own government had created: the budget deficit, the booby-trapping of U.S. Marines enmeshed in a civil war in Lebanon, his own open-ended commitment to insurrectionist terrorism in Nicaragua.

He made unfair statements, if not outright lies, about his opponents. He said, for example, that "Democratic candidates have suggested that [the invasion of Grenada] be likened to the Soviet invasion of Afghanistan, the crushing of human rights in Poland, or the genocide in Cambodia." This sweeping claim fit Reagan's purpose, to demonstrate that the Democrats lacked proper patriotism, but it was a Big Lie. Walter Mondale, at least, had said no such thing.* Four years of absolute power and six months of intoxicating poll results had taken Reagan out of the realm of political reality: he was telling stories of the kind he used to offer on the campaign trail, lifted from his index file of *Reader's Digest* clips and half-attributed anecdotes, without regard to their accuracy, assuming none but the faithful would be there to hear and tell.

Most unsettling was the ending of his speech. It meandered on about the Olympics and a new spirit of national pride. It invoked the virtues of optimism. But it had no real point, no message. For all the deft management of the convention, all the love-feasting in the hall, Reagan sounded at that moment like an old man who was not quite sure what he wanted to say.

✱ HART AND JACKSON DID

IX

Four More Years

L_ABOR DAY is the traditional beginning of any general election campaign. Summer is considered over, whatever the calendar may say. Families send their children back to school, offices and businesses resume the customary pressure, thoughts turn from ease and indulgence to an awareness that the long year is dwindling into mere weeks. Only then do voters become ready in earnest to consider the choice they must make. The political process shifts from attempts to define each party to an attempt to define and direct the country, and tens of millions who played no role in the partisan debates of spring and summer prepare to exercise their right to choose. No poll taken before Labor Day is given full faith and credit by professional politicians, no matter how one-sided the people's preference seems to be. Whatever their offhand opinion, their impulse, the voters have not yet really made up their minds.

In the heyday of the labor movement, the presidential campaign used to begin in Detroit, the home of the United Auto Workers, the quintessential image of the noble union, working in the archetypal American industry. Either or both parties' candidates would make a public speech to a rally of tens of thousands, and simultaneously to a radio audience of tens of millions. In those not-so-distant times, Labor Day was really a celebration of labor, as Independence Day was truly a celebration of independence. But in 1984 the auto industry was battered, almost discredited, and the labor movement had become more of a political burden than a coveted ally. With the help of the modern technology of aviation, and to attract the attention of the modern technology of television, Walter Mondale hopscotched across America on Labor Day. But he did not stop in Detroit.

He began in New York City, where at his insistence a union-sponsored parade began at 9:00 A.M. The hour was convenient for his master plan for the day, but too early for city dwellers who were returning from a weekend away, or even for those who wanted only to savor sleeping in on a holiday. The crowd was embarrassingly small — CBS News called it "puny." Even New York City Mayor Edward Koch could not be bothered to come in from the beach and so was not there to welcome Mondale and march by his side.

Mondale next headed to Merrill, Wisconsin, a midwestern village of the kind he grew up in, a meticulously chosen contrast to Detroit. His host, Representative David Obey, warmed up the crowd by saying, "When the sun comes out in Merrill, the Democrats are going to win." Moments later, it began to drizzle.

Then Mondale flew out to Long Beach, California, a town in Ronald Reagan's home territory, to demonstrate that the Democrats would concede nothing to him at the outset of the race. As Mondale tried to speak, his sound system failed three times. Humiliated by their own bad planning on the East Coast and by a stroke of pure chance in the Midwest, Mondale's frustrated staffers were ready to believe that sabotage had caused the day's third calamity. Their dark suspicions were never proved.

But whatever the causes of Mondale's misspent day, it was all the more galling because for Reagan everything went right. He felt no need to dissipate his energies on some grueling coast-to-coast display. He made one major appearance, in San Jose, at the southern end of the prosperous peninsula in California that calls itself Silicon Valley. The nickname derives from the chemical element that is essential to the making of computer microchips; the region has luxuriated in a high-tech boom economy, offering jobs galore for the skilled and educated. Behind Reagan a giant signboard proclaimed, SILICON VALLEY CELEBRATES / AMERICA IS WORKING AGAIN / LABOR DAY 1984. That exuberant sentiment did not apply, of course, to the many native-born semiliterates, nor to many of the immigrants from Mexico, nor to the other Americans not mentally equipped to adapt to the new order of things; but then, those misfortunates were not much in evidence around Silicon Valley. The area paid for its prosperity with some of the highest housing prices and lowest vacancy rates in America. The poor, the unemployable, those whom the future was leaving behind, had long since left. To the fifty thousand people at the rally, Reagan claimed credit for the nation's renewed prosperity. And he promised an even brighter light to come. Smiling that crinkly grin of a grandfather with a present behind his back, Reagan shouted, "You ain't seen nothin' yet."

Reagan's advisers had come out of Dallas more sure than ever that their man would saunter to victory, less because of what he was doing right than because of what the Democrats were doing wrong. Ferraro's troubles, climaxing in her press conference on the second day of the Republican convention, had slammed the brakes on Mondale's momentum. Her anguish, moreover, had prompted Mondale virtually to drop from sight until her fate was resolved. Thus he wasted valuable time and, worse, lost the appearance of courage and leadership. Once again, he had dared to be cautious.

At the convention, a succession of Reagan operatives had told reporters on the record that they anticipated a "landslide." Richard Wirthlin, who was the President's official pollster (although Robert Teeter was doing much of the campaign work), said he believed Reagan was ahead by as much as forty percentage points in most of the South, and seemed comparably uncatchable in the West. Wirthlin ticked off Midwest and Northeast states that Reagan seemed likely to carry, and described none as beyond his reach. White House political director Ed Rollins had much the same message. And independent sources confirmed they were right. In Massachusetts, for example, which in 1972 had been the one state that had stayed loyal to the Democrats under McGovern, the 1984 polls consistently had shown Reagan significantly ahead. In New York, in Pennsylvania, even in Michigan, where unemployment was probably the worst in the nation, Reagan was either leading or only marginally behind. Mondale had no more secret weapons, the Reagan team reasoned: Ferraro and the tax-raising gambit had caught them off guard, but they doubted Mondale had the cunning or originality to come up with some further telling stroke.

Mondale's side conceded the difficulty of beating Reagan, but had at least five theories of how it could happen. First was the gut conviction Mondale had felt ever since deciding to run in 1980 — that in its soul, America remained a Democratic nation, and thus would sooner or later come home to its natural party. Second was the belief that women would desert Reagan and the Republicans by the millions, because in the privacy of the voting booth they would not be able to resist the pleasure of voting for Ferraro, one of their own. Third was the calculation that the millions of newly registered black and Hispanic voters deeply feared Reagan's budget policies and hard line on immigration, and therefore would be motivated to vote in a higher ratio than the white average, even though historically minorities tended to vote less often. Fourth was a hope, at times a near certitude, that Mondale could reach beyond the poor into the prosperous middle class by sounding the alarm on budget and trade deficits and on nuclear arms control. Even prosperous people who looked to government for little, if any, material help would count on their leaders to preserve a healthy business climate and a secure future. Fifth was an unexpressed hope that Reagan might do something disastrous, or have something disastrous befall him: he was nearly seventy-four, he had been losing touch with the world outside the White House, and he had not had to campaign vigorously for four years. Particularly if he agreed to debate, Mondale might catch him off step.

None of these calculations was based strictly on a state-by-state analysis. Traditionally, politicians have thought of a national election as fifty different state elections, each conducted on a winner-take-all basis when it came to the real point of the matter, the electoral college vote. To dope out the likely result of a presidential race, they typically draw up a list of states and methodically denote each as belonging to one or the other candidate, or as undecided. Mondale's strategies meant that he would not be running geographically, but demographically. State by state, he needed far too many lucky breaks to have a chance to win. Only some transforming event, cutting across the nation, seemed likely to save him. But each of the transforming events he envisioned was plausible enough to come to pass. Conversely, some transforming demographic event that worked in Reagan's favor could put the election totally beyond reach.

———✧———

Of all the consequences that Mondale envisioned when he chose Geraldine Ferraro, an Italian and a Roman Catholic, to join him on the ticket, surely the one he never imagined was that she would involve his party in a slanging match with the hierarchy of her church, and thus in all likelihood lose rather than gain Catholic votes. But just that grim situation faced Mondale immediately after Labor Day, as the campaign began with a full-scale debate on pluralism, particularly in religion.

Mondale believed that Reagan had been allowed for too long to have it both ways in his dealings with Jerry Falwell and other fundamentalists. If Reagan wished to curry their favor and tacitly endorse their plan to make America a Christian nation, so be it; but in Mondale's view Reagan then deserved to be called to account before the majority of Americans who prefer religion to be a private, noncoercive matter. Mondale spoke up partly from political calculation, but also from personal conviction. He described himself as deeply religious, but he viewed with mistrust people who wore their piety as a sort of vainglorious public display; to him, such people were not practicing religion, but committing a particularly repellent form of the sin of pride. Mondale admired the tradition that made local churches consciences of the community: counselors to the troubled and sick and poor, ministers of material help to the needy, centers of fellowship and sharing. He seemed repelled by the religious figures Reagan had gathered around him: television evangelists, pulpit entertainers, advocates of a "personal relationship with God." In the view of the organized churches that Mondale admired, these TV preachers diverted money and time and attendance from humble parish chapels to religion practiced as a feel-good corporate enterprise. Mondale regarded their theology as singularly lacking in good works.

Mondale chose carefully the scene of his confrontation with Reagan: an international convention of the Jewish fraternal and service group B'nai B'rith. Jews had long mistrusted the Bible Belt evangelicals whom Reagan favored. Most of the evangelicals preached that Jews were unenlightened, even doomed to Hell. Of late, Falwell and some other fundamentalists had backed Israel on the grounds that it was anti-Communist and, in the post–Iran crisis era, desirably anti-Islamic. But some of the very preachers who urged aid to Israel did so in the fanatical conviction that a literal, biblical day of Armageddon would come soon, probably in the Middle East, and that this final battle would wipe out the Jews anyway, leaving a Christian planet. Mondale played deftly on the Jewish fear, instilled through centuries of peril and exclusion, of being counted as undesirable or even seditious merely because they were different. "No President should attempt to transform policy debates into theological disputes," Mondale said. "He must not let it be thought that political dissent from him is un-Christian. And he must not cast opposition to his programs as opposition to America." He quoted from a letter by Senator Paul Laxalt, Reagan's close friend and campaign chairman. Laxalt told Christian leaders that Reagan's backers in the faith were "leaders under God's authority." Mondale twisted the literal meaning — but not the spirit — of Laxalt's letter to claim that Reagan had indeed merged church and state. "Most Americans would be surprised," Mondale said, "to learn that God is a Republican." He quoted from the politicized homiletics of various "Christian" and "family" groups, which imposed a religious judgment on such plainly secular issues as the proposed nuclear arms freeze, and recommended how the faithful should vote. Then Mondale brought the argument back to the emotional anxieties of Jewish leaders: he reminded them that Reagan wished to restore school prayer, which meant, undeniably, Christian prayer. Many of those listening had attended public schools in the days of prayer, and most of them had felt shamed and excluded in their school days because they did not participate in prayer, or worse, had felt faithless to their inner convictions because they had succumbed to peer pressure and joined in.

Reagan appeared before the B'nai B'rith just hours later. Characteristically he tried to maintain that he had not been saying what all America had heard him say. Claiming credit not only for economic health and peace but also for a "new spiritual awareness in this country," Reagan asserted that heightened religious involvement would lead to greater mutual respect among faiths. He praised the traditional separation of church and state: "Every single American is free to choose and practice his or her religious beliefs or to choose no religion at all. Their rights shall not be questioned or violated by the state." As if in indirect acknowledgment of the inconsistency between what he had been saying to evangelicals and what he was saying to Jews, Reagan sidestepped any mention of the school-prayer amendment he sought to attach to the Constitution. Perhaps Reagan had been at his most honest a few days before, when attempting to explain away his pulpit-thumping at the Republican convention. Questioned by journalists, he said, "Well, I was only talking about it because I was speaking at a prayer breakfast." The remark all but amounted to a confession from a cynical old performer that he suited every performance to his audience, and never expressed his own true feelings at all.

———

Most observers, particularly in the secular media, thought Mondale had much the better of the exchange with the B'nai B'rith. And on narrow debater's grounds, he did. But his instruction to the religious world to stay out of politics was exactly what the Democrats' erstwhile allies in the Catholic hierarchy had not wanted to hear. After years of publicly admonishing parishioners to "render unto Caesar what is Caesar's" — the early Christian phrase that had latterly been interpreted as an instruction to abide by temporal authority, so long as it permits free practice of religion — the Roman Catholic bishops and their priests had become increasingly assertive during the past decade or two. Priests had joined the fight against the Vietnam war, had confronted right-wing oligarchies in Latin America, had lobbied for social services for the poor. Toward this avowedly political activity, the church had at first been neutral, then actively supportive. In the mid-1970s, Boston's Humberto Cardinal Medeiros, among other church leaders, had testified before the Massachusetts legislature on behalf of school busing for racial integration and, even more surprising, civil rights protection for homosexuals in housing and employment. During Reagan's first term, the Catholic bishops had collectively endorsed nuclear arms control and a whole host of specific peacekeeping measures, including aspects of the proposed nuclear freeze. Like most liberals, Mondale had tacitly welcomed this involvement on the part of the church, even though it threatened to violate the traditional presumption of separation between church and state.

Balanced against these liberal gestures, however, was the church's increasing intransigence on two matters the Democratic party could not accommodate. One was the church's inflexible opposition to abortion, except as a by-product of saving the prospective mother's life. The other, only slightly less fervently advocated, was some sort of tuition subsidy for students in Catholic and other religious schools. Opposition to abortion was to Catholics a matter of fundamental theology. But both it and the tuition subsidy were also vitally important organizing tools for preserving the church. As American Catholics had assimilated into suburban life in the postwar era, many of them had fallen away from the church. They rarely resigned. They simply stopped attending Mass. The church seemed less relevant to them, and it set them apart from Protestant neighbors. Church officials had worried openly about the slippage in attendance, and about a decline in what they called "vocations" — the choice by young people to become priests or nuns. Then, almost by accident, the church had discovered that opposition to abortion still aroused fervor among many otherwise indifferent Catholics. Part of the reason was a direct belief in the sanctity of life. But another part was a deep resentment and disgust at the whole sexual revolution, at the notion that intimacy was free and easy, and that pregnancy, the traditional "price" to be paid for dalliance, no longer need trouble a woman who sinned. The use of abortion as a form of *post facto* birth control embarrassed even the advocates of choice; in the eyes of the beleaguered defenders of chastity, it appeared as an abomination.

The proposed tuition tax credit for sending children to parochial schools had far less emotional immediacy than the abortion issue. But the tax credit would help parents who already sought to perpetuate the church through the indoctrination of their children, and it might encourage others, particularly in areas where the public schools were laggard, to bring their children into classrooms where the church could induct them into the faith. Some church officials candidly admitted that the tax credit would amount to a state subsidy of religion. But they added that the Catholic schools, which enrolled a significant percentage of the total school population in many East Coast cities, were already in effect subsidizing the state by performing its educational duty for it.

Catholic politicians often departed from the church's teachings on abortion and, less consequentially, on aid to parochial schools. If they represented multifaith districts or aspired to higher office, they commonly found it prudent to echo the formula offered by Senator Edward Kennedy: he personally opposed abortion, he said, but he felt that both procreation and religion were private matters, and he would not presume to impose his belief on someone else. This theoretical neutrality had unavoidable practical implications, however. Kennedy and those who agreed with him not only opposed a constitutional amendment to ban abortion; they also favored spending public money to enable abortions for the poor, on the egalitarian theory that rich and poor alike should have the same medical opportunities. Up until 1984, the church had tolerated such voting in laypersons, although not in the clergy. Father Robert Drinan, a Jesuit who represented suburban Boston in Congress for several terms, had eventually been forced to resign by the church authorities in Rome, ostensibly as part of a larger drive against electioneering by the clergy, but in fact to rebuke him for countering the church's dictum on abortion.

By 1984, the Catholic hierarchy seemed ready to extend its harassment to the laity who held public office. New York City's Archbishop John O'Connor had begun to contend in public that it was inconsistent, even "irresponsible," for Catholic officeholders to claim they endorsed church teachings if they failed to reflect them in their public conduct.

Just after Labor Day, seventeen New England bishops released a statement expressing similar sentiments. Its crucial line: "To evade this issue of abortion under the pretext that it is a matter pertaining exclusively to private morality is obviously illogical." O'Connor took matters a step further: he said that he did not see how Catholics could in good conscience vote for church members whose public records contravened the teachings of the church. O'Connor may have been motivated by worldly matters as well as ecclesiastical. An arrogant, humorless, and excessively ambitious conservative, he had long enjoyed dabbling in the politics of the country as well as those of the church. He had ardently supported Richard Nixon and made scant secret of his comfort with the idea of another Republican in the White House.

Ferraro plainly thought he was trying to sandbag her for partisan purposes. She barely controlled her anger the next week when O'Connor told reporters at an anti-abortion convention in Altoona, Pennsylvania, that she had "said some things about abortion relative to Catholic teaching which are not true." He made the charge worse by failing to clarify it at first. It turned out that his attack was prompted by a letter that Ferraro had sent to other House members in 1982, quoting various Catholic scholars and activists to demonstrate that there was a wide variety of opinion about abortion within the church. To O'Connor, "the church" consisted solely of the hierarchy in which he played such a prominent role. No mere parishioner, or even a theologian or priest, was entitled to speak out against the divinely ordained view of the church leadership, and Ferraro was to be chastised for pretending that such dissent could be valid. Ferraro demanded, "Why is this letter coming out now of all times?" O'Connor's lack of a candid answer amounted to admitting the obvious: because he hoped to wreck her campaign, and thereby scare all other Catholic officeholders into lockstep compliance with the church. That same week, as if to prove beyond doubt that the church officially preferred a nonmember whose views were congenial to a Catholic who dared to think for herself, O'Connor's colleague John Cardinal Krol of Philadelphia cohosted an exuberant reception for Reagan at a shrine in Doylestown, Pennsylvania, where he applauded the President for urging aid to religious schools.

Some of Ferraro's fellow Catholic officeholders leaped to her defense. Edward Kennedy and New York Governor Mario Cuomo recognized that the church harassment she faced might soon be visited upon them, and both spoke on her behalf. Cuomo journeyed to the emotional center of American Catholicism, the University of Notre Dame in South Bend, Indiana, to debate for nearly an hour the pros and cons of attempting to make America by law a more Catholic society. Cuomo argued for government by coexistence and consensus, for stability of law and for individual conscience. Above all he contended that the church best serves its own interests by tolerating laws, for example those permitting divorce and birth control, that may be more permissive than its own beliefs, but that reflect the general moral norm. To seek greater restriction would be to risk, at worst, backlash; at best, massive defiance of the law. Either way, both church and state would be diminished. Cuomo contended that he, not O'Connor, represented the wisdom of tradition and history: "The church in this country has never retreated into a moral fundamentalism that will settle for nothing less than total acceptance of its views." He implied, but did not say directly, that the major difference between abortion, which the church found unbearable, and divorce and birth control, to which it was reconciled, had little to do with the received word of God but much to do with self-interest and organizing tactics. To insist that church teaching be translated into civil law, Cuomo noted, has always been "not a matter of doctrine [but] a matter of prudential political judgment."

Once again, the Democrats were judged to have had the better of the intellectual debate. But the utter, irredeemable failure was that the confrontation had taken place at all. The Catholic "ethnics" whom Ferraro was supposed to help attract had been led by O'Connor to think of her as a disobedient churchwoman, presuming to defy the patriarchal leadership. In effect they had been made to think that Ferraro was not a "real" Catholic. The Democrats, who had set out to portray themselves as the true friends of traditional religious freedom against a cynical and expedient President, found themselves instead being viewed as the enemies of religion in public life. They were already the party of the pot smokers, the homosexuals, the couples living together without matrimony — all those whom down-home Americans thought of as sinners. In asserting that God should not dominate politics and that government is a separate kingdom, the Democrats had once again ceded to Reagan the spiritual realm in national public life. The faith that America was God's chosen nation had long been a bipartisan belief. The whole sorry debate on religion in early September helped convince all too many Americans that the Democrats no longer cared whether the country enjoyed God's protection. Even the inert, nonchurchgoing majority in America might not be quite ready emotionally for the end result — accepting that the United States was, spiritually, just another country among many.

Having failed to damage Reagan by pleading for religious pluralism, Mondale shifted his focus back to the mainstay Democratic case, the case for fairness. Faced with an election that seemed by conventional measures unwinnable — three post–Labor Day polls showed him trailing by thirteen to sixteen percentage points — Mondale decided to defy conventional political wisdom. The most basic tenet of campaigning dictates that candidates must vow to hold the line on taxes, and to protect any and all beloved social programs, if only as an earnest sign of good intentions. Should it be inescapably apparent that new taxes must be levied, the candidate is supposed to foster the illusion that some shadowy, unnamed other people, not the common citizenry, will be the ones to pay. Mondale would have none of it. He believed the American people wanted to be asked for sacrifice, yearned to be summoned to show common sense and restraint. So he unveiled a deficit-cutting plan and challenged Reagan to do the same.

The preoccupation with deficits was a newfound Democratic concern. For decades, the Democrats had been the party of Keynesian economics, regarding government overspending as a humane, even healthy way to stimulate job development. It was the Democrats who had devised the shell-and-pea game of the "full employment balanced budget" — a bit of number-crunching to prove that a sizable deficit would really amount to a surplus if only "normal" (that is, unattainably low) unemployment levels were prevailing. As a senator, Mondale had happily voted year after year for unbalanced budgets. So had nearly all of his partisan colleagues. What made the Reagan deficit so different? The Democrats commonly cited four factors.

First was its sheer size. Even allowing for inflation, the total had reached record proportions for peacetime; the fastest-growing item in the federal budget was "debt service," the interest owed on the accumulated national debt. Without some sort of intervention, the deficit threatened in time to change basic relationships between the public and private sectors, both in the percentage of gross national product consumed by government and in the availability and cost of loans to business enterprises that had to compete with government in the credit markets.

Second was the nature of the deficit: most of its growth was attributed by Democrats to the tax cuts that Reagan had granted to middle- and upper-income taxpayers and to the increases he had ordered in the defense budget. By using the deficit as an excuse, the Democrats could attempt to supplant Reagan's policies and priorities with their own.

Third was the impact of the deficit on interest rates. Democrats had accepted the Republican axiom that budget deficits cause inflation, just at the moment when Republicans were abandoning that belief in the face of new evidence: while Reagan's administration had run up record deficits year after year, inflation had fallen to less than half its peak during the Carter years. Nonetheless, the Democrats envisioned a vicious cycle of self-perpetuation: higher deficits driving up interest rates, which would drive up the cost of debt service, which in turn would drive the deficit up further. Cutting the deficit, the Democrats said, would set in motion a similar synergy, but in reverse.

Fourth was a conviction that the budget deficit was somehow linked to the record shortfall in the balance of payments between imports to the United States and exports from it. The weakness in exports meant a loss of American markets abroad; the strength of imports meant foreign competition for American products; both translated into a loss of jobs, as Mondale's union supporters tirelessly pointed out.

There was at best scant evidence that the general public shared Mondale's worry about the deficit. Perhaps the only group comparably exercised about it were far-right-wing Republicans, who would never consider voting for Mondale. Polls indicated that voters found the deficit an abstraction; to them, the more meaningful measures of prosperity were prices in the stores and at the gasoline pump, the stability of jobs, the frequency and size of salary rises, the cost of interest on loans to buy a house or car. Mondale tried in speech after speech to explain how the federal budget deficit connected to all these other concerns. But it was like teaching a surgical anatomy chart to kindergartners.

Mondale's proposal renewed the pledge in his convention acceptance speech to raise taxes: he proposed to do so for more than half the U.S.

population. He simultaneously vowed to clamp down on previously sacrosanct aid to farmers and to elderly recipients of Medicare health funding.
(He also proposed wiping out the three most celebrated new weapons sys-
tems for the Pentagon: the B-1 bomber, which had been under debate
since Jimmy Carter had first run for President, eight years before; the MX
missile installation, which even proponents acknowledged might well be
obsolete before it was ever completed; and Reagan's pet proposal, a
space-based antimissile defense system vernacularly known as "Star
Wars." None of these proposals attracted much critical attention from
Reagan or the press, who remained preoccupied with Mondale's star-
tlingly specific, and punitive, tax plan.) In all, Mondale's proposed budget
changes amounted to a theoretical two-thirds cut in the projected deficit
by fiscal year 1989, and even allowed for substantial new spending on traditional Democratic concerns, education and make-work jobs programs.

There were two hitches to the Mondale plan. One was that by far his
biggest "spending cut" was a presumed drop in the cost of debt service as
a result of a projected decline in interest rates on government borrowing.
His calculations were plausible enough — but they were still guesswork.

The other shortcoming of his plan was the widespread and substantial
amount of tax increase that he put forward. His levy had three facets. The
first was a proposal to take back some of the "indexation" protection that
Congress had enacted to keep taxpayers from being pushed by inflation
alone into higher-percentage tax brackets, without any increase in real income. The indexation law had been meant to eliminate the government's
self-interest in preserving inflation as an unending source of ever-increasing
revenue, which had been heavily exploited during the Carter years. Mondale proposed instead to permit full indexation only for families whose incomes fell below $25,000 a year, roughly the national average — families
who do not normally pay much in taxes anyway. For incomes beyond that
modest level, indexation was to be limited to the amount by which inflation exceeded 4 percent. This constituted a steepening of the graduation
in income-tax rates, at a time when the innovative thinkers of both parties
were exploring the idea of flattening the graduation rate instead, in hopes
that allowing people to keep more of their earnings would stimulate them
to produce more.

Mondale's other two proposals were classic liberal Democratic bids to
"soak the rich." He proposed another tax increase of two to three percentage points on adjusted gross incomes of more than $60,000, a sum gar-
nered by only about 5 percent of all households, and a further surcharge
of 10 percent of the tax liability on all adjusted gross incomes of more
than $100,000.

Mondale's proposals were intended to polarize the populace, to aggravate resentment toward the haves among the have-nots. The candidate hoped to stimulate the poorer half of the country's citizens by giving them a chance to burden the rich half. But there were several distinct disadvantages to this strategy. Class resentments had diminished considerably during Reagan's tenure, perhaps because of his rhetoric about America as an "opportunity society." Moreover, the poorer half of the country was by and large likely to vote for Mondale fairly solidly, if it voted at all. The Democrats' chief hope for gain lay among middle-class voters who were disaffected from the Republicans on social issues. One of the largest subgroups in this category was Gary Hart's erstwhile "Yuppies." Because they were generally college educated and living in two-income households, the Yuppies often had incomes high enough to be hit by Mondale's tax proposals — and if they were not yet in that elite bracket, many hoped or dreamed that they soon would be. Mondale's plan had a philosophical shortcoming beyond its lack of appeal for the rising well-to-do: it once again conceded to Reagan the high ground of optimism. He permitted Reagan to be the advocate of solving economic problems through growth and job development. Mondale assumed for himself the traditional Democratic posture of resolving problems through redistribution, through robbing Peter to pay Paul.

Reagan deftly conveyed this message in a campaign swing just after the tax proposals were offered. At a high school in Endicott, New York, Reagan asserted, "The American people aren't undertaxed. The government in Washington is overfed. The main difference between ourselves and the other side is: we see an America where every day is the Fourth of July. They see an America where every day is April 15." This perception of the election as a choice between pleasure and duty was already widespread. In a much-quoted line that alluded to the indomitable cheerfulness of a beer advertising campaign, *New Republic* political analyst Sydney Blumenthal had written, "Reagan is Miller Time, Mondale is the factory whistle." Mondale went on calling people back to the hard work of solving the nation's problems. But they did not seem ready to punch the clock.

———

Phase three of Mondale's assault was to have shifted to the issue of peace. He had found crowds responsive all year to his lament at the lack of progress toward nuclear arms control. He believed that people feared Reagan's belligerence, especially if he became a second-term President, unbound from the political constraints of having to seek reelection. Mondale sensed that the repeated horrors in Beirut — three fatal bombings of

U.S. facilities in eighteen months, each aggravated by inadequate security precautions — could persuade people that Reagan was mismanaging the nation's defenses. And he was heartened by polls showing that the public believed the Pentagon budget could safely be cut without encouraging Soviet misbehavior abroad. In all, the peace plank seemed the most viable basis for challenging Reagan.

But no sooner had Mondale prepared his onslaught than the Kremlin and the White House announced news that took some of the fight out of him: Reagan was going to upstage anything Mondale could say by holding his first-ever meeting as President with a senior Soviet official. Foreign Minister Andrei Gromyko, who had bypassed the United Nations General Assembly meeting the year before because of deteriorating relations with the United States, had decided to come in 1984. He would meet with Reagan, who planned to visit New York City to address the General Assembly. Gromyko would then journey to the White House for a substantive, lengthy meeting to discuss the possible resumption of assorted arms negotiations.

This news astonished most of the world. It was not surprising that Reagan, an astute politician, should want to make a gesture of amity during the final weeks of a presidential campaign. But it was utterly unexpected that the Soviet Politburo, who were widely believed to fear and despise Reagan, should agree to a diplomatic encounter that could only help his chances for reelection. One explanation was that the Soviets might find Reagan in a more conciliatory mood, might even extract real concessions in exchange for a specific starting date for negotiations. Another was that the Soviets simply wanted to reestablish a working relationship and judged that this gesture would win Reagan's gratitude. Either way, the message from Red Square to the American electorate seemed clear: even Reagan's enemies in the Kremlin assumed he was bound to win the election.

Mondale put in a bid for his own meeting with Gromyko and received a commitment for the day before the White House session. But that could hardly compensate for the favorable publicity that the visit would bestow on Reagan as the incumbent. Indeed, Mondale had to be careful not to appear to impede the talks between Reagan and Gromyko, or he, not the President, would be accused of subordinating world peace to personal political ambition.

Weeks one and two of the campaign had focused above all on religion; week three, on money. Week four revolved around Gromyko. It began with the arrival of Reagan at the United Nations to host a Sunday-night reception for delegates to the fall general session — a period when major officials of dozens of countries, particularly in the Third World, come to mingle, make speeches, and enjoy the expense-account life in Manhattan. Among the more than two hundred guests at Reagan's reception, Gromyko was the ninth to pass through the receiving line; he and Reagan shook hands and chatted for twenty-three seconds. Gromyko referred to Reagan's scheduled speech to the General Assembly the next day and asked, half joking, half belligerent, "How many arrows will you shoot at me tomorrow?" Reagan assured him there would be none.

The President proved true to his word. His speech was conciliatory and almost above the fray. It was also probably his best speech of the year, and in some ways the most remarkable of his presidency: after decades of berating the accommodationist tone of the customary bipartisan American foreign policy, Reagan endorsed it. After long condemning détente, he proposed a virtually total program of collaboration between the United States and the Soviet Union to achieve arms control, quell regional wars, apportion security interests in the world's tension spots, and even exchange "five-year military plans for weapons development." In effect he urged joint administration of the affairs of the rest of the world — a partnership in which the superpowers would ensure their own security at the potential expense of the freedom of smaller, restive nations. He made scarcely any reference to Soviet aggression. Rather than lambaste the Kremlin's financing of revolutionary governments in Cuba and Nicaragua, or its ties to rebel groups in El Salvador, Reagan simply quoted disciples of peace, including Mahatma Gandhi and Saint Ignatius Loyola. The closest he came to genuine confrontation with Gromyko, who sat stonefaced in the audience throughout the speech, was to call for "a negotiated outcome" to the conflict in Afghanistan; even then, Reagan did not mention the fact that the Soviets had been occupying the country since 1979. In one passage, Reagan appealed to Gromyko directly, almost by name. "There is not a great distance between us," he said. "There is every reason why we should do all that is possible to shorten that distance."

The delivery was vintage Reagan: the soft voice and gently shaking head for grandfatherly passages, the jut-jawed frown and staccato rhythm for the phrases reminding the world that America had begun to rearm. He read smoothly, mellifluously from the TelePrompTer, without a fluff or miscue. He made every word fit the natural cadences of his speech, and it all sounded as if it came from the heart. He had rarely if ever been more persuasive, more inspiring. He seemed to have the stature of the Leader of the Free World, the traditional epithet bestowed on Presidents. He reminded the world that it was the Soviets, not the Americans, who had walked out on arms negotiations, and he affirmed that the United States waited welcomingly for their resumption.

Journalists might reasonably have raised questions about Reagan's authenticity. What had happened to the rhetoric about the Evil Empire? What had happened to the admonitions that negotiation with the Soviets was all but pointless, because Communists could not be trusted to keep their agreements? What had happened to that joshing proposal just a few weeks before, in a warm-up for a speech — when Reagan thought the microphone hookup was off in the pressroom — that he just declare the Soviet Union had no right to exist, and start bombing five minutes later? Perhaps, as his aides suggested, he simply felt that the United States had been too weak before to consider serious arms control, but could now bargain effectively, from a position of strength. It seemed more likely that he was either intellectually inconsistent or emotionally insincere; that he was expediently talking about peace to a peace organization, just as he had talked about religion at a prayer breakfast. If ever there had been a moment to disbelieve in Reagan's fundamental integrity, to wonder aloud whether he was simply a cynical power-seeker who would sacrifice ideology to enhance a sales pitch, it was that day at the United Nations. Yet that was not the news as reported by the networks; it was not even the emphasis in the main story of the *New York Times,* incomparably the shrewdest American news organization on foreign policy. The story, instead, was that Reagan had spoken for cooperation and peace.

Mondale made a speech the next day in which he questioned Reagan's honesty: "After four years of sounding like Ronald Reagan, six weeks before the election he is trying to sound like Walter Mondale. . . . My dad was a Methodist minister and he once told me, 'Son, be skeptical of deathbed conversions.' I asked why. And he said, 'Because sometimes they get well on you.' " Even this deft thrust failed to popularize the idea that Reagan was a fraud: what had worked against Gary Hart, the unknown, would not work against Reagan, the familiar and beloved.

Two days after Mondale's retort, Gromyko gave his own United Nations speech, and he made plain that he either ignored or disbelieved most of Reagan's friendly approaches. "The tug-of-war between the groups that determine U.S. foreign policy," he said, "has been won by the militarily minded. . . . All we hear is that strength, strength, and above all strength is the guarantee of international peace. In other words, weapons, weapons, and still more weapons." In negotiations, he said, "everything the U.S. side says is intended to secure unilateral advantages for the United States. Therefore, from the very outset things are doomed to failure."

Despite this rhetoric, Mondale professed to find Gromyko predisposed toward resuming negotiations. After meeting with him for ninety minutes, Mondale said, "I believe there is an opportunity to make significant progress." By this device, Mondale hoped to suggest to reporters and voters that there was a real chance for specific accomplishments to be made during Reagan's meeting with Gromyko, and that the absence of such advances would be proof of Reagan's inflexibility or ineptitude. Mondale made sure to point out that he had told Gromyko that Reagan spoke for all Americans; he dared not risk being accused of sabotaging the negotiations by hinting of the possibility of a better deal after November.

According to reports in *Time* and elsewhere, attributed to unnamed sources, the White House meeting between Gromyko and Reagan had much of the character of a running debate, or even an argument. The two men were alone for only eight minutes, and were described as "gesticulating" by observers who saw them through a window. Much of the rest of the time, they were exchanging formal positions before a dozen or more senior diplomats and aides. Reagan told Gromyko that the Soviet Union was an aggressive, expansionist nation; Gromyko told Reagan that the United States was the source of most of the tension in the world. If any agreement was reached to resume negotiations on arms issues, no hint of it leaked from the participants, then or later. In his weekly radio address, Reagan called the talk "useful," which is diplomatic jargon for "combative and dubiously productive." That was not much of an achievement. But it was more than enough to overshadow Walter Mondale.

A minor foreign policy coda reverberated through the news during the week. On the night he gave his United Nations party, Reagan committed a gaffe that could easily have turned into a central issue of the campaign, except that it was supplanted — in a further proof of Reagan's characteristic luck — by the sustained focus of the press on his dealings with Gromyko. The problem started when Reagan met briefly with reporters and answered questions about security provisions at the United States embassy in East Beirut, which had just been bombed. Scheduled improvements in protection had not been in place, Reagan conceded, when a truck loaded with explosives pulled past concrete barriers to within thirty feet of the embassy's front door; the truck blew up and at least thirteen people were killed. Explaining away the apparently fatal delay in securing the embassy, Reagan said, in a typically homely analogy, "Anyone that's ever had their kitchen done over knows that it never gets done as soon as you wish it would."

A couple of days later, in answer to questions from a student at a campaign rally in Bowling Green, Ohio, Reagan appeared to blame the security snafus on the alleged "near destruction of our intelligence capability" by his predecessor, Jimmy Carter. The callousness and unfairness of these remarks prompted attacks from Mondale and Ferraro. Mondale said, "That's the problem right there. Being President and countering terrorists is a much more difficult task than fixing up the kitchen." Ferraro said Reagan had failed in his duties as commander in chief.

For once, the Democrats did not stand alone. Journalists hit harder at Reagan than any Democrat could. Syndicated columnist George Will, at whose home Reagan had four times been a guest, wrote, "The President's laconic, complacent comparison to home improvements misses a few points: the Commander in Chief has more leverage over his forces than the rest of us have over carpenters. And if carpenters are dilatory, the kitchen is inconvenient; if the Commander in Chief's employees are dilatory, people die." William Safire, the conservative columnist of the *New York Times*, fumed that Reagan's attempt to deflect blame had been "even more pusillanimous than Jimmy Carter's protracted hand-wringing at the seizure of hostages in Teheran." If Reagan did not have "the means or the guts" to protect the embassy, Safire said, he should close it down. The *Wall Street Journal* editorialized that holding someone accountable for the fiasco offered the only hope of averting a similar "avoidable tragedy" in the future. But all those printed words could not compete with the dramatic pictures of Reagan declaiming peace at the United Nations, Reagan breaking bread with Gromyko at the White House.

After the frustrations of the first four weeks of the campaign, Mondale went into seclusion for much of the fifth week to prepare for his first televised debate with Reagan, on a Sunday night, October 7. Having struck out in efforts to diminish Reagan on the Democrats' issues of pluralism, fairness, and peace, Mondale was reduced to trying to surprise Reagan in the arena in which he was an acknowledged master, the use of television. Mondale was not accorded much of a chance to score off Reagan by anyone except his own aides, but he also calculated that no amount of campaigning could possibly match the impact of the debate. Some 80 percent of likely voters said they would watch the ninety-minute encounter, and if past elections were any indication, many would be heavily influenced in their voting by their impression of who won.

Mondale knew that he had much more to gain than Reagan. Voters expect a President to look and act presidential; they are not so sure about his opponent. The public would especially expect Reagan to be glib and adroit, while Mondale had built up a reputation for being dull; measured against those expectations, Mondale had every chance to offer a pleasant surprise to the electorate. It was, moreover, a fact of American political history that in every previous presidential debate — Kennedy versus Nixon in 1960, Carter versus Ford in 1976, and Reagan versus Carter in

1980 — the member of the incumbent administration had lost and the insurgent had won.

⟶

As it turned out, nothing Mondale might have done on the stump could have produced headlines as dramatic as those that cropped up in midweek before the debate. Secretary of Labor Raymond Donovan, who had raised $600,000 for Reagan's 1980 campaign and had been rewarded with a cabinet post, was indicted for larceny. No sitting cabinet officer had ever been indicted before. Faced with indictment, Donovan, unlike most appointive officials who are charged with criminal activity, flatly refused to resign. He took a leave of absence instead.

Donovan had been the subject of rumors and allegations of impropriety since before he had taken office. He had been formally investigated by the FBI and by a special prosecutor. He had been accused, mostly by gangsters, of ties to organized crime. A reputed potential witness against him had been found slain. When Donovan was indicted, his codefendants included: a convicted criminal who had newly been charged with a murder; an alleged accomplice in that killing; a black Democratic state senator; and assorted executives of Donovan's erstwhile employer, the Schiavone Construction Company. According to the indictment, Schiavone created a dummy corporation, nominally owned by the state senator, the purpose of which was to circumvent laws requiring that a percentage of federally funded construction business be given to minority-owned companies; Schiavone then fabricated fraudulent billing to inflate the value of the work farmed out, and totally falsified the distribution of equity in the dummy company. The nominal 51-percent owner, the state senator, had in fact been only a salaried employee, the indictment said.

Donovan pleaded innocence; Reagan expressed the confident hope that Donovan would not be found guilty. Then, oddly, the scandal began to recede into the shadows. Mondale decided not to make an issue of it, thinking that an attack would be unfair and undignified, and that it would likely backfire. He also feared a counterattack on his running mate, who remained relatively untainted in the eyes of the general public but who was beginning to face problems from the persistent digging of a handful of news organizations: the *Wall Street Journal* editorial pages and Australian publisher Rupert Murdoch's assorted U.S. tabloids, including the *New York Post*, all motivated by ideological zeal for Reagan, and the liberal *Philadelphia Inquirer*, apparently prompted by true doubt about Ferraro's integrity and candor, or about her husband's, at least. Mondale seemed to believe that there was no smoking gun to be exposed, no real liability. (Indeed, the worst thing ever uncovered about Ferraro during the campaign was that her parents had been charged with gambling, but not convicted, when she was a child.) But Mondale did not want to subject his running mate to further pain, nor his own campaign to the distraction of renewed debate about her decency. He also had found that the "sleaze factor" did not much arouse voters. They thought of Reagan as personally honest, without a breath of financial scandal in all his years in office. The President's aides seemed no more venal than the average in politics, and mistrust of them had considerably diminished after a special prosecutor had ruled in September that there was no basis for an indictment against Edwin Meese, Reagan's chief policy adviser and his nominee to succeed William French Smith as attorney general. Except for Donovan's problem, which dated to well before his time in public service, the Reagan administration had produced no major scandal — certainly nothing to compare with the unholy dealings between Billy Carter and Libya during the latter years of the Carter administration. Hence, Mondale held his tongue about Donovan.

So did the rest of America. Donovan's indictment was treated as secondary news by *Time* the following week. It was superseded by the presidential debate on the cover of *Newsweek*. The labor secretary's woes disappeared quickly from the nightly newscasts and morning newspapers.

And not one question in any of the presidential debates would ever refer to the cabinet member's historic shame.

The meeting came on October 7, four weeks and two days before the election. It took place officially in Louisville, but in reality in the nation's living rooms. The structure was elaborate, providing for duplicate questions to each candidate, follow-ups to each main question, rebuttal time for each side. But the purpose was pure, and simple: to help the public decide exactly what it would mean to have the best man win. The initial estimate was that 93 million Americans had watched, more people than had ever actually voted in a presidential election. The ninety minutes of colloquy between Walter Mondale and Ronald Reagan were the most influential moments of the campaign. The four-year crusade for office, the yearlong trudge around the country for Mondale and the trek around the world for Reagan, came down to this.

The evening opened with an announcement by moderator Barbara Walters of ABC that the two campaigns had been given a list of almost one hundred qualified journalists and had been able to agree on only three as questioners, not the customary four. This wholesale exclusion, which was unprecedented, had resulted from a tit-for-tat policy by both sides of striking out any reporter who was thought to be even mildly disposed toward either a liberal or a conservative ideology. The Reagan team had started the squabble, but in time the Mondale camp had become equally vindictive and extreme. The eventual choices, paradoxically, could not have been much more conservative, nor, as it turned out, more fair. Jim Wieghart of the Scripps-Howard newspaper chain previously had been a Washington correspondent and later editor of the *New York Daily News*, a conservative paper that generally backed Reagan; Diane Sawyer of the CBS newsmagazine show "60 Minutes" had worked for Richard Nixon at the White House and continued on his staff after his resignation in disgrace; Fred Barnes of the *Baltimore Sun* was a regular contributor to the archconservative magazine *American Spectator*, for which his "beat" was the alleged liberal bias of the press.

The opening sequence of questions, by Wieghart, dealt with the budget. From their first words, the candidates appeared to have reversed roles. Reagan looked nervous, overanxious, eager to demonstrate his fitness to be President. Mondale seemed relaxed, expansive, communicative. He talked into the camera and directly over the airwaves to the viewer, not, as is the customary mistake in debates, to the audience in the hall. Reagan, so successful when using anecdotes, analogies, and homespun language to explain his approach to government, peppered the air instead with statistics — sixteen of them in his first two answers. He showed off his knowledge of interest rates, tax rates, "recovery rates" for the economy, the "rate of increase in government spending." He said virtually nothing about goals or values, nothing about what all these numbers meant to the lives of average Americans.

Mondale used only six numbers in his first two answers, and devoted most of his time to talking about what was "fair," how "leadership" ought to be measured, how misinformed Reagan had been in his economic projections, what the cost of this error would be to "our rural and farm friends" and to the elderly who "depend upon all of us for the little security that they have." He referred scornfully to the "coffeepot that costs seven thousand dollars" because of sloppy Pentagon procurement.

In rebuttal, Reagan misspoke and said "win it" for "minute," then corrected himself, at the outset of a tortured and almost incomprehensible sentence about his commitment to Social Security. As Reagan finished, Mondale delivered a roundhouse right, almost a technical knockout: "That's exactly the commitment that was made to the American people in 1980: he would never reduce benefits. And of course what happens right after the election is they proposed to cut Social Security bene-

[245]

fits by twenty-five percent, reducing the adjustment for inflation, cutting out minimum benefits for the poorest on Social Security, removing educational benefits for dependents . . . trying to get . . . through college. Everybody remembers that. People know what happened."

Sawyer asked Mondale to prove his repeated claims that Reagan was merely a showman, and Reagan to justify Vice-President Bush's claim that Mondale's campaign was "one of whining and hoping for bad news." Mondale raised anew the budget deficit, brought up the failed embassy security in Beirut, and asserted, "There's a difference between being a quarterback and a cheerleader." Reagan meandered off into an incoherent and, it was later proved, incorrect attempt to nullify the facts about his proposed Social Security reductions by accusing President Carter of having effected a 25 percent Social Security cut. Then he faced up to the question: "Now, leadership. First of all, I think you must have some principles you believe in. In mine, I happen to believe in the people and believe that the people are supposed to be dominant in our society. That they, not government, are to have control of their own affairs to the greatest extent possible with an orderly society. Now having that, I think, also that in leadership, will, I believe that you find the people — positions such as I'm in — who have the talent and the ability to do the things that are needed in the various departments of government." This awkward ramble, this gabbling inability to discuss what Reagan himself did at the helm of government, continued for several paragraphs. By its end, people across America were beginning to look at each other with a dawning wonder: could this half-addled old man really be the warrior king?

Sawyer then asked Reagan a stinging question about his authenticity. She noted, "Recently you showed up at the opening ceremony of a Buffalo old-age housing project when in fact your policy was to cut federal housing subsidies for the elderly, yet you were there to have your picture taken with them." Reagan replied, with utter certitude but in defiance of the facts, "Our policy was *not* to cut subsidies. . . . We have no thought of throwing people out into the snow, whether because of age or need. We have preserved the safety net for the people with true need in this country and it has been pure demagoguery that we in some way shut off all the charitable programs, or many of them, for the people who have real need."

Mondale, entitled to rebut, then uttered the phrase that won the battle of the sound bite. What he said was to be by far the most quoted line of the night: "Well, I guess I'm reminded a little bit of what Will Rogers once said about Herbert Hoover. He said it's not what he doesn't know that bothers me, it's [that] what he knows for sure just ain't so.

"The fact is that the housing unit for senior citizens in Buffalo was only made possible through a federal assistance program for senior citizens that the President's budget sought to terminate. So if he'd had his way, there wouldn't have been any housing project there at all." Mondale, as it happened, had gone slightly astray in one of his own facts. The alleged Will Rogers quip was disavowed by Rogers scholars. Some researchers attributed it to alternative American humorists such as Artemus Ward; others suggested that Mondale had unknowingly corrupted Disraeli's witticism about the man who knew one thing, and that one was wrong. The slip was, in any case, apparently innocent, although it seemed characteristic of Mondale's New Deal mind-set, and his desire to invoke the sins of the Republican past, that he found a way to link Reagan with Herbert Hoover.

Fred Barnes asked Mondale and Reagan whether they were born-again Christians. Both said no. Both, however, asserted their strong personal faith. Reagan used the balance of his time to remind voters of Ferraro's crack that he was not a good Christian. Mondale repeated the gist of the sermon on religious diversity that he had offered at the B'nai B'rith conference. He played upon the anxieties of moderate voters by quoting the fundamentalist preacher Jerry Falwell as saying that his faction had been granted control over the selection of at least two Supreme Court justices. This boast was certainly obscure, and it seemed later that Mondale might have wrenched it a bit out of context. But Reagan did not explicitly deny the possibility of a New Right veto over Court nominees. He mentioned only his popular appointment of the first woman justice, Sandra Day O'Connor.

Democrats were trying to make a major issue of Reagan's potential opportunity to appoint a total of as many as five or six justices by the end of his second term. For intellectuals, Yuppies, and other disaffected Democrats, the Court appointment issue was perhaps the single most compelling reason to stick with Mondale. Indeed, the controversy had been *Time's* cover story the preceding week. Said *Time:* "Assuming that the appointees are relatively young, the next President could set the Supreme Court's course through the end of the century."

Wieghart asked Mondale the question that had beleaguered the Democrats all year: "Polls indicate a massive change in the electorate, away from the coalition that has long made the Democratic party a majority. Blue-collar workers, young professionals, their children, and much of the middle class now regard themselves as independents or Republican instead of Democrats. And the gap, the edge the Democrats had in party registration, seems to be narrowing. I'd like to ask you, Mr. Mondale, what is causing this? Is the Democratic party out of sync with the majority of Americans?" Up to this point in the debate, only Reagan had been put on the spot. Matters had gone steadily Mondale's way. But this question needed to be answered, and it flew in the face of everything Mondale believed or wanted to believe. He simply could not see the Democrats as anything but the natural majority party. And he could not bring himself to consider thinking out loud about the party's future. So his answer was boilerplate about the deficit, the trade imbalance, the woes of farmers, the fear of nuclear war. The Democrats, he said, would win on the issues. Wieghart followed up deftly: "Isn't it possible that the American people have heard your message and they are listening but they are rejecting it?" Again, Mondale sidestepped real thought by repeating a couple of slogans about issues. If anything could have caused him to lose the debate against the befuddled Reagan, it would have been his unresponsiveness to the questions about who the Democrats hoped to be.

The next sequence of questions, from Sawyer, asked the candidates their views on abortion. Reagan likened it to murder. Mondale called it "a personal and private moral judgment," and declined to say more. In the subsequent sequence, which dealt with taxes, the candidates offered little beyond what they had said during September. Mondale insisted that increases were inevitable, and that he would administer them more fairly; Reagan again asserted that he would not permit any rise in taxes. After floundering throughout most of the debate, in the welter of statistics that his staff had supposedly dinned into him, Reagan at this point reached out for a familiar, comfortable locution. As if it were his rehearsed intention, he responded by invoking the catchphrase that had served him so well in the 1980 debate against Carter. "You know, I wasn't going to say this at all," he said in his sherry baritone, breaking into a smile, "but I can't help it. There you go again." But his self-congratulation was short-lived. For the second time that night, it turned out, Reagan had waded into Mondale's Sunday punch. For Mondale, too, had rehearsed: "Now, Mr. President, you said, 'There you go again.' Right. Remember the last time you said that?" Reagan, looking baffled and suddenly very old, said, "Mmm, hmmm." Mondale continued, "You said it when President Carter said that you were going to cut Medicare. And you said, 'Oh, no, there you go again, Mr. President.' And what did you do right after the election? You went right out and tried to cut $20 billion out of Medicare. And so, when you say, 'There you go again,' people remember this, you know. And people will remember that you signed the biggest tax increase in the history of California, and the biggest tax increase in the history of the United States. And what are you going to do? You've got a $260 billion deficit. You can't wash it away." Reagan replied, weakly, with yet another statistic, this time about the rate of increase of hospital care costs during the Carter administration. But Mondale's slashing challenge went largely unanswered, and Reagan seemed in a daze for the rest of the night.

Invited, in the final round of questions, to cite "the most outrageous thing your opponent said in this debate tonight," Mondale said he preferred to use his time to praise Reagan for having restored the country's optimism. He thus captured the essence of Reagan's appeal. But he added that Reagan was too passive, and the country too mired in self-congratulation, for the Republican administration to qualify as true leadership. At his turn, Reagan played the question straight: he said that Mondale really had been "outrageous" in implying that Reagan wanted to cut Social Security — even though Reagan undeniably had.

In the closing statement, Reagan tossed out still more statistics, at least one wildly wrong: he claimed erroneously that weapons consumed "only a small portion" of the military budget. Mondale, by contrast, used only one number in his finale: the fact that Reagan had tried to throw 400,000 people off disability payments. The rest of his speech was the litany, once more, of peace, pluralism, and fairness, with short pleas for the environment and education. His final paragraph hit the two key themes that might buoy him: he looked forward, while Reagan was tied to the past, and he believed that national self-criticism was not unpatriotic, but rather was a sign of pride and strength. "The question," Mondale said, "is our future. President Kennedy once said in response to similar arguments, we are great but we can be greater. We can be better if we face our future, rejoice in our strengths, face our problems and by solving them build a better society for our children."

The morning after the debate, pollsters for both sides said it would take three to four full days to determine who had won. In fact, opinion crystallized much sooner. At first analysts credited Mondale with a mild gain, because he had been funny and warm, had twice deflected Reagan, and had always held his own. He had seemed more at ease than people expected; he had regained, for the first time since the New York primary debate, his ingratiating public persona of the commonsensical family father. He had all but demolished Reagan several times during their exchanges, yet had always treated him with the utmost deference and respect. He had politely called Reagan back from the land of platitudes to deal with the disquieting facts on the table — the deficit, the trade imbalance, the continuing needs of the poor. He had shown wit and humor and flexibility and for once his piety had not seemed overbearing and self-righteous. On these grounds alone, Mondale might well have been declared the clear winner of the debate as opinion sifted down.

But something even more unexpected than a Mondale victory had happened: a Reagan defeat of such proportions that people began to wonder if the whole calculus of the election might change. It started on the Tuesday morning, a day and a half after the debate, with a *Wall Street Journal* story about what instantly became known as "the age issue." The *Journal* faced up to the questions that other reporters had been dealing with only obliquely: Reagan's health and vigor, the depth of his involvement in issues, the degree of genuine control he exerted over his White House staff, the apparent deterioration of his hearing, the fundamental matter of how well he knew what was going on. The *Journal*'s story legitimized the issue for the other major media. Within a day, the President's age and supposed decline were leading news on every network and in nearly every major newspaper.

The story was probably the right story. But it ran for the wrong reason. People had been startled by Reagan's poor performance because they were used to seeing him read from a TelePrompTer, as he had done in all his major speeches, most recently at the United Nations. Even his occasionally televised press conferences were semirehearsed; the questions he would be asked were predictable, and he practiced answering them with aides who impersonated reporters. Reagan's age had become an issue, as it should have been in the case of any candidate who would be only days shy of seventy-eight at the end of a new term, but it had arisen only because he appeared to have declined so abruptly. The contrast between the scripted Reagan and the impromptu Reagan had always been dramatic, and not much had changed; the public would have been equally aghast had it seen a similar display in the early days of his administration. Reporters knew this, but by and large failed to point it out, perhaps because they were reluctant, after years of virtual silence about his condition, to relinquish their only opportunity to counter the myth that Jack Kemp had evoked of a Reagan seeming to grow ever younger.

As the week wore on, polls showed Mondale being picked as the winner of the debate by steadily bigger margins, and that victory in turn was pushing him to within shouting distance of Reagan. For Mondale, even the narrowest of wins would still require a miracle. But miracles suddenly seemed imaginable. Indeed, it became conventional wisdom that a comparably crushing loss for Reagan in a second debate might well place the election-night outcome in doubt.

Four days after the Reagan-Mondale debate, just as the piquant possibility of a genuine contest was beginning to be savored by the press and public, attention shifted to the vice-presidential debate in Philadelphia.

The encounter was an oddity — the only previous televised meeting between vice-presidential candidates had been in 1976, between Mondale and Republican Robert Dole — and there had been substantial doubt about whether another would be held in 1984. Bush, ever the loyalist, had ducked the possibility for months, saying that the emphasis of the campaign ought to remain on the men at the top of the ticket. Some of this was deference, which he carried to an extreme even by the submissive standards of vice-presidents. Some of the reasoning was a practical calculation that Reagan was the stronger half of the Republican ticket, and Mondale the weaker half of the Democratic one. Bush also felt some hesitation about taking on a woman in debate; experience provided no ground rules as to how tough he could be without appearing to bully a female opponent. Measured against those considerations was the Reagan team's belief that Bush, the most diversely qualified vice-president of the twentieth century, could hardly fail to acquit himself better than Ferraro — and the worry that if he did not confront her before the cameras, he might be seen as intimidated by her formidable charm.

For Bush, the debate would also serve as an audition for the 1988 campaign. Based on his record as a congressional representative, two-time Senate candidate, Republican national chairman, Central Intelligence Agency director, diplomat in China, ambassador to the United Nations, formidable 1980 also-ran, and a presumed two-term vice-president, he would probably be entitled to lay an even stronger claim on his party's presidential nomination in the next election than Mondale had made in 1984. But Bush needed to prove that he was capable of grace under pressure. In 1980, he had seemed stiff and slow-footed on occasions when he had sought instead to be an adroit debater or nimble strategist.

For Ferraro, the debate was above all a chance to prove that a woman could hold her own with a man. She knew that a bad performance on her part would fracture not only her own career but the chances of other women to be nominated and elected to office. She would, after all, play no comparably substantive role at any other point in the campaign.

Bush set the tone with his opening remarks: he was vigorously, gleefully partisan, claiming that his boss had "brought America back," that "there's a new enthusiasm in this country," that "this President turned it around." He immediately linked Mondale with Carter, and Carter with despair. He also suggested at his first opportunity that Mondale and Ferraro were not an effective team because they differed on a number of issues, including busing to achieve school integration, tuition tax credits for parents of parochial school students, and the imposition of an embargo on grain sales to the Soviet Union as a means of applying pressure for change in that country's politics. Ferraro responded by reminding Bush of his 1980 reference to Reagan's "voodoo economics." She cited numbers and anecdotes to convey the problem of unemployment, especially in the industrial Midwest. Bush countered by reminding viewers of a scene they had heard described on television, or read about in their newspapers, just days before: Ferraro had asked a group of union workers why so many were voting for Reagan, and they had replied with what Bush called "a long deathly silence."

This rabbit-punching continued throughout the debate. Soon the reporters who were serving as panelists entered into the combative spirit. Jack White of *Time*, who is black, asked a question about civil rights that began, "Vice-President Bush, many critics of your administration say that it is the most hostile to minorities in recent memory." Robert Boyd of the Knight-Ridder newspapers asked Ferraro whether she had been guilty of a House ethics violation in claiming exemption from the disclosure requirements and noted that there had been dozens of errors in the paperwork she had released accompanying her press conference. He then pointed out to Bush that through taking advantage of legal tax deductions, the vice-president had paid 1983 income taxes at a rate of 13 percent, less than half the normal ratio for someone in his income bracket. Said Boyd: "Do you think it was fair?" Bush replied by talking about Mondale's high income and by accusing him of "telling the American people to try to divide [by] class — rich and poor." Ferraro feistily offered to lend Bush her accountant, but added, "He's expensive." Almost never did the tenor of discussion rise above bickering.

Ferraro won the battle of the sound bite; in the course of a discussion of international terrorism, she turned on her rival and said, "I almost resent, Vice-President Bush, your patronizing attitude that you have to teach me about foreign policy." The remark was aimed at every woman in earshot who had ever felt her intelligence was being belittled strictly because she was a woman, and it was repeated on newscasts for days afterward. Ferraro also castigated Bush for making a fraudulent claim worthy of Reagan at his most cavalier toward facts. He said that his "two opponents" had suggested that the Marines murdered by terrorists in Beirut had "died in shame." (Bush knew, or should have known, that the statement was a lie. It was immediately denied by Ferraro, and soon after the debate Mondale demanded an apology. But Bush never owned up to his apparently willful error.)

Ferraro also jumped into the fray with one of the reporters. When Boyd asked how she could prove to the American people that she was tough enough, despite being a woman, to deserve to be a potential President, she snapped, "Are you saying that I would have to have fought in the war to love peace?" That line, too, became a sound bite excerpted on newscasts.

Despite the acuity of Ferraro's rhetoric in a debate that rarely gravitated toward ideas from either side, and despite a considerably superior closing statement that reflected the concerns of ordinary citizens, while Bush was cheerleading vapidly for Reagan, Ferraro was generally judged to have lost the debate. Reporters may have wanted to avoid appearing biased by ceding a second consecutive victory to the Democrats. They may have been persuaded by Bush's crisp, unyielding assertion of what most people regarded as Reagan's generally good record. Yet the biggest reason for Ferraro's downfall in the debate was her demeanor. Her ready smile and quick humor had been replaced by a stern, slightly abrasive lawyerly manner and a thin-lipped, almost petulant grimace. She wore glasses much of the time, and frequently appeared to be reading from notes. She had not brought prepared cue cards in with her; that was not allowed, although the audience had little way of knowing. Any notes she used had been written during the course of the discussion. Her dependence on them, however, meant she was unable to make much eye contact with viewers. And so Ferraro, who had bowled over crowds with her warmth but left them uncertain about her brainpower, this time demonstrated her keen intelligence, but projected a distinctly unfeminine chill.

The next day, Bush gloated at his triumph. He bragged to workingmen in Pennsylvania that he had "kicked a little ass" the night before. The phrase was mild, but tasteless and widely criticized as sexist. Bush's wife, Barbara, incensed that her husband was being criticized, then referred to Ferraro in a reporter's presence as being "something that rhymes with rich." When that remark, too, became an issue, Mrs. Bush contended that she had meant to imply that Ferraro was a "witch," an unpleasant term but one acceptable in most circles. No one who knew of the incident had any doubt that she had instead meant "bitch," a word that it would be unwise for a white-haired, matronly wife of a vice-president to use.

———

After the initial burst of momentum from his debate with Reagan, Mondale had stalled by mid-October. Ferraro's standoff, to put the best face on it, with Bush had not added much to her popularity; polls continued to suggest that her presence neither significantly helped nor significantly hurt. Mondale's own message had not changed much since September, and his schedule was under constant debate between one faction of his aides, who thought he should try for victory everywhere, and another, who thought he should concentrate his time and money in the states where he had the best chance to win.

By this stage the campaign was being fought on five levels. There was

Mondale's actual stumping, rally by rally, state by state. There was the organizational work undertaken on his behalf by the party. There were the
stories that appeared on the nightly news, and secondarily in print. There
was the impending final debate. And there were TV commercials.

Mondale's commercials during the primaries had been generally nasty
and far from inspirational, with the exception of one ad that aired in the
early stages, when he did not think he would have to scrabble to win. It
pictured young children at a school, and talked about Mondale's concerns
for their future. A reworking of that theme became Mondale's signature
spot for the final weeks of the general-election campaign. It showed him
speaking to a group of mostly young people, apparently students at a university, about how good and fulfilling he hoped their lives would be. The
ad conveyed Mondale's essential decency. But it also captured his passivity, his lack of leadership. He was not promising anything, he was not
proposing anything, he was merely expressing a wish. The ad seemed almost like a premature plea that, after he was gone and on his way to being
forgotten, he be remembered, if at all, for being a nice and well-meaning
person.

For Reagan's commercials, he had turned again to what had worked in
1976 and 1980: after opening with feel-good ads so general that they
might have been used to sell toothpaste, Reagan reverted to the simplest
of formats, himself, alone, talking straight into the camera — straight into
the viewer's eyes — about his hard work, his accomplishments, and his
sense of having left his task unfinished. He asked for more time, not for
himself, but to complete the people's business.

Most of Reagan's commercials asserted his authority on the basis of his
incumbency itself. He stood on the White House grounds, or sat at his
Oval Office desk. He claimed credit for restoring economic health, rein-
vigorating the military, renewing national pride. Despite the universally
acknowledged incandescence of his smile, Reagan did not rely on grandfatherly charm; he looked calm and a little stern, and implied that his
weighty office demanded a counterbalancing strength of spirit. In one ad,
he spoke of what it meant to live and work in the nerve center of the Free
World. As he made a gesture meant to encompass all he surveyed, he
showed the kinetic wisdom acquired during half a century in the public
eye. He did not sweep his arm weakly out from his side, or glance furtively
over his shoulder, or flippantly point a thumb; his arm swept across his
own body and shoulder, in a show of strength and reserve and inner focus,
as if to remind his fellow citizens that this habitat, nominally theirs, was
actually his. Mondale's commercials barely spoke of the possibility of victory, because it would seem presumptuous; Reagan's commercials

touched only briefly on the matter of victory, because it seemed unnecessary.

—————✒—————

The second debate, held in Kansas City on October 21, was both climax and anticlimax to the campaign. Mondale came in needing another knockdown to have a chance of winning the election. Reagan, who continued to hold a substantial lead in polls and a place of honor in the hearts of his countrymen, had to demonstrate only that he was not too doddering or confused to retain his job. In theory, any result was possible. But the political dynamic at work practically guaranteed Reagan a victory.

Mondale had gotten his big push two weeks before because he had been so surprisingly good, and Reagan so surprisingly bad. The essential element in that debate had not been the objective quality of the performance of either candidate, but the surprise — the contrast between what happened and the expectations that voters had brought to it. Reagan had been supposed to be polished, witty, glib. Mondale had been supposed to be dull and ineffectual. In this second debate, Mondale could be every bit as clever as he had been in the first, and it would still seem that he had been radically less telling; because people's expectations had been raised, there was no longer the opportunity for him to seem spectacularly improved. Similarly, Reagan could fumble every bit as embarrassingly as in the first debate, and he would not attract anything like the same criticism; people's expectations had been lowered, so he could not seem spectacularly worse.

In the end, Reagan actually was a little better than he had been in the first debate, and Mondale was somewhat worse. Reagan's mind wandered and he stumbled over facts repeatedly. In his closing statement, as John Chancellor of NBC pointed out afterward, Reagan absolutely lost his way. But he showed less often than in Louisville the blank stare of confusion, and he got off the winning comic line of the night. Mondale suffered a more basic relapse: he lost the capacity to project himself on camera. He had trouble making eye contact with the lens, he had trouble remembering to smile, he put too little sense of himself into what he had to say. He seemed preoccupied with trying to embarrass and belittle Reagan. In place of the appealing message of the first debate, that Reagan had been a valuable President but it was time for a change, Mondale had adopted again the rhetoric of the self-righteous liberal.

The debate opened with discussion of Central America. Reagan's first question, from syndicated columnist Georgie Anne Geyer, asked him to justify a CIA-sponsored pamphlet that had instructed anti-Communist rebels in Nicaragua how to assassinate opponents — and even how to assassinate allies, in order to create "martyrs" for the movement. Reagan proceeded to tell a garbled, mostly inaccurate version of how the pamphlet had been prepared, to whom how many copies had been distributed, and what if any corrective censorship the CIA had imposed. He also referred to "the agency head of the CIA in Nicaragua," implying that the agency had a covert station there and was directing rebel operations through it. Once the significance of that statement was pointed out to Reagan by Geyer, he said he had "misspoken" himself and withdrew the remark. The odds, of course, were that his implication was true, and that he had just committed a major indiscretion. But Mondale chose not to pounce on it.

Moments later, Reagan brought up Mondale's repeated charge that the President did not understand the most basic facts about nuclear weaponry. It was established fact, as Mondale had claimed, that Reagan had once spoken of submarine-based missiles as less destabilizing, because they could be called back after launching (in truth, they could not). Reagan contended that he had merely been misunderstood — he had meant to say that it was possible to recall a plane or submarine, not the missiles it carried. That explanation made some sense in speaking about airplanes. But in a time of crisis, a missile-carrying submarine would almost certainly be maintained somewhere near a prospective target, not called back toward U.S. shores.

Reagan inaccurately described the Carter administration policy on weapons as one of "unilateral disarmament," an overstatement that was probably within the bounds of permissible rhetoric. He predicted that the most likely alternative government to the dictatorship of Ferdinand Marcos in the Philippines would be Communist, when in fact the major opposition forces were anti-Communist; but that, too, seemed within the purview of a campaigner. Reagan claimed that the problem of world population growth was "vastly exaggerated," an assertion pleasing to his right-wing supporters who oppose birth control and regulation of markets, but nonetheless reflecting either ignorance or willful blindness bordering on the irresponsible. In any case, all of Reagan's fluffs of fact were offset by his perfect delivery of a carefully rehearsed one-liner, the sound bite of the night if not the year. Asked whether his age gave him any doubts about his capacity to function without sleep during a crisis, Reagan said, "Not at all. And I want you to know that also I will not make age an issue of this campaign. I am not going to exploit for political purposes my opponent's youth and inexperience." Even Mondale laughed. The questioner, Henry Trewhitt of the *Baltimore Sun*, replied with a rueful, protracted metaphor about having pitched a ball that Reagan had hit for an out-of-the-park home run.

Mondale bobbled facts, too: he falsely implied that a proposed immigration bill would require people to carry a citizenship card. In an effort to work in one last reference to the deficit, even though this debate was supposedly devoted to foreign policy, he contrived to suggest that the deficit led to high U.S. interest rates, which led to high foreign interest rates, which led to difficulty for foreign government debtors in meeting their obligations, which led to increased illegal immigration.

Two strange events capped the night. First, Reagan said, more than once, that he wanted to share his beloved space-based "Star Wars" missile defense system with the Soviets, as a means of reducing tension and getting them to come to the bargaining table. This posture made almost no sense in conjunction with other things he said, nor with his career; and it was not heard again, ever. Then Reagan launched into a closing speech about heading down the scenic California coastal highway, pondering what to say about our era in a letter for a time capsule, and wondering what that future would think of us. He seemed to want to convey a message of peace. But time ran out while he was in the process of relieving his listeners' embarrassment by changing the subject, the time capsule story still unfinished.

———✧———

The second debate was unanimously judged a victory for Reagan, and with that, the President's team in effect declared the campaign over. Mondale had danced all his rain dances, and the mountain had never vibrated. Although Reagan was careful not to claim victory in advance, his closest aides began to speak of the possibility of a fifty-state sweep, something that had never been done before. (The largely black District of Columbia was conceded to Mondale.) Reagan venturesomely stumped in the Democratic industrial heartland of Pennsylvania and even in West Virginia; his staff spent advertising money in overwhelmingly Democratic, nonwhite Hawaii and in Mondale's home state of Minnesota. GOP pollsters stepped up the talk about how 1984 could prove to be a transforming election, one that marked the passage of the country into a protracted era of Republican dominance. After waves of anxiety verging on panic just two weeks before, in the aftermath of the Louisville debate, Reagan's men now felt so buoyantly optimistic that they virtually described the election itself as a mere formality.

Reagan carefully controlled his visibility, avoiding long days that might show him up as tired or lead him to make some careless, costly mistake.

He avoided press conferences, although he granted interviews to selected major news organizations. More overtly than ever, he tried to equate himself with optimism, fervor, patriotic joy. His rallies were like parades, or circuses, resplendent with giant flags and cascading balloons and bouncy music. His one-line joke had proved predictive: he did indeed seek to project a world in which every day was the Fourth of July.

His advertising reflected his shift in emphasis from combat to ratification, from seeking election to consolidating a mandate to govern. For a brief period he had used a perplexing, metaphorical ad that showed a man and a bear in the woods. The bear is, of course, the traditional symbol of the Soviet Union, and the punch line of the commercial was, "Isn't it smart to be as strong as the bear?" But when asked if the ad's aggressive undertone was meant to celebrate America's national defense gains, Reagan's aides waffled. They did not like to speculate on who the man was, who the bear was, what the whole elliptical little narrative meant. They preferred to let people read their own meanings into it — as to some extent they had read their own meanings into Reagan. The bear ad was dropped soon after the second debate, to be replaced by two explicitly celebratory sets of commercials. One was a revival of the ads aired in late spring, celebrating the "new day in America" that had been brought about by the President. The other showed the national grandfather himself, greeting the people in Ohio; they had, an announcer said, "just dropped by to say thanks" because he had so revivified the country.

Despite his party's purported interest in building a lasting superiority at all levels, Reagan poured most of his money into advertising time, not organization. His hard-pressed opponents were putting a greater share of their resources into grass-roots organizing, partly to exploit their edge in registration, partly to reward Mondale's kind of machine Democrat. As a result, the organizational budgets of the two parties were roughly akin. In buying network television time, however, Reagan was outspending Mondale two to one. The President and his admakers used television skillfully. But the investment in TV commercials reflected considerations beyond their effectiveness: Reagan's need to be loved; his competitive drive for a record victory; his belief that the right kind of triumph could empower him to work his way with Congress; the hope that a surge of happy emotion could lengthen the President's coattails, and allow him to work with a more strongly Republican Senate and a less strongly Democratic House.

As Reagan's ambitions expanded, Mondale's were contracting. Within a few days after the second debate, word leaked out to numerous reporters that Mondale had been told by his staff that his situation was hopeless. The gap in polls between him and Reagan, which had narrowed abruptly after the first debate, had opened again, to as much as twenty percentage points. Mondale was lagging, at the very best, a dozen points behind; worse, there were hardly any states where he appeared to have much of a chance to win. The schedule was therefore rewritten to take him to rallies in Democratic strongholds, where he could at least accumulate memories of tens of thousands of people cheering for him before he faced the humiliation of certain, and utter, defeat. Mondale did not accept his fate easily. The rallies, at which people applauded the things he believed so fervently himself, reinforced his hope that the greatest upset in American political history was somehow in the making. He had never drawn such a large and fervent following. "Those aren't loser's crowds," he said. But of course even a landslide loser in a presidential race attracts tens of millions of votes. It takes only a small percentage of them to fill street corners or stadiums to overflowing. The other thing that deceived Mondale was his own ideological certitude. Margaret Warner of *Newsweek*, who had covered him for a year and a half, sat interviewing him late one night in this final phase of the campaign. "He just kept saying over and over, 'I don't believe that the American people are selfish.' To him, those were the possibilities: to be selfish or to vote for his kind of Democrat. He could not recognize that something was changing in the relationship between individuals and government."

For a few days after the second debate, Mondale sustained his belligerent, dismissive tone toward Reagan. To a group of New Jersey students, he sneered at the incumbent, as seen in Kansas City, as "the most detached, the most remote, the most uninformed President in modern history." But he soon grasped that he could not by words persuade people to believe the opposite of what they had seen with their own eyes; Reagan had been unimpressive, but scarcely contemptible, and Mondale not much better. If Mondale hoped to gather undecided voters, he would have a stronger chance, he concluded, by emphasizing anew the virtues of his own party, rather than the supposed sins of the President. As his prospects for even a dignified loss receded, Mondale adjusted his itinerary further and devoted his energies more toward helping others in the party. He traveled to Texas, a state carried by every Democrat who had ever won the White House, and one where Mondale was a hopeless thirty percentage points behind, chiefly to aid a troubled Senate candidate. He journeyed to Des Moines — Iowa had been carried only once by a Democrat, Lyndon Johnson, since the days of Harry Truman — less in hope of victory for himself than to assist a Senate challenger in a tight race. At times he spoke of serendipity. During a "harvest tour" of farm villages in the Mississippi valley of Iowa, Illinois, and Missouri, he recalled how just such places had rescued Truman in 1948. But mostly he acknowledged by his very bearing that he would rather be righteous than President.

Mondale's advertising for a while had included a variant of the primary campaign standby "red phone," one that this time showed a flashing telephone while a voice warned that if Reagan stationed "killer weapons in space," then "computers [would] take control." The ads seemed ineffective, either because the "red phone" device was shopworn, or because the Star Wars space weapons proposal was too little understood to be mistrusted, or most likely because people refused to believe Reagan was dangerous. In polls, a consistent plurality judged the President better equipped than Mondale to achieve a workable arms treaty with the Soviets. Mondale nonetheless insisted on retaining the essence of the "red phone" message: his next group of ads used the rock tune "Teach Your Children" as background music for a montage of kids playing and nuclear missiles being launched. Like almost everything else in Mondale's strategy all year, his insistence on raining missiles on Reagan's parade was either a brave, bold gesture or, as it seemed more likely to prove, the pathetic, petulant wrong-headedness of a candidate less ready to say why he should win than why his opponent should lose.

During the two weeks between the second debate and election day, the press increasingly portrayed the race as over. The daily newspapers and nightly newscasts hinted strongly of Mondale's defeat. By election eve, liberal *Newsweek* and conservative *U.S. News & World Report* were both on the stands with covers virtually declaring Reagan's victory before a single voting booth had opened.

The end came quickly. Exit polls, which had been used all spring to forecast primary results, were used for the second straight election to foretell the outcome of the general balloting. The message from everywhere was the same: the Reagan runaway that had been foreshadowed in every advance poll was holding up, perhaps more strongly than anticipated. The only question was the magnitude of his triumph.

Under pressure from Westerners who did not want the national results to discourage voters from showing up to cast ballots in other, local races, the networks had debated at length whether or not to "call" the race officially before the polls closed in California. As it turned out, the returns were so lopsided that CBS and ABC and NBC all called the race before precincts had even closed in New York. The rejection of Mondale, the networks proclaimed, would be even more decisive than the downfall of Jimmy Carter in 1980. Network anchors speculated almost gleefully about whether Mondale would make history by losing every state.

Minnesota spared him. His home had never let him down, Mondale said gratefully. This time it had stayed loyal by the thinnest of margins, 3,761 votes out of almost 2.1 million cast. Mondale thanked his supporters humbly and disappeared — not depressed, he insisted later, but "bone-tired." Some 37,565,334 Americans had voted for him, just over 40 percent of the total. But in the election-night summaries and morning-after analyses, it seemed as though almost no one had. Mondale became an unperson, and so did the armies of his partisans. There was no room in all the vast land, it was asserted, for them and their bygone beliefs.

Ronald Reagan carried 54,451,521 votes, nearly 59 percent of the total cast. The turnout was more than ninety-two million voters, almost six million more than in 1980, and the percentage of Americans participating in the presidential election rose slightly for the first time in more than two decades.

Statistically, the President's victory embraced nearly everyone: he won a vast majority of first-time, mostly young voters, along with pluralities in many states among lifelong, lunchbucket Democrats. Reagan won by almost identical two-to-one margins among Gary Hart's "Yuppies" and among born-again Christians. His plurality among Catholics was nearly as wide as in the nation at large. He ran practically even with Mondale in union households.

For those who argued that his victory was largely personal, not partisan, there was ample evidence. While he was steamrolling to victory, his party was losing two seats in the Senate, and gaining only fifteen seats, less than half of what had been hoped, in the House. In Congress, the Republicans actually seemed numerically somewhat weaker than they had been after election day in 1980. Moreover, polls still indicated that majorities of Americans felt closer to the Democratic than the Republican positions on issues. Voters had opted for Reagan as a strong leader, tough and decisive against the Soviets, committed to a consistent plan for economic recovery, not always right but always determined.

Reagan did not believe in that emphasis on his character. Late in the campaign he had said, "People are crossing the lines to vote because they agree more with what we're proposing." There was some evidence that the crossover would endure. The registration gap between Democrats and Republicans has closed from almost two-to-one during the 1970s to a modest margin of 38 percent to 32 percent. Among voters under twenty-four years old, the Republicans actually hold a lead.

The news was more negative for the Democrats than positive for the Republicans. Among Catholics, whose trust the Democrats must regain if they are to prevail, the abortion issue and the Democratic party's conflict with the church hierarchy have proved costly already, and seem likely not to abate. New York's Italian-Americans were the group likeliest to have been swayed, first one way by Ferraro's accession, then the other way after her trouble with Archbishop O'Connor; Reagan won them by a breathtaking 63 percent to 37 percent. In the South, white men have virtually stopped being Democrats; they went to Reagan by 71 percent to 29 percent. As the Republicans had predicted, new registration for their party among whites outstripped new registration for the Democrats among blacks — in Florida, by a margin of two to one. Almost immediately, Democratic officials started talking about repositioning the party so that it would not be so plainly perceived as the natural haven for blacks. Jesse Jackson just as quickly countered by threatening to lead a walkout. The Democrats could not win without blacks, as they could not have in any election since the days of Roosevelt, with the sole exception of 1964. At least a quarter, perhaps a third of Mondale's votes had come from blacks, and his devastation would have been immeasurably worse if blacks had stayed home. Yet it seemed the Democrats could not win with the blacks, either, because of white resistance. The factions of the party that had warred in 1984 predicted an even more bitter struggle in 1988.

The election had been the first time since 1972, arguably the first since 1964, without a significant protest candidate. Still, in Nevada more than 1 percent of the voters cast their ballots for the designation "none of the above." In Massachusetts, about 1.5 percent left their presidential ballots blank. Not even the choice between a beloved President and a Democrat's Democrat can satisfy every voter's yearning.

———

Reagan told a cheering crowd of three thousand on election night, "Tonight is the end of nothing. It is the beginning of everything." The statement was as enigmatic as the man. If everything was just beginning, then what had his first four years meant? Did he truly intend to be the radical unleashed? Or was he merely firing up a crowd with a rousing but empty line?

Americans knew what they were voting for when they voted for Reagan: they were voting for optimism, for prosperity, for the strength of the individual and the stability of the national defense. But maybe they did not know for *whom* they were voting. If in truth only a second term would let Reagan be Reagan, then they would have to wait to see him whole.

In the balloting booths, voters had rejected chastening visions of the past, had been tantalized by factionalist visions of the future; they had considered hopes for a new America, and settled on affection for a fondly idealized old America. It seemed strangely apposite that Reagan had never ended his story of driving down the highway, at the edge of the unknown New World, the Pacific, pondering the time capsule. Americans can never know what the future will think of them, nor what the future may bring to the seemingly eternal American imperium. Yet they retain an urgent faith in their nation's manifest destiny, in its role as a moral beacon to mankind. It fascinated political scientists that Reagan, the oldest President, appealed intensely to the young. But it turned out that he appealed to a majority of almost every demographic group that anyone could name, including women. Mondale carried the blacks and Hispanics and, more narrowly, the Jews; he won widely among those with incomes below $5,000 a year, the hard-core poverty level, and prevailed, but less forcefully, among those with annual incomes between $5,000 and $10,000; every other income group opted for Reagan. Only those who may already have felt themselves to be outsiders, excluded from the continuity of American culture and the American economic dream, gave their hearts in majorities to the Democrats, the party that insisted on improving upon the past in purely material ways. Reagan believed himself a revolutionary, but of the spirit, not of the marketplace. Throughout 1984 he had invoked, again and again, the eighteenth-century liberationist Thomas Paine, who said that under American guidance the earth could be born anew. As Reagan had quoted Paine in his final words of the first debate: "We have it in our power to begin the world over again."

Reagan did not always convey a clear vision of the technological present nor of the mechanistically defined future, but he conveyed a vision of America. It was a vision more of pride than of purpose. But perhaps pride was the purpose. Perhaps the nation longed to be, not proud because of American achievement, but proud merely to be American — longed to feel what every previous generation of the twentieth-century had felt, that Americans were known instinctively by the rest of the world as their natural moral superiors. Perhaps the future needed no more precise definition than the aura of divinely ordained possibility implied in the roof-raising line of the warrior king on the march, "You ain't seen nothin' yet."

Ronald Reagan was sworn in at a private ceremony on January 20, a triple holiday: a Sunday, Inauguration Day, and the day of the professional football Super Bowl. Cold weather cancelled a scheduled parade the next day, but he nonetheless went ahead with formal ceremonies and delivered a speech proclaiming a "Second American Revolution," based on diminished government and greater individual responsibility. A few days later, he delivered a State of the Union message to Congress that opened with the declaration: "Four years ago we began to change, forever, I hope, our assumptions about government and its place in our lives."

Index